Berlitz® speaking your language

D1289776

Japanese
in 30 days

Course Book
by Kazuko Imaeda

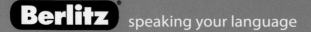

Berlitz® speaking your language

Japanese
in 30 days
Course Book
by Kazuko Imaeda

Berlitz Publishing
New York   London   Singapore

No part of this book may be reproduced, stored in a retrieval system or transmitted in any form or means electronic, mechanical, photocopying, recording or otherwise, without prior written permission from Apa Publications.

Contacting the Editors
Every effort has been made to provide accurate information in this publication, but changes are inevitable. The publisher cannot be responsible for any resulting loss, inconvenience or injury. We would appreciate it if readers would call our attention to any errors or outdated information. Please contact us at: comments@berlitzpublishing.com

All Rights Reserved
© 2006 Berlitz Publishing/APA Publications (UK) Ltd.

Original edition: 2001 by Langenscheidt KG, Berlin and Munich

Second edition: 2014
Printed in China

Berlitz Trademark Reg. U.S. Patent Office and other countries. Marca Registrada.
Used under license from Berlitz Investment Corporation

Senior Commissioning Editor: Kate Drynan
Design: Beverley Speight
Picture research: Beverley Speight
Japanese editor: Eri Nishikawa

Cover photos: © Ming Tang Evans and istock
Interior photos: © all photos by Ming Tang Evans except for: istockphoto p21, 53,71,83,112,164,174,193, 201,226,235,244; APA Bev Speight p131; Apa Corrie Wingate p143.

Distribution

Worldwide
APA Publications GmbH & Co. Verlag KG
(Singapore branch)
7030 Ang Mo Kio Ave 5
08-65 Northstar @ AMK, Singapore 569880
Email: apasin@singnet.com.sg

US
Ingram Publisher Services
One Ingram Blvd, PO Box 3006
La Vergne, TN 37086-1986
Email: ips@ingramcontent.com

UK and Ireland
Dorling Kindersley Ltd
(a Penguin Company)
80 Strand, London, WC2R ORL, UK
Email: sales@uk.dk.com

Australia
Woodslane
10 Apollo St
Warriewood, NSW 2102
Email: info@woodslane.com.au

Contents

How to Use this Book

Japanese in 30 Days is a self-study course which will provide you with a basic knowledge of everyday Japanese in a very short time. The course is divided into 30 short, manageable daily lessons. This book will familiarize you with the main grammatical structures of Japanese and provide you with a good command of essential vocabulary. The writing sections throughout, and the final 3 lessons in their entirety, will teach you how to read and write Japanese characters. In 30 days you will acquire both an active and a passive understanding of the language, enabling you to function effectively in day-to-day life.

Each chapter is an episode in a journey that takes place over 30 days, from your arrival to your final departure, with the main focus on typical, day-to-day situations. Each day has a similar pattern: first, there is a short intro into what you will learn as well as some country and culture information about Japan. You will then have a text in Japanese – generally a dialogue – followed by a grammar section and a number of exercises to help reinforce what you have learned. At the end of each lesson you will find a list of vocabulary. The quick grammar and vocabulary tests, together with the answer key at the back of the book, will enable you to check your progress.

Every lesson (except the first two lessons) begins with a dialogue to introduce the grammar and vocabulary that will be taught in the lesson. These are marked by a CD symbol. Some lessons have several dialogues to demonstrate different themes or grammar points. You will notice that the Japanese spoken language can vary greatly from the written language. This is because when people talk, they omit parts of a sentence that may be understood from context. The dialogues reflect this natural style of speech, but you will see the omitted parts in parentheses in the book, to avoid confusion.

For supplementary learning materials, including an appendix of particles and information about addressing people in Japanese, visit the free downloads section of our website at **www.berlitzpublishing.com**.

Welcome to Japan!

Japanese sentences are written with a combination of characters called **kanji**, **hiragana** and **katakana**. **Kanji** consists of old Chinese characters, and each **kanji** symbol represents a full word, phrase or idea. **Hiragana** and **katakana** are two "alphabets". Each character represents a syllable without any individual meaning, just like English letters. **Hiragana** is used to write **Japanese**, **Katakana** is used for **foreign words** that are now part of the Japanese vocabulary.

Because you are not yet able to read any of these characters, this book uses **rōmaji**; a way to write Japanese using the English alphabet.

Using **rōmaji**, the chart on page 8 shows all of the syllables included in **hiragana** and **katakana**. Each syllable is equivalent to one **hiragana** or **katakana** symbol. Study the following chart and listen to the CD until you are familiar with the syllables and their pronunciation.

Syllables and their pronunciation

First third

a	i	u	e	o
ka	ki	ku	ke	ko
sa	shi	su	se	so
ta	chi	tsu	te	to
na	ni	nu	ne	no
ha	hi	fu	he	ho
ma	mi	mu	me	mo
ya		yu		yo
ra	ri	ru	re	ro
wa				wo
n				

Second third

ga	gi	gu	ge	go
za	ji	zu	ze	zo
da			de	do
ba	bi	bu	be	bo
pa	pi	pu	pe	po

Third third

kya	kyu	kyo
sha	shu	sho
cha	chu	cho
nya	nyu	nyo
hya	hyu	hyo
mya	myu	myo
rya	ryu	ryo
gya	gyu	gyo
ja	ju	jo
bya	byu	byo
pya	pyu	pyo

Exercises

Exercise 1

Listen to the sound of each syllable, and write down the rōmaji for that syllable. Refer to the syllable table on page 8.

1 .... 11 ....

2 .... 12 ....

3 .... 13 ....

4 .... 14 ....

5 .... 15 ....

6 .... 16 ....

7 .... 17 ....

8 .... 18 ....

9 .... 19 ....

10 .... 20 ....

How to read Japanese

The easiest way to pronounce a Japanese word is to break it up using a slash (/) after every vowel (a, i, u, e, o) and to read each syllable separately.

Good night   O/ya/su/mi/na/sa/i/

I am back (now)   Ta/da/i/ma/

When the characters between the two slashes start with n, you must do a test. If this n is not followed by a vowel or a y, it is a syllabic n—pronounced separately—and you put a slash after the n.

e.g. Good evening   Ko/nba/nwa/

The n is not followed by a vowel or a y, so you put a slash after the n. Ko/n/ba/n/wa/

Similarly, Go/me/nna/sa/i/ Sorry, becomes Go/me/n/na/sa/i/.

Long vowels

When a vowel has a bar over it, the effect is to lengthen it to almost double the length of the regular vowel. The difference between a long vowel and a regular vowel is important in Japanese, since the meanings of many words change according to the lengths of the vowels.

aunt obasan	grandmother obāsan
bird tori	street tōri
uncle ojisan	grandfather ojīsan

The following system is used to indicate long vowels.

ā is pronounced as a/a/

ī is pronounced as i/i/

ū is pronounced as u/u/

ē is pronounced as e/e/

ō is pronounced as o/o/

ohayōgozaimasu   good morning
is pronounced as O/ha/yo/o/go/za/i/ma/su/.
arigatō   thank you
is pronounced as A/ri/ga/to/o/.
obāsan   grandmother
is pronounced as o/ba/a/sa/n/.
ojīsan   uncle
is pronounced as o/ji/i/sa/n/.

Exercise 2

Listen to the words, and write them in rōmaji. Refer to the syllable table on page 8.

1 ....

2 ....

3 ....

Double consonants

Double consonants (kk, pp, tt, ss) are given twice the length of single consonants. The first consonant is a momentary silent pause, and the second consonant is pronounced as usual.

Japan Nippon	Ni/(short pause)/po/n/
magazine zasshi	za/(short pause)/shi/
school gakkō	ga/(short pause)/ko/o/
ticket kippu	ki/(short pause)/pu

The vowels i and u are whispered (barely pronounced) when they occur between a pair of f, h, k, p, s, t, ch, sh and ts, or when they occur at the end of a sentence after f, h, k, p, s, t, ch, sh and ts. The most noticeable whispering sounds are for the verbs V•masu and desu when they occur at the ends of sentences.

Exercise 3

Listen to each word, find it in the list to the right and write the corresponding letter in the blank.

1 .... a Nippon

2 .... b tōri

3 .... c ojisan

4 .... d obasan

5 .... e gakkō

6 .... f ojī⁻san

7....................................... g tori

8 .... h obāsan

9 .... i zasshi

Exercise 4

Rewrite the following words adding slashes (/) and short pauses to indicate the syllables.

1 hajimemashite...

2 okaerinasai...

3 konnichiwa ....

4 sumimasen ....

5 otōsan ....

6 okāsan ....

7 koppu ....

8 kitte ....

day:2

Getting started

Day 2 starts with simple greetings and phrases. You will be surprised by the power of these simple greetings and phrases accompanied by a smile: in no time, you will have plenty of Japanese friends and will have begun to build your vocabulary.

BOWING...

The Japanese may bow to one another on occasions when Westerners shake hands, as well as when greeting someone or saying goodbye, and when expressing gratitude or an apology. When you bow, bend from the waist, and don't change the angle of your head: your eyes should be looking slightly downward. The legs are kept straight and the heels together. A man's arms should be held close to his sides and a woman's hands should be held in front, palms lightly touching. The lower ranking person (age, social/business status determine this) should hold the bow lower and longer.

Vocabulary

Below is a list of vocabulary encountered in this chapter.

Ohayōgozaimasu	*Good morning*	**Hai genki desu**	*I'm fine*
Konnichiwa	*Good afternoon/*	**Hai okagesamade**	*I'm fine, thank you*
Konbanwa	*Good evening*	**Dōzo**	*Please*
Oyasuminasai	*Good night*	**Gomennasai**	*Sorry*
Sayōnara	*Goodbye*	**Sumimasen**	*Excuse me/Pardon me/*
Dewa mata	*See you*		*Sorry*
Hajimemashite	*How do you do?*	**Arigatō**	*Thank you*
Dōzo yoroshiku	*Pleased to meet you*	**Dō itashimashite**	*You are welcome*
(O)genki desu ka	*How are you?*		

Grammar

Tadaima

Whenever you come home from work, school, shopping, traveling etc., you say tadaima (*I am back (now)*), as a greeting. Whoever is there will acknowledge you by saying okaerinasai (*welcome back*).

Whenever you start to eat or drink something, you say itadakimasu, implying gratitude to the person who prepared or offered it, good fortune for being able to afford it, etc. When you finish, you say gochisōsama (*thank you, it was delicious*) to the person who prepared or offered it.

Itadakimasu is also used when you accept a gift, implying both acceptance and gratitude.

Meeting and greeting

Whenever you are introduced, you say hajimemashite, dōzo yoroshiku. This phrase expresses desire for a friendly relationship in the future and may be thought as *please be good to me* in the future or *pleased to meet you*.

After you ask a favor, you say dōzo yoroshiku by itself. It means please take good care of this matter. It is also used after ni (*to*) to express kind regards to a person or persons not present, and it is translated as please give my regards to....

Dōzo yoroshiku. Pleased to meet you (in introductions).
Please do as I requested (after asking for a favor).

... ni dōzo yoroshiku. Please give my regards to ....

Exercises

Exercise 1

Listen to the phrases on the recording, and say the appropriate response aloud. Check your answers on the CD.

Exercise 2

Listen to the phrases on the CD and choose the context in which each greeting should be used.

1 ....   5 ....

2 ....   6 ....

3 ....   7 ....

4 ....   8 ....

a greeting in the morning

b when you are introduced to a stranger

c greeting in the afternoon

d when you come home from school

e greeting in the evening

f when you go to bed

g after eating

h when you part from a friend

Eating out

Day 3 is all about food. You will learn how to order items and build your knowledge of common Japanese dishes. You will learn about the singular and plurals of nouns, particles and how they affect the meaning of words and sentences, and you will become more accustomed to listening to, speaking and writing Japanese.

IRASSHAIMASE

As soon as you step into a restaurant, you will hear irasshaimase. *It is sometimes said gently with a deep bow by the waiter in charge; more often though it is said loudly by many of them, one after another.* Irasshaimase *is a greeting to a customer when he or she comes into a restaurant or a shop. It is translated as Hello and welcome! or Come in! You usually don't reply unless you know them. You may also be greeted with* irasshaimase *when you visit someone's home.*

Japanese conversation: Tenpura o kudasai.

Waitress:	Irasshaimase.
Tom:	Konnichiwa. Tenpura o kudasai.
Waitress:	Hai.
Waitress:	Dōzo.
Tom:	Arigatō.

English conversation: May I have tempura please?

Tom, an American, has just moved to Japan with his family. This is his first visit to a Japanese restaurant.

Waitress:	Hello and welcome!
Tom:	Good afternoon. May I have tempura please?
Waitress:	Certainly (Yes).

The waitress comes back with a dish of tempura.

Waitress:	Here you go.
Tom:	Thank you.

Grammar

Singular and plural nouns

Japanese nouns have no special forms to show whether they are singular or plural, and there are no articles (the, a, an) in Japanese.
Ringo can mean *an apple, apples, some apples, the apple* or *the apples*.

Similarly, most Japanese pronouns have no special forms to show whether they are singular or plural. For example, although the plural form of **kore** is **korera**, this is mainly used in academic texts and in formal writings and is not common in everyday conversation. In this book **kore** (singular form) is consistently used.

Particles

Consider the English sentence *The cat chases the mouse.* The action word, or verb, is *chases*. The subject is the person or thing doing the chasing: *the cat*. What is being chased is the direct object: *the mouse*. The meaning of the sentence is very different if the cat and the mouse are interchanged, that is: *the mouse chases the cat.*

Japanese has little words called particles, usually made out of one or two syllables (such as **wa, ga** and **o**). Particles, not word order, indicate subjects and objects in sentences. For example, **o** is placed after direct objects and **wa / ga** is placed after subjects.

Regardless of word order, it is always clear in a Japanese sentence which word is the subject and which word is the direct object. Only verbs have fixed locations: the verb comes at the end of the sentence or just before if **ka / ne / yo** follows the verb. Japanese prepositions and conjunctions are also considered particles.

Requests: Kudasai

The simplest way to ask for something is to use the sentence structure: direct object + **o kudasai**.
Kudasai is the verb meaning *May I have____ please?*
O is the particle that indicates that the preceeding word is the direct object.

May I have an apple please?	**Ringo o kudasai.**
May I have an orange please?	**Orenji o kudasai.**

Vocabulary

Below is a list of vocabulary encountered in this chapter.

fruits	kudamono		
banana	*banana*	**orange**	*orenji*
grape	*budō*	**pineapple**	*painappuru*
strawberry	*ichigo*	**apple**	*ringo*
tangerine	*mikan*	**cherry**	*sakuranbo*
peach	*momo*	**watermelon**	*suika*
pear	*nashi*	**tomato**	*tomato*

vegetables	yasai		
large white radish	*daikon*	**cucumber**	*kyūri*
Chinese cabbage	*hakusai*	**carrot**	*ninjin*
potato	*jagaimo*	**onion**	*tamanegi*

Exercises

Exercise 1

Listen to the food items, and match each with its English translation.

1 .... **a** sandwich

2 .... **b** watermelon

3 .... **c** apple

4 .... **d** coffee

5 .... **e** bread

6 .... **f** tangerine

7.. **g** potato

8 .... **h** steak

The Particles *to* and *ka*

The particle to, when used between nouns, is translated as *and* or *both*.

an apple and a tangerine	ringo to mikan
a banana and a tangerine	banana to mikan
May I have both an apple and a tangerine please?	Ringo to mikan o kudasai.

The particle ka, when used between nouns, acts like the English *either/or*.

an apple or an orange	ringo ka orenji
vegetables or fruits	yasai ka kudamono
May I have either an apple or an orange please?	Ringo ka orenji o kudasai.

Restaurants

In front of some restaurants in Japan, you will find a window display showing various dishes. The names for the dishes and their prices are displayed beside them. The displays are helpful, but it's best to know what's actually in the dishes.

Typical items on the menu

bowl of cooked rice with toppings of meat, fish, eggs and vegetables	donburi
hamburger	hanbāgā
juice	jūsu
curry	karēraisu
coffee	kōhī
meat and vegetable pancake	okonomiyaki
bread	pan
ramen (hot soup with noodles)	rāmen
sandwich	sandoicchi
salad	sarada
buckwheat noodles eaten either with a cold dipping sauce or in a hot broth	soba
meat and vegetables cooked in sweetened soy sauce	sukiyaki
raw fish placed on top of vinegared rice balls or rolled with vinegared rice	sushi
steak	sutēki
tempura (pieces of food coated with thin batter and then deep fried)	tenpura
pork cutlet	tonkatsu
thick noodles in hot soup, garnished with meat and vegetables	udon
fried noodles with meat and vegetables (Chinese chow mein)	yakisoba
small chicken pieces skewered and barbequed with sauce	yakitori

Exercise 2

Translate into English:

1 *Banana o kudasai.* ....

2 *Sushi o kudasai.* ....

3 *Sutēki to pan* ....

4 *Sutēki to pan o kudasai.* ....

5 *Kōhī ka jūsū* ....

6 *Kōhī ka jūsū o kudasai.* ....

7 *Ringo to mikan to banana o kudasai.* ....

Translate into rōmaji:

8 *May I have apples please?* ....

9 *May I have a curry please?* ....

10 *A banana or an orange* ....

11 *May I have a banana or an orange please?* ....

12 *Tempura and soba* ....

13 *May I have tempura and soba please?* ....

14 *May I have a pork cutlet, bread and coffee please?* ....

Exercise 3

You are in a restaurant. Ask a waiter for the following dishes, using the sentence structure _ o kudasai.

Say each sentence aloud, and check your answers on the CD.

1 hamburger

2 juice

3 salad

4 steak

5 coffee and sandwich

Introductions

Day 4 discusses people and introductions. You will learn how to start a basic conversation, describe yourself and your family and learn how to use the different words to mean this and that. Finally, you will build up some vocabulary and learn how to use *san* as sign of respect.

RESPECT...

Japanese has two distinct words for brother and two for sister meaning "older brother" and "younger brother", "older sister" and "younger sister". In Japanese culture, it is important to distinguish between older and younger siblings as elders automatically gain respect. That is why **san** *is used as a mark of respect. When talking to or refering to an older person, they can be called* **ojīsan, otōsan, onīsan,** *and so forth. A younger family member is referred to only by their name, without* **san***.*

Japanese conversation: Hajimemashite.

Tom:	Konnichiwa (Makoto-kun).
Makoto:	Konnichiwa (Tom-kun).
	Kore wa Sachiko desu.
	(Kore wa) imōto desu.
Sachiko:	Hajimemashite.
	Dōzo yoroshiku.
Tom:	Hajimemashite.
	(Boku wa) Tom desu.
	Dōzo yoroshiku.

English conversation: How do you do?

Tom meets Makoto who is walking with his sister Sachiko.

Tom:	Good afternoon, Makoto.
Makoto:	Good afternoon, Tom.
	This is Sachiko.
	This is (my) younger sister.
Sachiko:	How do you do?
	Pleased to meet you.
Tom:	How do you do?
	I am Tom.
	Pleased to meet you.

Grammar

Basic conversation

When Japanese people speak, they omit parts of sentences that may be understood from the context or situation. To help you understand the conversations clearly in this book, such parts are included in parentheses. While practicing the conversations, omit the parts in parentheses. Note that when a word is omitted from a conversation, the particle defining the purpose of the word in the sentence is omitted with it. For example, if a subject is omitted from a sentence, the particle wa is omitted also.

Linking verbs: is, am, are

To link subjects with complements in Japanese you use the intransitive verb desu*.

subject wa **complement** desu

The particle wa follows a subject and the complement is placed before the intransitive verb desu, which comes at the end of the sentence.
Because Japanese verbs have no special forms to show whether their subjects are singular or plural, or whether they are of the first, second or third person, desu is translated as *is, am* or *are*.

Although desu is defined as an auxiliary verb in Japanese grammar, we define it here as a linking verb since its main function is to equate one thing with another, like the English linking verb "to be".

Personal pronouns

Here are some important personal pronouns.

I, me (for boys)	boku
I, me (except boys)	watashi
you	anata

You may notice that boys use boku (*I/me*) while everybody else uses watashi (*I/me*).

To introduce yourself, just use watashi (or boku) for the subject and your name for the complement, in the sentence structure _ wa _ desu.

I am Tom.	Watashi wa Tom desu.
I am Tom.	Boku wa Tom desu.

-jin, -tachi: describing yourself and others

Jin is a suffix added to the name of a country to stand for its person/people. Although Japanese nouns have the same form for singular and plural (both *an apple* and *apples* are **ringo** in Japanese), an exception applies to people. For people, we put **tachi** after nouns and personal pronouns to make them plural.
e.g. **watashi-tachi** means *we*
Amerika-jin-tachi means *American people*

Vocabulary

Below is a list of vocabulary encountered in this chapter.

American person	*Amerika-jin*	**physician, medical doctor**	*isha*
German person	*Doitsu-jin*	**office worker**	*kaishain*
French person	*Furansu-jin*	**nurse**	*kangofu*
British person	*Igirisu-jin*	**student**	*seito*
Canadian person	*Kanada-jin*	**teacher**	*sensei*
Japanese person	*Nihon-jin*	**waiter**	*uētā*
foreigner	*gaijin*	**waitress**	*uētoresu*
baby	*akachan*		
child	*kodomo*		
adult	*otona*	**I am an American.**	*Watashi wa Amerika-jin desu.*
friend	*tomodachi*		
student (of a school)	*gakusei*	**I am a student.**	*Watashi wa gakusei desu.*
dentist	*ha-isha*		

Suffixes

A Japanese person has two names, a family name and a first name, and uses them in that order (for example, Hepburn *Audrey*). You may address a person by their family name or first name, according to your degree of acquaintance, but the following suffixes must be added to either name:

-chan is added after the names of small children and especially after girl's names
e.g. **Amy-chan**, *Amy*.

-kun is added after boy's names
e.g. **Bob-kun**, *Bob*.

-san is added after names; it is comparable to Mr. or Ms.
e.g. **Smith-san**, *Mr./Ms. Smith;* **Betty-san**, *(Ms.) Betty*.

-sensei is added after the names of teachers (of any kind) and medical doctors
e.g. **Kelly-sensei**, *Mr./Ms./Dr. Kelly*.

Suffixes should never be used when you are speaking about yourself. Teachers and medical doctors have a high social status in Japan. In a culture where showing respect for one another is important, it would be rude not to add **sensei** after their names.

You are Mr. Tom Kelly.	**Anata wa Kelly Tom-san desu.**
You are Makoto.	**Anata wa Makoto-kun desu.**
Hanako is a baby.	**Hanako-chan wa akachan desu.**

Exercises

Exercise 1

Someone is introducing herself/himself to you. Listen carefully and answer the following questions in rōmaji by filling in the blanks.

1 Who am I?

Anata wa Hanako-san desu.

Am I Japanese, American or Canadian?

Anata wa .... desu.

Am I a teacher? A student?

Anata wa .... desu.

2. Who am I?

Anata wa .... -kun desu.

Am I Japanese, American or Canadian?

Anata wa .... desu.

Am I a teacher? A student?

Anata wa .... desu.

Exercise 2

How should you address these people? Write chan, san, kun or sensei in the blanks.

1 Mr. Kelly, your school teacher

Kelly ....

2 Hiroshi, a 12-year old boy

Hiroshi ....

3 Noriko, a 5 year old girl

Noriko ....

4 Dr. Nakamura, your physician

Nakamura ....

This, that, and (that) over there: *kore*, *sore* and *are*

To introduce and talk about things or people, you need to learn pronouns such as *this* and *that*.

When you refer to things you use kore, sore and are.

this	kore	*indicates a thing/person near the speaker.*
that	sore	*indicates a thing/person near the listener.*
that	are	*indicates a thing/person away from the speaker and the listener.*

Note: it is fine to use the above to refer to younger siblings or your sons and daughters as on page 22.

This is Mr. Smith.	Kore wa Smith-san desu.
This is Hanako.	Kore wa Hanako-san desu.

When you refer to people (especially those to whom you should show respect, such as teachers, medical doctors or elders), you use **kochira, sochira** and **achira.**

this	kochira	*a person near the speaker*
that	sochira	*a person near the listener*
that	achira	*a person away from the speaker and the listener*

Vocabulary - Family

To introduce your family, use the following vocabulary.

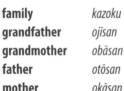

family	*kazoku*
grandfather	*ojīsan*
grandmother	*obāsan*
father	*otōsan*
mother	*okāsan*
older (elder) brother	*onisan*
older (elder) sister	*onēsan*
younger brother	*otōto*
younger sister	*imōto*
uncle	*ojisan*
aunt	*obasan*

This is (my) father.
Kochira wa otōsan desu.

(My) father is a teacher.
Otōsan wa sensei desu.

This is (my) younger brother.
Kore wa otōto desu.

(My) younger brother is a student.
Otōto wa gakusei desu.

Husband and wife

Japanese has different words for wife and husband, depending on whose husband and whose wife, as may be seen below.

my wife	kanai
my husband	shujin
somebody else's wife	okusan
somebody else's husband	goshujin

Both shujin and goshujin mean master as well as husband.

Exercise 3

Listen to Tom as he introduces a member of his family. Who did he introduce? Write the answer in English.

1 ....

2 ....

3 ....

Exercise 4

Listen to the track for Exercise 3 again, and fill in the blanks with the correct words in rōmaji.

1 **What does Tom's father do?** Otōsan wa.......................................desu.

2 **What does Tom's mother do?** .... wa...................................desu.

3 **What nationality is Tom's mother?** ....wa ....desu.

4 **Are Tom and his brother Ken both students?** Hai, ... to .... wa gakusei desu.

5 **How do you know that Ken is older than Tom?** Ken wa ....desu.

Vocabulary - Animals

To talk about animals, use the following vocabulary.

animals	*dōbutsu*	**This is a cow.**
duck	*ahiru*	*Kore wa ushi desu.*
squirrel	*risu*	**That is a dog.**
pig	*buta*	*Sore wa inu desu.*
monkey	*saru*	**That (over there) is a cat.**
snake	*hebi*	*Are wa neko desu.*
racoon dog	*tanuki*	**These are a dog and a cat.**
dog	*inu*	*Kore wa inu to neko desu.*
tiger	*tora*	
giraffe	*kirin*	
bird	*tori*	
bear	*kuma*	
horse	*uma*	
cat	*neko*	
rabbit	*usagi*	
mouse, rat	*nezumi*	
cow	*ushi*	
lion	*raion*	
elephant	*zō*	

This, that and (that) over there for places: *koko*, *soko* and *asoko*

Unlike English, Japanese has many different words for this and that. When you talk about a thing or person, you use **kore, sore** and **are** (or **kochira, sochira** and **achira**). When you talk about this and that related to a place, you must use **koko, soko** and **asoko.**

this (place)	**koko**	*a place near the speaker*
that (place)	**soko**	*a place near the listener*
that (place)	**asoko**	*a place away from both the speaker over there and the listener*

Exercise 5

Imagine yourself visiting a zoo. Listen to the descriptions, and answer the following in English.

1 What animals are nearby? ....

2 What animal is in the distance? ....

3 What animal is very far away? ....

Vocabulary - Places

Use any of these words in the sentence structure _ **wa** _ **desu** to describe location.

bus stop	*basu-sutoppu/basu-tei*	**washroom**	*toire*
hospital	*byōin*	**apartment**	*apāto*
department store	*depāto*	**house, home**	*ie*
zoo	*dōbutsuen*	**high-class apartment**	*manshon*
(railway) station	*eki*	**house, home**	*uchi*
school	*gakkō*	**river**	*kawa*
bank	*ginkō*	**lake**	*mizūmi*
airport	*hikōjō/kūkō*	**sea**	*umi*
hotel	*hoteru*	**mountain**	*yama*
bookstore	*hon-ya*		
shrine	*jinja*		
park	*kōen*	Example sentences:	
toy shop	*omocha-ya*		
restaurant	*resutoran*	**This (place) is a department store.**	
Japanese inn	*ryokan*	*Koko wa depāto desu.*	
temple	*(o)tera*		
kindergarten	*yōchien*	**That (place) is a zoo.**	
post office	*yūbinkyoku*	*Soko wa dōbutsuen desu.*	
kitchen	*daidokoro*		
bathroom	*furoba*	**That (place over there) is a (railway) station.**	
family room	*ima*		
garden	*niwa*	*Asoko wa eki desu.*	
washroom (polite)	*otearai*		

Exercise 6

Write the correct pronoun in the blanks: kore, sore, are, koko, soko or asoko.

1 To describe the cat you are holding:

....wa neko desu.

2 To describe the station you are in:

....wa eki desu.

3 To describe the dog near you, but not too close:

....wa inu desu.

4 To describe the toilet near you, but not too close:

....wa toire desu.

5 To describe the horse far away from you:

....wa uma desu.

6 To describe the airport far away from you:

....wa kūkō desu.

Exercise 7

Translate into English:

1 *Watashi wa Hanako desu* ....

2 *Kochira wa Amy-san desu.*...

3 *Kore wa neko desu.* ....

4 *Are wa imōto to otōto desu.* ....

5 *Achira wa sensei desu.* ....

Translate into rōmaji:

6 *I am Betty.* ....

7 *We are students.* ....

8 *This is (my) mother.* ....

9. *These are pigs and cows.* ....

10. *Betty is (my) younger sister.* ....

Exercise 8

Translate the following using the _ wa _ desu sentence structure. Say each sentence aloud. Check your sentences against the correct answers on the CD.

1 **Your younger sister who is beside you** ....

2 **Your older sister who is near you**...

3 **Your father who is far away** ....

4 **The cat you are holding** ....

5 **The bird in the sky** ....

6 **The bank we are in** ....

7 **The mountain far away** ....

Writing Exercise

For each Japanese character, there is a standard order in which the different parts of the character should be drawn, as well as a standard way of drawing each part. For the writing exercises in this book, follow the boxes from left to right for the order of the strokes. There are three basic rules for each part of a character:

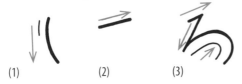

1. If the part is vertical or nearly vertical, it is drawn from top to bottom.
2. If the part is horizontal or nearly horizontal, it is drawn from left to right.
3. If, the part is strongly curved, it is usually drawn from the higher end to the lower end.
Remember that once you start to draw part of a character, you continue it until the end of that part.

Practice the five hiragana characters **a, i, u, e, o**:

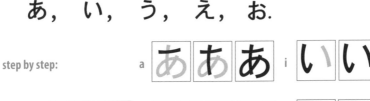

step by step:

Family

Day 5 is all about the family. You will learn to talk about people and ask questions. You will also learn how to say yes and no, and further practice writing *hiragana*. Practice speaking Japanese by following the audio CD and through the exercises.

PERSONAL SEALS

In Japan, people do not sign their names as in the West. Instead, they use personal seals, which have exactly the same significance as a signature. Every time you want to withdraw or deposit money at a counter at a bank, you must use your personal seal.

Japanese conversation 1: Hajimemashite.

Hanako:	(Anata wa) Tom-kun desu ka.
Tom:	Hai sō desu. Anata wa (dare desu ka).
Hanako:	(Watashi wa) Hanako desu.
	Dōzo yoroshiku.
Tom:	Dōzo yoroshiku.
Hanako:	(Anata wa) Kanada-jin desu ka.
Tom:	Iie (boku wa) Kanada-jin de wa arimasen.
	(Boku wa) Amerika-jin desu.
Hanako:	(Kore wa) chizu desu.
	Amerika wa doko desu ka.
Tom:	(Amerika wa) koko desu.

English conversation 1: How do you do?

This is Tom's first day at his new college. He meets Hanako, who is eager to make conversation.

Hanako:	Are you Tom?
Tom:	Yes, I am. And you are?
Hanako:	I'm Hanako.
	Pleased to meet you.
Tom:	Pleased to meet you too.
Hanako:	Are you Canadian?
Tom:	No, I'm not Canadian. I'm American.
Hanako:	This is a map.
	Where is America?
Tom:	America is here.

Japanese conversation 2: Kore wa kazoku desu.

Tom:	Konnichiwa.
Hanako:	Konnichiwa. Dōzo.
***	
Tom:	(Kore wa) purezento desu.
Hanako:	Arigatō. (Kore wa) nan desu ka.
Tom:	(Kore wa) sakuranbo desu.
***	

Hanako:	Kore wa kazoku desu.
Tom:	(Kore wa) okāsan desu ka.
Hanako:	Iie (sore wa) okāsan de wa arimasen.
	(Sore wa) onēsan desu.
	Onēsan wa gakusei desu.
Tom:	(Kore wa) imōto-san desu ka.
Hanako:	Hai (sore wa) imōto desu.
Tom:	Namae wa (nan desu ka).
Hanako:	(Namae wa) Mari desu.
Tom:	Koko wa doko desu ka.
Hanako:	(Soko wa) kōen desu.

English conversation 2: This is (my) family

Tom visits Hanako with a present.

Tom:	Good afternoon.
Hanako:	Good afternoon. Please come in.

Tom takes his shoes off and enters the family room.

Tom:	This is (a present) for you.
Hanako:	Thank you. What is it?
Tom:	These are cherries.

Hanako shows Tom her family photograph.

Hanako:	This is my family.
Tom:	Is this your mother?
Hanako:	No, that's not my mother.
	That's my older sister.
	My older sister is a student.
Tom:	Is this your younger sister?
Hanako:	Yes, it is.
Tom:	What's her name?
Hanako:	Her name is Mari.
Tom:	Where is this (place)?
Hanako:	That (place) is a park.

Grammar

Questions

In Japanese, the particle **ka** at the end of a statement converts it into a question; no question mark is used. **Ka** is pronounced with slightly higher pitch.

This is tempura.   **Kore wa tenpura desu.**
Is this tempura?   **Kore wa tenpura desu ka.**

You are Makoto.   **Anata wa Makoto-kun desu.**
Are you Makoto?   **Anata wa Makoto-kun desu ka.**

This (place) is a (railway) station.   **Koko wa eki desu.**
Is this (place) a (railway) station?   **Koko wa eki desu ka.**

* When an interrogative sentence is abbreviated and ka is omitted, the last syllable of the last word is pronounced with slightly higher pitch, to denote that it is a question.

Yes and No

To answer questions, use *yes* or *no*.
hai yes   **iie** no

Now, you may answer questions as follows.

Hai kore wa tenpura desu.   Yes, this is tempura.
Iie kore wa yakitori desu.   No, this is yakitori.

Quite often, people abbreviate replies by saying just **hai sō desu**, which should be translated accordingly.

Anata wa Tom-kun desu ka.   Are you Tom?
Hai sō desu.   Yes, I am.
Asoko wa eki desu ka.   Is that the station?
Hai sō desu.   Yes, it is.
Are wa Hanako-san desu ka.   Is that Hanako?
Hai sō desu.   Yes, it is.

Hai

When you are talking to a Japanese person, you will hear **hai** regulary. If you think that he/she is agreeing with you about everything, you are probably mistaken. **Hai** in this case means "I am hearing you". Some people may nod or utter approving sounds instead of saying **hai**.

Exercises

Exercise 1

You will hear a statement in Japanese. Convert it into a question and say it back.
Check your replies against the answers recorded on the CD. Then translate the
questions into English and write them below.

1 ....

2 ....

3 ....

4 ....

5 ....

Negative statements

A negative statement for *subject* wa *complement* **desu** is:
 subject wa *complement* **de wa arimasen.**

This is a pencil.	**Kore wa enpitsu desu.**
This is not a pencil.	**Kore wa enpitsu de wa arimasen.**
Are you Makoto?	**Anata wa Kakoto-kun desu ka.**
No, I am not Makoto.	**Iie boku wa Makoto de wa arimasen.**
I am Hiroshi.	**Boku wa Hiroshi desu.**
Is this (place) Tokyo?	**Koko wa Tōkyō desu ka.**
No, this (place) is not Tokyo.	**Iie koko wa Tōkyō de wa arimasen.**
This (place) is Nagoya.	**Koko wa Nagoya desu.**

Exercise 2

Listen to the statements. Convert what you hear into negative statements and
check your answers on the CD.

Exercise 3

Translate into English:

1 *Sumimasen. Koko wa yūbinkyoku desu ka.* ....

Iie koko wa yūbinkyoku de wa arimasen. ....

Koko wa ginkō desu. ....

2 *Tom-kun wa Furansu-jin desu ka..* ....

Iie Tom-kun wa Furansu-jin de wa arimasen. ....

Tom-kun wa Amerika-jin desu.. ....

Translate into rōmaji:

3 *Are you Amy?* ....

No, I am not Amy. ....

I am Betty. ....

4 *Are you American?* ....

No, I am not American. ....

I am German. ....

Interrogative pronouns

| who | dare | where, which place | doko |
| which one | dore | what | nan/nani |

By replacing nouns with interrogative pronouns for simple statements, you can convert them into questions. Let's suppose that you want to make the sentence *What is this?* Start by considering one possible answer to the question *"What is this?"*

Start with the statement:	**Kore wa hon desu.**	This is a book.
Since *What is this?* is a question, put **ka** at the end:	**Kore wa hon desu ka.**	Is this a book?
Since **hon** is what you are asking about and it is a "thing," replace **hon** with **nan**, *what*:	**Kore wa nan desu ka.**	What is this?

Now you can go one step further.

What is this?	Kore wa nan desu ka.
Replace **kore** with **tenpura** to get:	
What is tempura?	Tenpura wa nan desu ka.

By changing **nan**, *what*, to **dore**, *which one*, in the above sentence, you get:

Which one is tempura?	Tenpura wa dore desu ka.

Let's do the same thing with another sentence, using **dare**, *who*. **Dare** replaces a "person" as follows:

You are Makoto.	Anata wa Makoto-kun desu.
Are you Makoto?	Anata wa Makoto-kun desu ka.
Who are you?	Anata wa dare desu ka.
Who is the teacher?	Sensei wa dare desu ka.

Let's try one more example using the question word **doko**, *where*. **Doko** replaces a "place" as follows:

This (place) is a post office.	Koko wa yūbinkyoku desu.
Is this (place) a post office?	Koko wa yūbinkyoku desu ka.
Where is this (place)?	Koko wa doko desu ka.
Where is the toilet?	Toire wa doko desu ka.

* Japanese grammar classifies **dare** as a pronoun and **nan** as a demonstrative pronoun. We have followed the classification of English grammar.

Exercise 4

Listen to the questions and look at the picture. Reply to each question aloud in a full sentence and write it below.

1 ....

2 ....

3 ....

(1)

(2)

(3)

Exercise 5

a Make a statement by writing *rōmaji* in the blank space.

b Turn the statement into a question.

c Write *nan/dare/doko* in the blank to ask *what/who/where*.

1a. Kore wa .... desu. This is (my) grandmother.

b. Kore wa .... desu ka. Is this (my) grandmother?

c. Kore wa .... desu ka. Who is this?

2a. Kore wa .... desu. This is a carrot.

b. Kore wa .... desu ka. Is this a carrot?

c. Kore wa......................... desu ka. What is this?

3a. Koko wa......................... desu. This is a park.

b. Koko wa......................... desu ka. Is this a park?

c. Koko wa .... desu ka. Where is this?

Exercise 6

Listen to the statements and questions on the CD, and answer below in rōmaji.

1 ....

2 ....

3 ....

4 ....

Exercise 7

Say the following sentences aloud in Japanese. Check your answers on the CD.

1 What is this (beside me)?

2 What is that (near you)?

3 What is that (far away)?

4 Who is this (beside me)?

5 Who is that (near you)?

6 Who is that (far away)?

7 Where is this place (we are in)?

8 Where is that place?

9 Where is that place (far away)?

Exercise 8

Translate into English:

1 *Are wa nan desu ka.* ....

 Are was hon desu. ....

2 *Koko wa doko desu ka.* ....

 Koko wa kōen desu. ....

3 *Ie wa doko desu ka.* ....

Translate into rōmaji:

4 *Who is that (over there)?* ....

 That (over there) is a teacher. ....

5 *Where is this (place)?* ....

 This is a department store ....

6 *Who are you?* ....

 I am Peter ....

Exercise 9

You will hear some questions about Dialogue 2. Reply to the questions
aloud in Japanese, in full sentences. Check your answers against the CD.

Writing exercise

Practice the five hiragana characters ka, ki, ku, ke and ko.

か, き, く, け, こ.

step by step: ka か か か ki き き き

ku く ke け け け ko こ こ

Mine or yours?

Day 6 introduces the word *no* and explains how it can be used to make personal pronouns, adjectives, etc. You will also build your vocabulary and become more practiced at writing hiragana and understanding Japanese.

HOLIDAYS...

*A working person usually has three one-week holidays a year in Japan: New Year's Holiday, **Golden-Week** (a string of national holidays from April 29 to May 5) and **O-Bon** in mid August. **O-Bon** is a Buddhist festival to commemorate deceased family members. According to Japanese tradition, spirits of the deceased return home once a year to be reunited with their families. Homes are decorated with **chochin** laterns and offerings of food are left out.*

Japanese conversation: (Kore wa) anata no (nōto) desu ka.

Hanako:	(Kore wa) watashi no (nōto) desu
	(Kore wa) anata no (nōto) desu ka.
Tom:	Iie (sore wa) boku no (nōto) de wa arimasen.
	(Sore wa) Makoto-kun no (nōto) desu.

English conversation: Is it yours or mine?

Tom and Hanako sort through a pile of notebooks to find theirs.

Hanako:	This is mine.
	Is this yours?
Tom:	No, it's not mine.
	It's Makoto's.

Vocabulary

Here is some new vocabulary that you'll use in this lesson.

pencil	enpitsu	umbrella	kasa
book	hon	eyeglasses	megane
notebook	nōto	wallet/ purse	saifu
pen	pen	chair	isu
handbag	handobaggu	table	tēburu
briefcase	kaban	desk	tsukue

Grammar

The particle *no*

The idea of possessive adjective (my, your, etc.) is expressed using the personal pronoun watashi, anata, etc., followed by no.

For example:

Hanako-san no hon   Hanako's book

It may be easier to think that **no** has the same function as **'s** in English, with the **'s** signifying posession.

Tom's book	Tom no hon
my book	watashi no hon
your book	anata no hon
my father	watashi no otōsan
your father	anata no otōsan

Note: The possessors do not have to be personal pronouns; they can be nouns, such as father, mother, dog, etc.

father's chair	otōsan no isu
mother's chair	okāsan no isu
dog's chair	inu no isu

Exercises

Exercise 1

Say the following phrases aloud in Japanese. Check your answers on the CD.

1 my book

2 your book

3 (my) younger brother's book

4 my father

5 your father

6 Tom's father

Using *no* to describe locations

name of a place no noun

No between two nouns can also express something other than possession. If the first noun is a name of a place, it describes the origin or location of the second noun.
In other words, **no** turns the **place** or **noun** into an **adjective**.

Italian handbag	Itaria no handobaggu
Japanese apple	Nihon no ringo
Tokyo station	Tōkyō no eki
London airport	Rondon no kūkō

Vocabulary

countries	*kuni*	**Japan**	*Nippon*
China	*Chūgoku*	**abroad**	*gaikoku*
Germany	*Doitsu*	**capitals**	*shuto*
France	*Furansu*	**Washington**	*Washinton*
Britain	*Igirisu*	**Paris**	*Pari*
Italy	*Itaria*	**London**	*Rondon*
Canada	*Kanada*	**Tokyo**	*Tōkyō*
Japan	*Nihon*		

Using *no* to describe nouns

A (noun) no   B (noun)

No is also used between two nouns where the first noun describes the second. In this case, the first noun is neither a person nor a place, and **A no B** is translated as *B of/for/in/on A*.

school teacher (teacher of school)	gakkō no sensei
book on sport	supōtsu no hon

Using *no* more than once

No can be used more than once in a sentence:

watashi no Eigo no hon
Consider eigo no hon first. It means an *English book*.
Then consider watashi no *English book: my English book*.

watashi no gakkō no sensei
Consider watashi no gakkō first. It means *my school*.
Then consider *my school* no sensei: *teacher of my school*.

watashi no otōsan no hon
Consider watashi no otōsan first. It means *my father*.
Then consider *my father* no hon: *my father's book*.

Koko wa watashi no sensei no ie desu.
This (place) is my teacher's house.

Japanese conversation 2: (Kore wa) Eigo no hon desu ka.

Hanako:	(Kore wa) anata no (hon) desu ka.
Tom:	Hai (sore wa) boku no (hon) desu.
Hanako:	(Kore wa) Eigo no hon desu ka.
Tom:	Iie (sore wa) Eigo no hon de wa arimasen.
	(Sore wa) Furansu-go no hon desu.

English conversation 2: Is it a book in English?

Tom and Hanako are going through a pile of books to find Tom's book.

Hanako:	Is this yours?
Tom:	Yes, it's mine.
Hanako:	Is it a book in English?
Tom:	No, it's not a book in English.
	It's a book in French...

The suffix -*go*

The suffix **-go** is added to the name of a country for its language (just as **-jin** is used for its people). e.g. **Furansu-go** *French language*. Note that there are exceptions to the rule such as **Eigo** *English*.

German language	**Doitsu-go**
English language	**Eigo**
French language	**Furansu-go**
Italian language	**Itaria-go**
Japanese language	**Nihon-go**
Japanese language student *(student of the Japanese language)*	**Nihon-go no gakusei**
English language school *(school for the English language)*	**Eigo no gakkō**
English book *(book in the English language)*	**Eigo no hon**

Exercise 2

Listen to the phrases on the CD. Repeat the Japanese, then write the English translation.

1 teacher's pen

2 ....

3 ....

4 ....

5 ....

6 ....

Exercise 3

Write rōmaji in the blanks to translate the following phrases.

1. Hanako's sister: Hanako-san no imōto

2. our table: ....no ....

3. Tom's country: ....no ....

4. British capital: ....no..

5. magazine in the English language:

....no ....

6. books on food: ....no..

Japanese conversation 3: Kore wa nan no hon desu ka.

Hanako:	(Kore wa) dare no megane desu ka.
Tom:	(Kore wa boku no) okāsan no (megane) desu.
	(Kore wa) Itaria no (megane) desu.
Hanako:	Kore wa nan no hon desu ka.
Tom:	(Kore wa) kudamono no hon desu. (Kore wa) okāsan no (hon) desu.

English conversation 3: Whose glasses are these?

Hanako visits Tom's house and sees many things that interest her on a table.

Hanako:	Whose glasses are these?
Tom:	They're my mother's.
	They're Italian.
Hanako:	What kind of book is this?
Tom:	It's a book on fruit. It's my mother's.

Interrogatives + *no*

You can ask more questions using the interrogative pronouns **dare**, *who*; **nan**, *what* and **doko**, *where*. Let's suppose that you want to make the sentence *Whose book is this?* Remember to make interrogative sentences by starting with a simple statement and changing it into a question. To do this, consider a simple statement that could be an answer to the question *Whose book is this?*

You start with the statement:	**Kore wa watashi no hon desu.**	This is my book.
Put **ka** at the end to form a question:	**Kore wa watashi no hon desu ka.**	Is this my book?
Since **watashi** is a **person**, replace it with **dare** *(who):*	**Kore wa dare no hon desu ka.**	Whose book is this?

Let's do the same thing with another sentence, using **nan** *what (kind of)*. **Nan** replaces a **thing**.

Kore wa Eigo no hon desu.	This is an English book.
Kore wa Eigo no hon desu ka.	Is this an English book?

Replace **Eigo** with **nan** to get:

Kore wa nan no hon desu ka.	What (kind of) book is this?

Let's try one more example using the question word doko *(where)*. Doko replaces a place:

Koko wa Tōkyō no eki desu.   This is Tokyo station.
Koko wa Tōkyō no eki desu ka.   Is this Tokyo station?

Replace Tōkyō with doko to get:
Koko wa doko no eki desu ka.   Which station is this?

Exercise 4

Listen to the various replies to the question: Kore wa dare no hon desu ka.

Write down whose book it is in English.

1 father's

2 ....

3 ....

4 ....

5 ....

Exercise 5

Write wa, o, ka, to or ni in the blanks, and translate the sentences into English.

1 Koko ....gakkō desu.   <u>This is a school.</u>

2 Koko ....gakkō desu ka. ....

3 Koko...............................anata .... gakkō desu ka................................

....

4 Koko...............................anata ....onēsan ....

gakkō desu ka. ....

5 Pen...............................kudasai...

6 Pen...............................enpitsu .... kudasai.

<u>May I have a pen and a pencil please?</u>

7 Pen...............................enpitsu ....kudasai.

<u>May I have a pen or a pencil please?</u>

Exercise 6

Write **nan, doko** or **dare** in the blanks so that the replies are appropriate.

1 Question: Koko wa ....no shuto desu ka.

Reply: Koko wa Chūgoku no shuto desu.

2 Question: Kore wa .... no handobaggu desu ka.

Reply: Kore wa onēsan no handobaggu desu.

3 Question: Kore wa .... no shashin desu ka.

Reply: Kore wa Itaria no isu no shashin desu.

Exercise 7

Translate these sentences into English.

1 *Sensei no isu* ....

2 *Okāsan no saifu* ....

3 *Hanako-san no otōsan* ....

4 *Kore wa watashi no okāsan desu.* ....

5 *Sore wa watashi-tachi no inu desu.* ....

6 *Koko wa doko no kuni desu ka.* ....

   Koko wa Itaria desu. ....

Translate into rōmaji:

7 *My Friend* ....

8 *Your family* ....

9 *This is (my) mother's umbrella* ....

10 *May I have my notebook please?* ....

....

11 *I am a student of the English language.* ....

....

12 *What kind of fruit is this?* ....

   This is a watermelon. ....

Writing exercise

Practice the five hiragana characters sa, shi, su, se **and** so.

さ, し, す, せ, そ.

Step by step:

sa

shi

su

se

so

Eating out

Day 7 takes you to a restaurant. You will learn all about Japanese verbs and how to order, as well as how to ask questions and pick up essential vocabulary. Finally, you will pick up some more information about Japanese culture.

SAKE...

Sake is a drink made from fermented rice. Sometimes known as "rice wine". When you drink sake with other people, you should never pour your own drink. Instead, make sure you pour your companions' drinks, and they will return the favor.

Japanese conversation: (Hanako-san wa) nani o nomimasu ka.

Tom:	(Hanako-san wa) nani o nomimasu ka.
Hanako:	(Watashi wa) orenji-jūsu o nomimasu.
	(Tom-kun wa) nani o nomimasu ka.
Tom:	(Boku wa) tomato-jūsu o nomimasu.
	(Anata wa) nani o tabemasu ka.
Hanako:	(Watashi wa) tenpura o tabemasu.
Tom:	Tenpura wa niku desu ka.
	(Tenpura wa) sakana desu ka.
Hanako:	(Tenpura wa) sakana desu.
Tom:	Boku wa karēraisu to pan o tabemasu.

English conversation: What will you drink?

Tom and Hanako look at the show window of a restaurant to decide what to order.

Tom:	What will you drink?
Hanako:	I'll drink orange juice.
	What will you drink?
Tom:	I'll drink tomato juice.
	What will you eat?
Hanako:	I'll eat tempura.
Tom:	Is tempura meat
	or (is it) fish?
Hanako:	It is fish.
Tom:	I'll have curry and bread.

Grammar

V•masu verbs

Japanese verbs can be separated into two groups: **desu** and **V•masu** verbs. **V•masu** verbs are a verb form + an auxillary verb **masu**. They are used for the polite style of speech, which is the most commonly used style and the one you should use. Below is a list of **V•masu** verbs. You will notice that every verb ends in **masu**. The verbs listed below are transitive verbs (verbs which may have direct objects).

wash	araimasu
speak	hanashimasu
buy	kaimasu
write, draw	kakimasu
listen to, hear, ask for	kikimasu
see, watch	mimasu
learn	naraimasu
drink	nomimasu
send	okurimasu
eat	tabemasu
take	torimasu
make	tsukurimasu
sell	urimasu
read	yomimasu

Nouns

Since these are transitive verbs, you need to learn nouns that may be direct objects.

drinks	nomimono
Japanese green tea	(o)cha
English tea	kōcha
milk	miruku
water	mizu
Japanese rice wine	sake
wine	wain
candy	ame
candy, sweet	okashi
meat	niku
pork	buta-niku
beef	gyū-niku
chicken (meat)	tori-niku
fish	sakana
voice, cry	koe
music	ongaku
radio	rajio
song	uta
newspaper	shinbun
letter	tegami
magazine	zasshi
picture, painting	e

movie	eiga
television	terebi
direction	hōkō
stamp	kitte

Forming sentences

A transitive **V·masu** verb has the sentence structure:

subject wa **direct object** o **V·masu**

I wash a dog.	Watashi wa inu o araimasu.
A dog sees a cat.	Inu wa neko o mimasu.
The younger brother eats an apple.	Otōto wa ringo o tabemasu.
Mother writes a letter.	Okāsan wa tegami o kakimasu.
Father reads a newspaper.	Otōsan wa shinbun o yomimasu.
The dog drinks water.	Inu wa mizu o nomimasu.
Father buys a newspaper.	Otōsan wa shinbun o kaimasu.
I learn English.	Watashi wa Eigo o naraimasu.
The younger sister makes bread.	Imōto wa pan o tsukurimasu.

Note:

A Japanese verb can be translated into more than one verb in English, and vice versa.
For instance, **kikimasu** can be translated as *hear, ask for* and *listen to*.

I hear a bird's cry.	Watashi wa tori no koe o kikimasu.
I ask for directions.	Watashi wa hōkō o kikimasu.
I listen to the music.	Watashi wa ongaku o kikimasu.

Exercises

Exercise 1

Say the following sentences aloud in Japanese, and check your answers against the CD.

1 *I eat fish.*

2 *I drink milk.*

3 *I speak English.*

4 *I read newspapers.*

5 *I buy candy.*

6 *I listen to the music.*

7 *I learn Japanese.*

Exercise 2

Listen to the phrases and write in English who does what.

1 ....

2 ....

3 ....

4 ....

5 ....

6 ....

7 ....

Questions

To ask a question using V•masu verbs, just as with desu verbs, add the particle ka at the end of the statement.

You eat an apple.	**Anata wa ringo o tabemasu.**
Do you eat an apple?	**Anata wa ringo o tabemasu ka.**

The next step is to ask questions such as *What do you eat?*, *What do you drink?* and *What do you read?* nan *(what)* is used before a word starting with n/d/t. Note that nan comes before desu and *no*.

Is this a book?	Kore wa hon desu ka.
What is this?	Kore wa nan desu ka.
Is this an English book?	Kore wa Eigo no hon desu ka.
What (kind of) book is this?	Kore wa nan no hon desu ka.

nani is used before a word starting with **any other letter**. Note that nani comes before o.

Do you buy apples?	Anata wa ringo o kaimasu ka.
What do you buy?	Anata wa nani o kaimasu ka.
What do you drink?	Anata wa nani o nomimasu ka.
What do you eat?	Anata wa nani o tabemasu ka.

You can add suffixes such as -jin *(people)* and -go *(language)* to nani directly:

| nani-jin | what nationality? |
| nani-go | what language? |

Exercise 3

Write either nan or nani in the blanks and then translate the sentences into English.

1 Anata wa .... *no niku o tabemasu ka.*

What meat do you eat?

2 Anata wa .... *-go o hanashimasu ka.*

....

3 Anata wa .... *o nomimasu ka.*

....

Exercise 4

Translate into English:

1 *Watashi wa terebi o mimasu.* ....

2 *Watashi to otōto wa Nihon-go o naraimasu.* ....

....

3 *Otōsan wa shinbun to zasshi o yomimasu.* ....

4 *Watashi-tachi wa ongaku o kikimasu.* ....

....

5 *Anata wa Nihon-go o hanashimasu ka.* ....

....

6 *Anata wa nani o tabemasu ka.* ....

....

7 *Anata wa nan no hon o yomimasu ka.* ....

....

8 *Anata wa nani o kaimasu ka.* ....

....

9 *Anata wa nani o tsukurimasu ka.* ....

....

Translate into rōmaji**:**

10 *We read Japanese books.* ....

11 *We learn English.* ....

12 *I listen to Japanese music.* ....

....

13 *Does your father drink sake?* ....

....

14 *What language do you speak?* ....

....

15 *What do you drink?* ....

....

16 *What (kind of) fruit do you eat?* ....

....

17 *What (kind of) book do you read?* ....

....

18 *What movie do you watch?* ....

....

Future tense

In Japanese, **V-masu** verbs have the same form for both the present and future tenses. This is not the case for **desu**.

Watashi wa ringo o tabemasu may be translated as *I eat an apple* or *I will eat an apple*.

There is rarely any confusion as to which translation to choose because the context usually makes the tense clear. Vocabulary, such as the words shown below, may also be used to indicate the future tense.

tomorrow	ashita
next year	rainen
next week	rai-shū

Education

Day 8 teaches you how to answer questions and also make negative statements. You will also learn how to accept or decline food and will learn about the Japanese education system.

THE SCHOOL SYSTEM...

Elementary schools and secondary schools are compulsory, and enrollment and literacy rates are essentially 100%. More than 90% of secondary school graduates go on to high school.

Japanese society judges people by the schools they attend, and careers depend greatly on the university from which one graduates. Because of this, the competition to get into a good university is fierce. To get into a good university, one has to get into a good high school, and to do that one has to first get into a good secondary school.

Japanese conversation: Amerika

Hanako:	Amerika no kodomo-tachi wa Nihon-go o naraimasu ka.
Tom:	Iie naraimasen.
Hanako:	(Amerika no kodomo-tachi wa) nani o naraimasu ka.
Tom:	(America no kodomo-tachi wa) Eigo to Furansugo to chiri to kagaku to sansū o naraimasu.
Hanako:	Amerika-jin wa nani-go o hanashimasu ka.
Tom:	(Amerika-jin wa) Eigo o hanashimasu.
Hanako:	Amerika-jin wa nani o tabemasu ka.
Tom:	(Amerika-jin wa) niku to yasai to pan o tabemasu.

English conversation: America

Hanako asks Tom about America.

Hanako:	Do American children learn Japanese?
Tom:	No, they don't.
Hanako:	What do they learn?
Tom:	They learn English, French, geography, science and arithmetic.
Hanako:	What language do Americans speak?
Tom:	They speak English.
Hanako:	What do Americans eat?
Tom:	They eat meat, vegetables and bread.

Grammar

Answering questions

You can answer a question with hai + a positive verb (for a positive reply) or iie + a negative verb (for a negative reply).

Question	Answer
Anata wa Nihon-go no hon o yomimasu ka. Do you read Japanese books?	Hai yomimasu/ hanashimasu. Yes, I do.
	or
Anata wa Itaria-go o hanashimasu ka. Do you speak Italian?	Iie yomimasen/ hanashimasen. No, I don't.

Negatives

For the verbs ending with masu, you can make negative statements by changing masu into masen.

I wash a dog.	Watashi wa inu o araimasu.
I do not wash a dog.	Watashi wa inu o araimasen.
(My) younger brother speaks English.	Otōto wa Eigo o hanashimasu.
(My) younger brother does not speak English.	Otōto wa Eigo o hanashimasen.
Mother makes bread.	Okāsan wa pan o tsukurimasu.
Mother does not make bread.	Okāsan wa pan o tsukurimasen.

Negative V•masu + *ka*

The negative V•masu verb + ka, meaning *Would you like to. . . ?*, is primarily used in one-to-one conversations. The subject, which is always the person to whom you are speaking, is usually dropped.

Question	Answer
Eiga o mimasen ka. Would you like to see a movie?	Hai mimasu/yomimasu. Yes, I would.
Kore o yomimasen ka. Would you like to read this?	*or*
	Iie mimasen/yomimasen. No, I would not.

Offering food

When the expression _masen ka is used with respect to food or drinks, replies are a little tricky. Let us look at the following example in which someone offers you a coffee.

Question	
Would you like to drink coffee?	Kōhī o nomimasen ka.

Replies	
Yes, I would.	Hai nomimasu.
No, I would not.	Iie nomimasen.

In the example, a speaker suggests coffee without specifying who will provide it. For instance, when you are walking on a street with a friend, he may suggest having a coffee. You do not know whether he is thinking of buying coffee for you, or going Dutch. If that is the case, the above replies are appropriate.

When it is obvious that someone is offering you a coffee, such as when you are in his home, more polite replies are appropriate. You may recall that **itadakimasu**, *thank you,* is the phrase used to accept an offer with gratitude. To refuse with gratitude, use the phrase below.

Yes, thank you.	Hai itadakimasu.
(accepting with gratitude)	
No, thank you.	Iie kekkō desu.
(rejecting with gratitude)	

Exercises

Exercise 1

Fill in the table below.

Meaning	Positive verb	Negative verb
read	yomimasu	yomimasen
	torimasu	
sell		
		okurimasen
	nomimasu	

Exercise 2

Listen to the speaker describing her younger sister. Answer the following questions in rōmaji, using only hai or iie and a verb, e.g., hai tabemasu, iie tabemasen.

1 *Watashi no imōto wa miruku o nomimasu ka.* ....

....

2 *Watashi no imōto wa (o)-cha o nomimasu ka.* ....

....

3 *Watashi no imōto wa shinbun o yomimasu ka.* ....

....

4 *Watashi no imōto wa Nihon-go o naraimasu ka.* ....

....

5 *Watashi no imōto wa terebi o mimasu ka.* ....

....

6 *Watashi no imōto wa Eigo o hanashimasu ka.* ....

....

Exercise 3

Translate into English:

1 *Boku wa inu o araimasen.* ....

2 *Onēsan wa niku o tabemasen.* ....

3 *Okāsan wa kudamono o kaimasen.* ....

....

4 *Imōto wa pan o tsukurimasen.* ....

5 *Otōto wa otōsan no hon o yomimasen.* ....

....

6 *Watashi wa Eigo o hanashimasen.* ....

7 *Anata wa Doitsu-go o naraimasu ka. Iie naraimasen.* ....
....

Translate into rōmaji:

8 *I do not write letters.* ....
....

9 *(My) mother does not drink milk.* ....
....

10 *Makoto does not eat udon.* ....
....

11 *Tom does not read newspapers.* ....
....

12 *I do not listen to the music.* ....
....

13 *I do not speak Japanese.* ....
....

14 *Are you going to buy this? No, I am not.* ....
....

Japanese conversation 2: Bideo o mimasen ka.

Hanako:	Bideo o mimasen ka.
Tom:	(Bideo wa) nan no bideo desu ka.
Hanako:	(Bideo wa) inu no eiga desu.
	(Eiga wa) Dizunī no manga desu. Eiga wa Eigo desu.
Tom:	Hai mimasu.

Dizunī	Disney
manga	cartoon
bideo	video

English conversation 2: Would you like to watch a video?

Hanako suggests that Tom watch a video with her.

Hanako:	Would you like to watch a video?
Tom:	What kind of video is it?
Hanako:	It's a movie of a dog.
	It's a Disney cartoon. The movie is in English.
Tom:	Yes, I'll watch it.

Exercise 4

The speaker will suggest an activity. Write down the suggestion in English.

1 ....

2 ....

3 ....

4 ....

5 ....

Exercise 5

Say the following sentences aloud in Japanese and check your answers on the CD.

1 Would you like to drink?

2 Would you like to watch?

3 Would you like to buy?

4 Would you like to learn Japanese?

5 Would you like to eat chow mein?

Exercise 6

Translate into English:

1 *Kore o mimasen ka.* ....

2 *Furansu-go o naraimasen ka.* ....

3 *Ongaku o kikimasen ka.* ....

4 *Nihon-go o hanashimasen ka.* ....

5 *Sushi o tabemasen ka.* ....

    Hai itadakimasu. ....

6 *Mizu o nomimasen ka.* ....

    Iie kekkō desu. ....

Translate into rōmaji:

7 *Would you like to speak English?* ....

....

8 *Would you like to draw a picture?* ....

....

9 *Would you like to listen to Japanese music?* ....

....

10 *Would you like to learn German?* ....

....

11 *Would you like to drink Japanese green tea? Yes, thank you.*

....

Writing exercise

Practice the five hiragana characters ta, chi, tsu, te and to.

た， ち， つ， て， と.

step by step: ta た た た た   chi ち ち

tsu つ   te て   to と と

Vocabulary

Here is some of the vocabulary you have encountered in this chapter.

geography	*chiri*	the national	*kokugo*
history	*rekishi*	language	
science	*kagaku*	mathematics	*sūgaku*
arithmetic	*sansū*		

day:9

Food

Day 9 continues to talk about food and also introduces some new activities. You will learn how to make more complicated sentences, expanding on what you have already learnt, further build your vocabulary and be able to practice what you have learned.

CHOPSTICKS AND TABLE MANNERS...

A traditional Japanese meal consists of small servings of many different colorful dishes, all served together on separate trays. Japanese use chopsticks to eat, and food is served in bite-sized pieces. Remember to use one hand to hold chopsticks and the other to pick up bowls and plates. Never dig chopsticks into rice or any other food. It is regarded as very bad manners: sticking chopsticks into rice is only done at funerals. When you are not using chopsticks, rest the "eating end" on a plate or on a chopsticks-rest.

Japanese conversation: tabemasu

Hanako:	Yakisoba o tabemasen ka.
Tom:	Hai itadakimasu.
Hanako:	(Anata wa yakisoba o) (o)hashi de tabemasu ka.
	Hōku de tabemasu ka.
Tom:	(Boku wa yakisoba o) hōku de tabemasu.
Hanako:	(Anata wa) nani o (o)hashi de tabemasu ka.
Tom:	(Boku wa) sakana o ((o)hashi de) tabemasu.

English conversation: Eat

Hanako offers Tom yakisoba.

Hanako:	Would you like to eat yakisoba?
Tom:	Yes, thank you.
Hanako:	Do you eat it with chopsticks or a fork?
Tom:	I will eat it with a fork.
Hanako:	What do you eat with chopsticks?
Tom:	I eat fish.

Grammar

The Particle De

Using the V•masu-verbs you have learned in the previous lesson, you can say many simple sentences such as *I eat an apple, I read a book, etc.* By using the particle **de**, you can expand on those sentences. The particle **de** following a noun has two uses. One is to indicate "how", or "with what instrument", something is done. Translated according to context, it can mean *in/with/by.* Be careful not to confuse this with the "with" of accompaniment *(I go to school with Makoto)*.

I wash a dog with water. (with what?)	Watashi wa inu o mizu de araimasu.
I wash a dog by hand. (with what?)	Watashi wa inu o te de araimasu.
Father writes a letter with a pen. (with what?)	Otōsan wa tegami o pen de kakimasu.
Father writes a letter in English. (how?)	Otōsan wa tegami o Eigo de kakimasu.

Vocabulary

To describe the instrument you use to do something, you will often need to mention parts of the body, eating utensils or modes of transportation. The vocabulary below will be useful for describing how or with what instrument you do many things.

body	*karada*	**stomach, abdomen**	*onaka*
leg	*ashi*	**hand**	*te*
head	*atama*	**arm**	*ude*
nose	*hana*	**finger**	*yubi*
hair	*kami*	**chopsticks**	*hashi*
face	*kao*	**fork**	*hōku*
shoulder	*kata*	**knife**	*naifu*
mouth	*kuchi*	**spoon**	*supūn*
eye	*me*	**bus**	*basu*
ear	*mimi*		

De to describe a place

The second use of **de** is to **express action in a place**.
Translated according to context, it can mean *in/at/on*.

I wash a dog in the garden	**Watashi wa inu o niwa de arimasu.**
I read a magazine on a bus.	**Watashi wa zasshi o basu de yomimasu.**
Father draws a picture at a mountain.	**Otōsan wa e o yama de kakimasu.**

De with the verb *desu*

One of the first things you will do when you get friendly with a Japanese person is to ask for words in Japanese. It's a great way to build your vocabulary.

De is used with the verb **desu** when you want to ask for words in Japanese.
Consider **Kore wa nan desu ka** *What is this?*
By inserting **Nihon-go de**, you get **Kore wa Nihon-go de nan desu ka**, *What is this in Japanese?*

Similarly, let's consider **Kore wa RINGO desu**, *This is "RINGO".* By inserting **Nihon-go de**, *in Japanese,* you get **Kore wa Nihon-go de RINGO desu**, *This is "RINGO" in Japanese.* By changing **Kore** with *APPLE,* you get **"APPLE" wa Nihon-go de RINGO desu**, *APPLE is "RINGO" in Japanese.*

What is TOKEI in English?	**TOKEI wa Eigo de nan desu ka.**
It's WATCH.	**(TOKEI wa Eigo de) WATCH desu.**
What is SANGURASU in English?	**SANGURASU wa Eigo de nan desu ka.**
It's SUNGLASSES.	**(SANGURASU wa Eigo de) SUNGLASSES desu.**

Exercises

Exercise 1

You will hear a Japanese word for a body part. Write the English for each one, in order as they appear on the CD.

1 ....

2 ....

3 ....

4 ....

5 ....

6 ....

7 ....

8 ....

9 ....

10 ....

11 ....

12 ....

13 ....

Exercise 2

Say the following sentences aloud in Japanese. Write your answers below and check your pronunciation against the CD.

1 I write a letter with (my) hand. [not with a computer] ....
....

2 I write a letter in the garden. ....

3 I write a letter with a pen. ....

4 I write a letter in English. ....

5 I eat steak in the kitchen. ....

6 I eat steak with knife and fork..

Exercise 3

Translate into English:

1 *Watashi wa udon o (o)hashi de tabemasu.* ....
....

2 *Onēsan wa Eigo no uta o rajio de kikimasu.* ....
....

3 *Anata wa tegami o nan de kakimasu ka.* ....
....

4 *Otōsan wa hon o heya de yomimasu.* ....
....

5 *Watashi-tachi wa Eigo o gakkō de naraimasu.* ....
....

6 *Okāsan wa kudamono o niwa de tsukurimasen.* ....
....

7 *Ojī san wa pan o doko de kaimasu ka.* ....
....

Translate into rōmaji:

8 *Hanako washes a cat with water.* ....
....

9 *We eat meat with knife and fork.* ....
....

10 *Grandmother reads books with glasses.* ....
....

11 *Elephants eat bananas with (their) trunks (noses).* ....
....

12 *I do not write a letter in Japanese.* ....

....

13 *Do you learn music at school?* ....

....

14 *I do not speak Japanese at home.* ....

....

Exercise 4

Translate into English:

1 *Kore wa Nihon-go de nan desu ka.* ....

....

2 *Kore wa Eigo de nan desu ka.* ....

....

Exercise 5

Make sentences by putting appropriate words in the blanks.

1 .... *wa Nihon-go de MIZU desu.*

2 *ASHI wa Eigo de* .... *desu.*

3 *NEKO wa Eigo de* .... *desu.*

4 *DOG wa Nihon-go de* .... *desu.*

5 .... *wa Eigo de BOOK desu.*

Exercise 6

When you hear a question, reply to it aloud in a full sentence in Japanese.

Write your answers below and check your pronunciation on the CD.

1 ....

2 ....

3 ....

4 ....

Word order

Day 10 focuses on the importance of word order in Japanese to give you a solid foundation on which to build your knowledge of the language. You will also learn to write some more *hirigana* characters.

YO...

Yo *at the end of a sentence highlights what the speaker is saying. It acts like an exclamation mark in English.*

That is our bus! **Are wa watashi-tachi no basu desu yo.**

We will eat (meals)! **Watashi-tachi wa (gohan o) tabemasu yo.**

Japanese conversation: Are wa Kazuko-san desu ne.

Tom:	Are wa Kazuko-san desu ne.
Hanako:	Iie (are wa) Yōko-san desu yo.
	(Yōko-san wa) Kazuko-san no onēsan desu yo.
	(Yōko-san wa) watashi no onēsan no tomodachi desu.

English conversation: That's Kazuko, isn't it?

Tom sees a familiar face and asks Hanako who she is.

Tom:	That's Kazuko, isn't it?
Hanako:	No, that's Yoko!
	Kazuko's older sister!
	She is (my) older sister's friend.

Grammar

The Particle *ne*

You will often hear ne at the end of a sentence. This particle at the end of a sentence solicits agreement from the listener. According to the context, it can mean *Isn't it?, Don't you?,* etc.

| That is a book, isn't it? | Are wa hon desu ne. |
| You'll eat an apple, won't you? | Anata wa ringo o tabemasu ne. |

The Particle *to*

When the particle to follows a person, it means *together/ along with.*

| I watch a movie with Hanako. | Watashi wa eiga o Hanako-san to mimasu. |
| Would you like to eat lunch with me? | Ranchi o watashi to tabemasen ka. |

Word Order

Particles may be separated into three categories, depending on where they appear in sentences.

1. **Ka, ne, yo:** placed at the end of a sentence, after the verb, meaning *Isn't it?*

2. **To, ka, no:** put between words, meaning *and*, *or*, and in the case of **no**, *possessive*, *origin of*, or *of/for/in/ on*. These particles always stay between words.

3. **Wa, o, de, to, (ni, ga, e, kara):** describe and follow nouns/pronouns. They make a noun/pronoun the subject, the direct object, the adverb clause, etc. A **noun/pronoun + its particle** can be put anywhere in a sentence before a verb.

Note that **ka** appears in two different locations for two different purposes in sentences: one for questions at the end of sentences, and another to mean *or* between words. **To** also appears in two different locations: one between nouns/pronouns meaning *and* and another after nouns/pronouns meaning *with*.

Verbs always come either at the end of sentences or just before **ka/ne/yo** (placed at the end of sentences). Complements, which are not followed by any particle, must come before the verb **desu**.

The following sentences all mean the same thing:

Anata wa inu o niwa de araimasu ka.   Do you wash the dog in the garden?
Anata wa niwa de inu o araimasu ka.
Inu o anata wa niwa de araimasu ka.
Inu o niwa de anata wa araimasu ka.
Niwa de anata wa inu o araimasu ka.
Niwa de inu o anata wa araimasu ka.

To make learning easier, we will basically stick to the sentence structure SUBJECT + DIRECT OBJECT + OTHERS + V·MASU-VERB + KA/NE/YO. That is, we write Anata wa inu o niwa de araimasu ka, rather than any other forms shown above.

Word order with *desu*

The following sentences both mean the same thing:
APPLE wa Nihon-go de RINGO desu yo.   APPLE is RINGO in Japanese!
Nihon-go de APPLE wa RINGO desu yo.

You can see that the verb **desu** always comes before the particle **yo**. The complement RINGO, which is not followed by any particle, comes before **desu**. The noun/pronoun + its particles (APPLE wa and Nihon-go de) are interchangable. As with V·masu verbs, we will keep to the sentence structure:
SUBJECT + OTHERS + COMPLEMENT + DESU + KA/NE/YO.

The noun/pronoun + to/ka/no + noun/pronoun is treated as one unit.

Watashi wa <u>inu to neko</u> o araimasu.   I wash the dog and the cat.
<u>Inu to neko</u> o watashi wa araimasu.

Watashi wa <u>otōsan no hon</u> o yomimasen.   I do not read (my) father's book.
<u>Otōsan no hon</u> o watashi wa yomimasen.

Watashi wa terebi o <u>Hanako-san ka Makoto-kun</u> to mimasu. I watch TV with Hanako or Makoto.
<u>Hanako-san ka Makoto-kun</u> to watashi wa terebi o mimasu.

Exercises

Exercise 1

You will hear a sentence. Convert it into a sentence that solicits an agreement from the listener. Say it out loud and write it in rōmaji, then check your answers against the CD.

1 ....

2 ....

3 ....

4 ....

5 ....

Exercise 2

Say the following sentences aloud in Japanese.
Check your answers against the CD.

1 I drink coffee with a friend.

2 I watch TV with my family.

3 I speak Japanese with my older brother.

4 I learn Japanese with my younger brother.

5 I listen to the music with my mother.

Exercise 3

Translate into English:

1 *Watashi wa ongaku o Makoto-kun to kikimasu.* ....

....

2 *Sukiyaki o watashi-tachi to tabemasen ka.* ....

....

3 *Anata wa Eigo o dare to hanashimasu ka.* ....

....

4 *Anata wa Hanako-san desu ne.* ....

....

5 *Are wa boku-tachi no basu desu yo.* ....

....

Translate into rōmaji:

6 *What do you make with Makoto?* ....

....

7 *Would you like to watch a video with me?* ....

....

8 *I will not speak with Hanako.* ....

....

9 *That is the hospital, isn't it?* ....

....

10 *This is mine!* ....

....

Exercise 4

Rewrite the following sentences in as many different orders as possible.

1 Tom-kun wa Nihon-go to Eigo o hanashimasu yo...

....

....

....

2 Watashi wa Hanako-san to ranchi o tabemasu..

....

....

....

3 Anata no namae wa Hanako-san desu ka. ....

....

....

....

Writing exercise

Practice the five hiragana characters na, ni, nu, ne and no.

な, に, ぬ, ね, の.

Step by step: na   ni

nu ne   no

Numbers

Day 11 talks about numbers, including money and dates. You will also learn the days of the week and the months. Listen carefully to the audio to become accustomed to deciphering numbers.

EYE CONTACT...

When Japanese people talk face to face, they do not make direct eye contact. This is considered intimidating; it is interpreted not as a sign of interest and respect, but as an indication of the speaker's defiance. Japanese people may smile not just when they are happy or amused, but also when they are sad or embarrassed. They generally refrain from showing negative emotions in public so as not to make others feel uncomfortable.

Japanese conversation: Kore wa ikura desu ka.

Tom:	Kore wa ikura desu ka.
Clerk:	(Kore wa) go-hyaku kyū-jū-en desu.
Tom:	Kore wa (ikura desu ka).
Clerk:	(Kore wa) roppyaku san-jū-en desu.
Tom:	Kore o kudasai.

English conversation: How much is this?

Tom goes shopping.

Tom:	How much is this?
Clerk:	It's 590 yen.
Tom:	How about this?
Clerk:	It's 630 yen.
Tom:	May I have this please?

Numbers

0	zero		
1	ichi	9	kyū/ku*
2	ni	10	jū
3	san	100	hyaku
4	yon/shi*	1,000	sen
5	go	10,000	man
6	roku	100,000	jū-man
7	nana/shichi*	1,000,000	hyaku-man
8	hachi		

* Note that 4, 7 and 9 have two forms in Japanese. The second forms given for 4, 7 and 9 are not used as multipliers.

Grammar

Forming large numbers

Multiple-digit numbers are formed the same way in Japanese as they are in English.
For instance, 2,457 is expressed as **2 sen** *(thousand)* + **4 hyaku** *(hundred)* + **5 jū** *(ten)* + **7**
The 2, 4 and 5 are called multipliers and the 7 is simply called the last digit.

A five digit number is expressed as:

multiplier -man + multiplier -sen + multiplier -hyaku + multiplier -jū + last digit

↑	↑	↑	↑	↑
ten thousands	thousands	hundreds	tens	ones

Some numbers change spelling when **hyaku** and **sen** are combined with multipliers: they are **sanbyaku**, *300;* **roppyaku**, *600;* **happyaku**, *800;* **sanzen**, *3000* and **hassen**, *8000*. The multiplier **ichi**, *1,* is used only for **ichi-man**, *10,000*, and not used for **sen**, *1,000*, **hyaku**, *100* and **jū**, *10*. Hence 11,111 is **ichi-man sen hyaku jū ichi**. You can now say any number from 1 to 1,000,000 in Japanese.

5,263   **go-sen ni-hyaku roku-jū san**
7,928   **nana-sen kyū-hyaku ni-jū hachi**

Money

The suffix **-en** is used to tell an amount of money.
-en, also written as **¥_**, is translated as _ *yen*.
For example, **ni-hyaku-en**, *¥200*, means *200 yen*.

Ikura: How much?

Ikura is used to ask *how much.*
Let's try to make the sentence *How much is this?* Start with the statement **Kore wa ni-hyaku-en desu**, *This is 200 yen.* Put **ka** at the end to form a question, *Is this 200 yen?* Then replace **ni-hyaku-en** with **ikura,** to get **Kore wa ikura desu ka**, *How much is this?*

Exercises

Exercise 1

Say the numbers from 1 to 10, and then 100, 1,000, and 10,000 aloud.

Check your answers against the CD.

Exercise 2

You will hear some Japanese telephone numbers. Write them down.
Japanese telephone numbers are expressed as "number for the area code –
number for the exchange – number." The numbers are said individually; no is used for
hyphens and ban, *number,* is put at the end; 2 and 5 are pronounced as nī and gō when
describing telephone numbers.

1 072-856-7211

2 ....

3 ....

Exercise 3

Translate into English:

1 ni-sen nana-hyaku san-jū ni ....

....

2 san-man yon-sen go-hyaku roku-jū hachi ....

....

3 yon-sen kyu-hyakū hachi-jū ichi...

....

Translate into rōmaji:

4 735 ....

5 5,241 ....

6 9,726 ....

Exercise 4

You have asked a shop clerk Kore wa ikura desu ka *How much is this?*
Listen for the replies. Write down the amount you hear in English.

1 .... yen

2 .... yen

3 .... yen

4 .... yen

Days and Months

It is very easy to express months in Japanese, just put the suffix -gatsu after a number to indicate the month. Yon, *4;* nana, *7* and kyū, *9,* are not used to indicate the months; instead, the alternate forms of 4, 7, and 9 (shi, shichi and ku, respectively) are used. The numbers associated with the month, day, hour and minutes are written without hyphens. That is, instead of jū-ni, *12,* jūni is used to write jūni-gatsu, *December;* instead of san-jū-ichi, *31,* sanjūichi is used to write sanjūichi-nichi, *31st.*

Months

January	ichi-gatsu	July	shichi-gatsu
February	ni-gatsu	August	hachi-gatsu
March	san-gatsu	September	ku-gatsu
April	shi-gatsu	October	jū-gatsu
May	go-gatsu	November	jūichi-gatsu
June	roku-gatsu	December	jūni-gatsu

Dates

Dates within a month are slightly more complicated, and you must memorize the
1st to the 10th. The suffix -nichi is put after the numbers to form the rest of the days
of the month except the 14th, 20th and 24th. Note that shi, *4;* nana, *7* and
kyū, *9,* are not used to indicate dates.

1st	tsuitachi	18th	jūhachi-nichi
2nd	futsuka	19th	jūku-nichi*
3rd	mikka	20th	hatsuka
4th	yokka	21st	nijūichi-nichi
5th	itsuka	22nd	nijūni-nichi
6th	muika	23rd	nijūsan-nichi
7th	nanoka	24th	nijūyokka*
8th	yōka	25th	nijūgo-nichi
9th	kokonoka	26th	nijūroku-nichi
10th	tōka	27th	nijūshichi-nichi/
11th	jūichi-nichi		nijūnana-nichi
12th	jūni-nichi	28th	nijūhachi-nichi
13th	jūsan-nichi	29th	nijūku-nichi*
14th	jūyokka*	30th	sanjū-nichi
15th	jūgo-nichi	31st	sanjūichi-nichi
16th	jūroku-nichi		
17th	jūshichi-nichi/		
	jūnana-nichi		

Days

The days of the week don't follow any rules except that they all carry the suffix -yōbi.

Monday	getsu-yōbi
Tuesday	ka-yōbi
Wednesday	sui-yōbi
Thursday	moku-yōbi
Friday	kin-yōbi
Saturday	do-yōbi
Sunday	nichi-yōbi

Dates

To say the date in Japanese, start with the year, followed by the month, followed by the day of the month, followed by the day of the week. This is written as year/month/date/day of the week. The suffix –nen, *year*, is put after a number for the year.

Nisen jūyo-nen go-gatsu nanoka getsu-yōbi

Monday 7 May 2014

Ni-sen jūgo-nen san-gatsu itsuka sui-yōbi

Wednesday 5 March 2015

The suffixes associated with dates are summarized below.

-gatsu is put after a number to tell the month.

-nen is put after a number to tell the year.

-nichi is put after some numbers to tell the date.

-yōbi denotes the day of the week.

Exercise 5

You will hear the birthday of each of Hanako's family members.

Write down the date for each of them in English.

The Japanese words for birthday are (o)tanjōbi/bāsudē.

1 Father's birthday is ....

2 Mother's birthday is ....

3 The older sister's birthday is ....

4 Hanako's birthday is ....

5 The younger sister's birthday is ....

Exercise 6

Following the example, write and then say the dates of the holidays in Japanese. Check your answers against the CD.

1 1 January (O)shōgatsu *New Year's Day*

Ichigatsu tsuitachi wa (o)shogatsu desu. January 1 is New Year's Day.

2 3 March (Hinamatsuri, *The Festival of Dolls,* **regarded as festival for girls**) ....

....

3 5 May (Kodomo no hi, *Children's Day,* **regarded as festival for boys**) ....

....

4 7 July (Tanabata, *The Festival of Stars,* **celebration of the annual tryst of stars Altair and Vega, separated by the Milky Way**) ....

....

5 25 December (Kurisumasu, *Christmas*)..

....

6 31 December (Ōmisoka, *New Year's Eve*) ....

....

Exercise 7

Translate into English.

1 *Ni-sen ni-nen san-gatsu itsuka sui-yōbi*

....

2 *Ni-sen-nen roku-gatsu nijūgo-nichi getsu-yōbi*

....

3 *Sen kyū-hyaku hachi-jū ichi-nen san-gatsu futsuka do-yōbi*

....

4 *Sen nana-hyaku ni-jū roku-nen hachi-gatsu jūku-nichi nichi-yōbi*

....

Translate into rōmaji:

5 *Saturday 14 February 2004*

....

6 *Wednesday 28 October 1579*

....

7 *Sunday 5 July 1400*

....

8 *Monday 1 January 2001*

....

Writing exercise

Practice the five hiragana characters **ha, hi, fu, he** and **ho**.

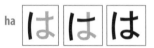

Step by step:

ha

hi

fu

he

ho

day: 12

Telling the time

Day 12 focuses on how to tell the time. You will also learn how to count items that are classified such as objects, animals and people. Finally, you will learn the difference between polite, plain and honorific speech in Japanese.

TIME...

The suffixes and nouns associated with time are collected below.

han   *half past hour*   **gogo**   *p.m.*

mae   *before(hour)/(minutes)to*   **gozen**   *a.m.*

sugi   *after(hour)/(minute)past*

-fun/pun   *is put after a number to tell minutes, and it is translated as minutes.*

-ji   *is put after a number to tell the hour, and it is translated as o'clock.*

Japanese conversation: Ima (wa) nan-ji desu ka.

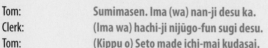

Tom:	Sumimasen. Ima (wa) nan-ji desu ka.
Clerk:	(Ima wa) hachi-ji nijūgo-fun sugi desu.
Tom:	(Kippu o) Seto made ichi-mai kudasai.
	(Kippu wa) ikura desu ka.
Clerk:	(Kippu wa) yon-hyaku hachi-jū-en desu.

***

Tom:	(Kore wa) sen-en desu.
Clerk:	(O)tsuri wa go-hyaku ni-jū-en desu.
Tom:	Densha wa nan-ji desu ka.
Clerk:	(Densha wa) ku-ji go-fun desu.
Tom:	Purattohōmu wa doko desu ka.
Clerk:	(Purattohōmu wa) ni-ban sen desu.

English conversation: What time is it now?

Tom buys a train ticket at a station.

Tom:	Excuse me. What time is it now?
Clerk:	It is just gone 8:25.
Tom:	May I have 1 ticket to Seto please?
	How much is it?
Clerk:	It is ¥480.

Tom puts money on the money-receiving tray.

Tom:	This is ¥1000.
Clerk:	The change is ¥520.
Tom:	What time is the train?
Clerk:	It's at 9:05.
Tom:	Where is the platform?
Clerk:	It's the (train) line number 2.

Hours

Hours are formed by putting the suffix -ji after the numbers, with the exception of yo-ji, *four o'clock,* which has gone through a phonetic change (from yon-ji).

1 o'clock	ichi-ji	7 o'clock	shichi-ji*
2 o'clock	ni-ji	8 o'clock	hachi-ji
3 o'clock	san-ji	9 o'clock	ku-ji*
4 o'clock	yo-ji*	10 o'clock	jū-ji
5 o'clock	go-ji	11 o'clock	jūichi-ji
6 o'clock	roku-ji	12 o'clock	jūni-ji

* Note that shi 4, nana 7 and kyū 9 are not used to indicate hours.

Minutes

The minutes are shown below. To form 2 to 9 minutes, add -pun or -fun after the numbers. Ip-pun, *1 minute,* and jup-pun, *10 minutes,* have gone through phonetic changes. Notice that there are two forms for 8 minutes and they are used interchangeably.

1 minute	ip-pun	7 minutes	nana-fun**
2 minutes	ni-fun	8 minutes	hachi-fun
3 minutes	san-pun	8 minutes	hap-pun
4 minutes	yon-fun**	9 minutes	kyū-fun**
5 minutes	go-fun	10 minutes	jup-pun
6 minutes	rop-pun		

** Note that shi (4), shichi (7) and ku (9) are not used to indicate minutes.

Minutes 10 to 60

When you put jū, *10;* nijū, *20;* sanjū, *30;* yonjū, *40* and gojū, *50* before the minutes 1 to 9, you can form *11 minutes, 12 minutes, 59 minutes, etc.* You obtain 20, 30, 40, 50 and 60 minutes by putting ni, *2;* san, *3;* yon, *4;* go, *5* and roku, *6,* in front of jup-pun, *10 minutes;* this forms nijup-pun, sanjup-pun, yonjup-pun, gojup-pun and rokujup-pun respectively.

Putting 10 in front of 1, 2, 3 and 4 minutes, you get:

jū-ip-pun	11 minutes
jū-ni-fun	12 minutes

jū-san-pun	13 minutes
jū-yon-fun	14 minutes

Putting 20 in front of 1, 2, 3 and 4 minutes, you get:

nijū-ip-fun	21 minutes
nijū-ni-fun	22 minutes
nijū-san-pun	23 minutes
nijū-yon-fun	24 minutes

Putting 30, 40 and 50 in front of 1 minute, you get:

sanjū-ip-pun	31 minutes
yonjū-ip-pun	41 minutes
gojū-ip-pun	51 minutes

Putting 50 in front of 5 and 6 minutes, you get:

gojū-go-fun	55 minutes
gojū-rop-pun	56 minutes

How to tell the time

In Japanese, you tell the time by saying the hour followed by the minute. It is written *hour:minute* just like it is in English.

2:15	ni-ji jūgo-fun
9:35	ku-ji sanjūgo-fun

Japanese has expressions such as *before/after* the hour just like English does. In these cases, **mae/sugi**, *before/after,* is put after the hour to indicate *before* or *after* as follows.

before 3 o'clock	san-ji mae
after 3 o'clock	san-ji sugi

Japanese has expressions such as *to/past* the hour just like English does. In these cases, **mae/sugi** is put after the minutes to indicate *to* or *past.*

5 minutes to 3 o'clock	san-ji go-fun mae
5 minutes past 3 o'clock	san-ji go-fun sugi

Although there is no special word for a quarter of an hour, Japanese has **han** for *half past,* which is put after the hour. For example, 9:30 can be expressed in the following ways:

9:30	ku-ji sanjup-pun
half past 9	ku-ji han

Gozen and gogo are used for *a.m.* and *p.m.*, and they come before the hour.

| 2:15 p.m. | gogo ni-ji jūgo-fun |
| 9:35 a.m. | gozen ku-ji sanjūgo-fun |

Other suffixes associated with numbers

One of the more difficult features of the Japanese number system is the concept of classifiers, special words that are attached after numbers to show categories of objects to which they belong. For instance, in English, you talk of *two sheets of paper* (rather than *two papers*), *three cups of water* (rather than *three waters*) or *two pieces of cake*.

The words *sheet, cup* and *piece* are called classifiers because they classify the category of things, namely papers, liquid and slices.

In the Japanese number system, most things are described in terms of classifiers. The following vocabulary lists the classifiers associated with counting animals, just to illustrate a few of the many classifiers that exist in Japanese.

-hiki is put after a number to count animals such as dogs, tigers, rabbits*, fish and insects.
-tō is put after a number to count animals such as whales, cows and horses.
-nin is put after a number to count people.
-wa is put after a number to count animals such as rabbits*, and birds such as ducks and chickens.

Classifiers go through some phonetic changes when they are combined with some numbers (e.g., ichi-hiki becomes ippiki).
Here are two more important suffixes.
-ban is put after a number to tell the order. For example, ichi-ban means number one; ni-ban means number two; etc.
-mai is put after a number to count thin flat objects such as stamps, papers, tickets, plates, blankets, etc.

Numbers are not followed by any particle.
| May I have three tickets please? | Kippu o san-mai kudasai. |
| Mother buys two fish. | Okāsan wa sakana o ni-hiki kaimasu. |

* Note that rabbits are counted with both -hiki and -wa.

How to ask the date and time

The prefix nan-, what, is put before nen, gatsu, nichi, yōbi, ji and fun to obtain the following expressions.

nan-nen	What year?
nan-gatsu	What month?
nan-nichi	What date (of the month)?
nan-yōbi	What day of the week?
nan-ji	What time?/What hour?
nan-fun	How many minutes?

You can ask the date and time using the following words.

now	ima
today	kyō

What day (month and day) is it today?
Kyō wa nan-gatsu nan-nichi desu ka.

It's the 20th of March.
(Kyō wa) san-gatsu hatsuka desu.

What day of the week is the 3rd of March?
San-gatsu mikka wa nan-yōbi desu ka.

What time is it now?
Ima (wa) nan-ji desu ka.

It is 3 o'clock.
(Ima wa) san-ji desu.

Japanese Speech Style

There are three levels of speech in Japanese: polite, plain and honorific.

Polite speech

Polite speech is used in formal situations, such as when you speak in public, in business, while shopping, and to strangers or superiors. It is characterized by the use of the polite verbal forms desu and V•masu. In this book, you will learn polite speech. It is safer to be polite than plain, and honorific speech is not called for on the part of a foreign speaker.

Plain speech

Plain speech is used in informal, everyday situations among family, friends, equals, or when addressing children. For example, if you replace desu with da in a polite-style sentence, it will become a plain-style sentence: kore wa inu da is a plain form of kore wa inu desu, *this is a dog*. Similarly, by changing the endings of V•masu-verbs, you may convert polite-style V•masu-verb sentences into plain-style sentences. For example, mizu o nomu is a plain form of (watashi wa) mizu o nomimasu.

Honorific speech

Use honorific speech to express respect. For example, a clerk in a shop would use honorific speech to a customer; if you were talking to your teacher or supervisor, you would use honorific speech. There are two ways to show your respect for others in honorofic speech.

Method 1: The most common form of expressing your respect is by using o or go as a prefix to nouns and adjectives when referring to the person or his belongings.
Kore wa boku no tegami desu.
This is my letter.
Kore wa sensei no (o)tegami desu.
This is the teacher's letter.

In some words, honorific prefixes have become so common that they have lost their honorific meaning and are thought of as a part of words. For instance, (o)cha is almost always used to mean *tea*: its plain form cha is rarely used. Not every noun or adjective takes an honorific prefix and there is no specific rule as to whether a word is prefixed by o or go. You should not try to make honorific words up by yourself until you have reached a more advanced level of proficiency in the language.

Another common way of expressing your respect is to add -san to a person's family, as shown below.
Kore wa anata no imōto-san desu ka.
Is this your younger sister?
Hai kore wa watashi no imōto desu.
Yes, this is my younger sister.

Method 2: You may show your respect by using humble terms for yourself and your belongings. Expressing deeper respect for the other person creates a greater distance between you both, and, unless you are advanced in Japanese, you should not try to use honorific speech.

Exercises

Exercise 1

You will hear some times in Japanese. Write down each time in English.

1 ....

2 ....

3 ....

4 ....

5 ....

6 ....

Exercise 2

Say the following times aloud in Japanese, and check your answers on the CD.

1 2:15

2 4:30

3 6:00

4 8:40

5 10:20

6 12:00

Exercise 3

Translate into English:

1 *jūichi-ji nijūgo-fun sugi* ....

2 *ku-ji jūnana-fun mae* ....

3 *gogo roku-ji sanjup-pun* ....

4 *go-ji han* ....

Write the times in rōmaji and say them aloud:

5 1:15 p.m. ....

6 12:30 p.m. ....

7 6:45 a.m. ....

8 7:23 p.m. ....

Writing exercise

Practice writing the five hiragana characters **ma**, **mi**, **mu**, **me** and **mo**

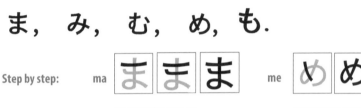

Step by step:

ma  me

mi mo

mu

Vocabulary

Below is a list of vocabulary encountered in this chapter.

electric train	densha	**change**	(o)tsuri
platform	purattohōmu	**until, till**	made
(train)line	sen		

day:13

Correspondence

Day 13 teaches you how to specify a certain time. You will also learn how to use the particle *mo*, to say that you do something too. Finally, you will continue to build on and improve your Japanese comprehension.

ADDRESSING CARDS

*In Japan, **hagaki** (plain post cards) are popular. You write the addresses and names of both the sender and the receiver on the front: larger characters are used for the receiver and smaller characters for the sender. The message should be written on the back. Special postcards are issued every year for New Year's and 'Summer Season' greetings. Japanese post offices are marked with 〒.*

Japanese conversation 1: Ima (wa) nan-ji desu ka.

Hanako:	Anata mo* kōhī o nomimasen ka.
Tom:	Hai (boku mo kōhī o) nomimasu.
Hanako:	Anata no otōsan to okāsan wa Nihon-go o hanashimasu ka.
Tom:	Hai (Boku no) otōsan mo okāsan mo (Nihon-go o) hanashimasu.
	(Boku no) otōsan wa Furansu-go mo hanashimasu.
Hanako:	Watashi no onēsan mo Furansu-go o hanashi-masu.

*Anata mo is put in the sentence to emphasize that the meaning is you too.

English conversation 1: My father speaks French, too

Hanako asks Tom about his parents' skill in Japanese.

Hanako:	Would you also like to drink coffee?
Tom:	Yes, I would.
Hanako:	Do your father and mother speak Japanese?
Tom:	Yes, both (my) father and (my) mother speak Japanese.
	My father speaks French too.
Hanako:	My older sister also speaks French.

Grammar

The particle *mo*

The particle mo means *also/too*. Mo is placed after the word to which it refers. If mo refers to a subject, it replaces the particle wa or ga (discussed later). If mo refers to a direct object, it replaces o. However, if the noun mo refers/to/a word that is followed by the particle de or ni/e (discussed in a later lesson), the particle remains, and mo comes after the particle.

| I read a book. | Watashi wa hon o yomimasu. |
| Father also reads a book. | Otōsan mo hon o yomimasu. |

| Father reads a book. | Otōsan wa hon o yomimasu. |
| Father reads a magazine also (as well as a book). | Otōsan wa zasshi mo yomimasu. |

This is a book.   Kore wa hon desu.
That also is a book.   Are mo hon desu.

I read a book in my room.   Watashi wa hon o watashi no heya de yomimasu.
I read a book in the living room also.   Watashi wa hon o ima de mo yomimasu.

If each noun in a list is followed by *mo*, this means *both _ and_*.
Both younger sister and older sister read books.   Imōto mo onēsan mo hon o yomimasu.

The cat eats both fish and meat.   Neko wa sakana mo niku mo tabemasu.

For negative verbs, _ mo _ mo means neither_ nor_.
Neither the younger sister nor the older sister reads books.   Imōto mo onēsan mo hon o yomimasen.

A rabbit eats neither fish nor meat.   Usagi wa sakana mo niku mo tabemasen.

The particle *ni* after a specific time

Time expressions may be separated into three different categories: **specific time, general time** and **relative time.**

Specific time is time that may be indicated as a point on a calendar or clock (1 o'clock, March 25).
Relative time is time that depends on when **now** is, such as *last month, next year* and *tomorrow.*
General time is time in general such as *everyday, morning* and *spring.*

When you use time expressions, the time expression is put at the beginning of a sentence or just after the subject (and its particle). The time expression must be followed by *ni, at/in/on,* if it indicates a specific time.

At 8 o'clock, I watch TV.
Hachi-ji ni watashi wa terebi o mimasu.

I watch TV at 8 o'clock.
Watashi wa hachi-ji ni terebi o mimasu.

In September, we shall learn Japanese.
Ku-gatsu ni watashi-tachi wa Nihon-go o naraimasu.

I drink coffee at 9 o'clock also (as well as at 8 o'clock).
Ku-ji ni mo watashi wa kōhī o nomimasu.

Specifying times

When discussing general time, you do not need to put any particle after the expression of time. However, you can use the particle **ni** with these expressions of time also.

morning	asa		spring	haru
afternoon	hiru		summer	natsu
evening	ban		autumn	aki
night	yoru		winter	fuyu

In summer, we will learn English.
Natsu watashi-tachi wa Eigo o naraimasu.
We will learn English in summer.
Watashi-tachi wa natsu Eigo o naraimasu.
Do you watch TV at night?
Yoru anata wa terebi o mimasu ka.

The particle *ni* after an indirect object

There are two types of action verbs: **transitive verbs** and **intransitive verbs.**
A transitive verb may have a direct object and an indirect object. A direct object is the person/thing/matter to which the verb directs its action. An indirect object is the person/thing for whom the action is taking place. In most cases, the words *to* or *for* can be inserted before the indirect object in English.

Consider the following two sentences:

The sentences 1 and 2 have the same meaning, but in different forms. *Letter* is what was *sent* and therefore it is the direct object; *Betty* is the person to whom the letter is sent and therefore it is the indirect object. An indirect object, which may be preceded by *to* or *for* in English, must be followed by **ni** in Japanese.

Exercises

Exercise 1

Combine the two sentences into one sentence.

1 Watashi wa tegami o kōkūbin de okurimasu. Imōto mo tegami o kōkūbin de okurimasu.

Watashi ....imōto.....................tegami o kōkūbin de okurimasu.

Both my sister and I send letters by airmail.

2 Ashita watashi wa ban-gohan o ie de tabemasen. Ashita otōto mo ban-gohan o ie de tabemasen.

Ashita watashi...............otōto..............................ban-gohan o ie de tabemasen.

Neither my younger brother nor I will eat dinner at home tomorrow.

Exercise 2

Write ni in the blanks wherever it is needed, and then translate the sentences into English.

1 Asa no hachi-ji...watashi-tachi wa asa-gohan o tabemasu.

We eat breakfast at 8 o'clock in the morning.

2 Roku-ji...otōsan wa ban-gohan o tabemasen.

....

3 Yoru... watashi-tachi wa terebi o mimasu.

....

4 Natsu...otōsan wa ie o urimasu.

....

Japanese conversation 2: Asa-gohan

Hanako:	Nan-ji ni (anata wa) asa-gohan o tabemasu ka.
Tom:	Asa no shichi-ji han ni (boku wa asa-gohan o) tabemasu.
Hanako:	(Anata wa) nani o (asa-gohan ni) tabemasu ka.
Tom:	(Boku wa asa-gohan ni) pan o tabemasu.
	(Boku wa) kōhī mo nomimasu.
Hanako:	Nan-ji ni (anata wa) ban-gohan o tabemasu ka.
Tom:	Roku-ji ni (boku-tachi wa ban-gohan o) tabemasu.
Hanako:	Yoru (anata wa) hon o yomimasu ka.
Tom:	Hai yomimasu.
	(Yoru boku wa) terebi mo mimasu.

English conversation 2: Breakfast

Hanako asks Tom about his daily eating habits.

Hanako:	What time do you eat (your) breakfast?
Tom:	I eat at 7:30 in the morning.
Hanako:	What do you eat?
Tom:	I eat bread.
	I drink coffee too.
Hanako:	What time do you eat (your) dinner?
Tom:	We eat at 6 o'clock.
Hanako:	Do you read books at night?
Tom:	Yes, I do.
	I watch TV too.

Exercise 3

You will hear some questions about Dialogue 2. Reply to each question aloud in Japanese. Write your answers below, and check them on the CD.

1 ....

2 ....

3 ....

4 ....

Exercise 4

Translate into English:

1 *Watashi wa mizu o nomimasu.* ....

Imōto mo mizu o nomimasu. ....

2 *Okāsan mo otōsan mo hon o heya de yomimasu.* ....

....

3 *Ashita anata mo watashi-tachi to bideo o mimasen ka.* ....

....

4 *Yoru watashi-tachi wa tegami o tomodachi ni kakimasu.* ....

....

5 *Ichi-ji ni Igirisu-jin wa ranchi o tabemasu.* ....

....

Translate into rōmaji:

6 *Hanako does not read French books.* ....

....

Makoto also does not read French books. ....

....

7 *In December, we send presents to (our) grandfather and grandmother.*..................................

....

8 *I speak both English and Japanese.*..

....

9 *Neither (my) father nor (my) mother speaks English.*...

....

10 *At twelve o'clock, we listen to Japanese music on the radio.*..................................

....

Vocabulary

Here are some more verbs that you can use in the sentence structure _ **wa** _ **o V·masu**

collect	*atsumemasu*		**stop (vehicles)**	*tomemasu*
choose	*erabimasu*		**forget**	*wasuremasu*
return	*kaeshimasu*		**resign from, quit**	*yamemasu*
(things borrowed)			**give (to somebody)**	*agemasu*
borrow	*karimasu*		**give (to me)**	*kuremasu*
lend	*kashimasu*		**put on**	*hakimasu*
wait for	*machimasu*		**(footwear, trousers)**	
invite	*manekimasu*		**put on (hat)**	*kaburimasu*
show	*misemasu*		**put on (dress)**	*kimasu*
lose	*nakushimasu*			

I stop (my) car here.
Boku wa kuruma o koko de tomemasu.
I give you this. (I give this to you.)
Watashi wa kore o anata ni agemasu.
Will you give me this?
Anata wa kore o watashi ni kuremasu ka.
Tomorrow, I will return you this. (return this to you)
Ashita watashi wa kore o anata ni kaeshimasu.
In September, the history teacher resigns from the school.
Ku-gatsu ni rekishi no sensei wa gakkō o yamemasu.
At 8 o'clock, I'll wait for you at the station.
Hachi-ji ni watashi wa anata o eki de machimasu.

The verb *wait* is followed by *for* in English. The Japanese equivalent **machimasu** is a transitive verb and is preceded by **o**. Similarly, the verb *resign* is followed by *from* in English. The Japanese equivalent **yamemasu** is a transitive verb and is also preceded by **o**.

Verbs: to put on

There are three different words for *put on* (clothing) in Japanese. Use **kaburimasu** for put on <u>on the head,</u> **kimasu** for put on <u>above the waist and below the head,</u> and **hakimasu** for put on <u>below the waist.</u>

The following vocabulary lists some clothing that you may put on your body.

Vocabulary

The following vocabulary lists some clothing items.

hat	*bōshi*	**skirt**	*sukāto*
shoe	*kutsu*	**suit**	*sūtsu*
blouse	*burausu*	**kimono**	*kimono*
sock, stocking	*kutsushita*	**one-piece dress**	*wanpīsu*
dress	*doresu*	**coat**	*kōto*
sweater	*sētā*	**trousers, pants**	*zubon*
clothes, clothing	*fuku*		

Exercise 5

You will hear the narrator talk about things she does. Respond to each phrase by saying that you do that thing too. Check your replies against the answers on the CD.

1 ....

2 ....

3 ....

4 ....

Exercise 6

Translate into English:

1 *Watashi wa kore o karimasu.* ....

....

2 *Haru sensei wa gakkō o yamemasu.* ....

....

3 *Natsu okāsan wa obāsan o Nihon ni manekimasu.* ....

....

4 *Otōsan wa kuruma o doko de tomemasu ka.* ....

....

5 *Anata wa fuyu bōshi o kaburimasu ka.* ....

....

Translate into rōmaji:

6 *My younger brother and I invite Robert to our house.* ....

....

7 *My older sister collects hats.* ....

....

8 *I will not forget you.* ....

....

9 *In winter, do you put on a coat?* ....

....

10 *I will not show (my) painting to (my) father.* ....

....

Writing exercise

Practice the three hiragana characters ya, yu and yo.

Step by step: ya

yu

yo

Vocabulary

breakfast	*asa-gohan*	**lunch**	*ranchi / hiru-gohan*
dinner	*ban-gohan*	**meal, boiled rice**	*gohan*

day:14

On the phone

Day 14 introduces you to making telephone calls in Japanese. You will also further develop your conversation skills by learning how to describe how you do things. You will learn the vocabulary for different modes of transport and places you might go to. You will also further practice your writing.

MOSHI-MOSHI

*When you talk to a person on the telephone, you always say **moshi-moshi** for hello. The person on the other line will also reply **moshi-moshi**, hello. **Moshi-moshi** is used only on the telephone.*

Japanese conversation 1: Watashi no bāsudē pātī

Tom:	Moshi-moshi.
Hanako:	Moshi-moshi. (Anata wa) Tom-kun desu ka.
Tom:	Hai (boku wa Tom desu). Hanako-san Konban-wa.
Hanako:	Konbanwa.
	San-gatsu nijūichi-nichi no hiru (ni) anata wa hima desu ka.
Tom:	(San-gatsu nijūichi-nichi wa) nan-yōbi desu ka.
Hanako:	(San-gatsu nijūichi-nichi wa) do-yōbi desu.
Tom:	(Boku wa) hima desu.
Hanako:	San-gatsu nijūichi-nichi wa watashi no bāsudē desu.
	Bāsudē pātī ni kimasen ka.
Tom:	Hai (Boku wa bāsudē pātī ni) ikimasu. (Bāsudēpātī wa)
	nan-ji kara nan-ji made desu ka.
Hanako:	(Bāsudē pātī wa) jūni-ji kara yo-ji made desu.

English conversation 1: My birthday party

Hanako calls Tom to invite him to her birthday party.

Tom:	Hello!
Hanako:	Hello! Is that (Are you) Tom?
Tom:	Yes. Good evening Hanako.
Hanako:	Good evening.
	Are you free in the afternoon of March 21st?
Tom:	What day of the week is it?
Hanako:	It's a Saturday.
Tom:	I'm free.
Hanako:	March 21st is my birthday.
	Would you like to come to (my) birthday party?
Tom:	Yes, I would.
	From what time to what time is it?
Hanako:	It's from 12 o'clock to 4 o'clock.

Japanese conversation 2: Hikōki de kimasu ka.

Tom:	Hanako-san Konnichiwa.
Hanako:	Tom-kun Konnichiwa. (O)genki desu ka.
Tom:	Hai genki desu. (O)genki desu ka.
Hanako:	Hai okagesama de. (Anata wa) doko e ikimasu ka.
Tom:	(Boku wa) yūbinkyoku e ikimasu.
	(Boku wa) tegami o ojīsan ni okurimasu.
Hanako:	(Anata wa) tegami o Nihon-go de ojīsan ni kakimasu ka.
Tom:	Iie (boku wa tegami o) Eigo de kakimasu.
	Ojīsan wa Nihon-go o yomimasen.
	Haru ojīsan wa Nihon e kimasu.
Hanako:	(Ojīsan wa Nihon e) hikōki de kimasu ka.
Tom:	Hai (ojīsan wa Nihon e hikōki de kimasu).
Hanako:	Ojīsan wa Nihon-go o hanashimasu ka.
Tom:	Iie hanashimasen.
Hanako:	Watashi wa Eigo o naraimasu.
	(Watashi wa) Eigo o ojīsan ni hanashimasu.
	Dewa mata. Sayōnara.
Tom:	Sayōnara.

English conversation 2: Is he coming by plane?

Tom meets Hanako on his way to a post office.

Tom:	Good afternoon, Hanako.
Hanako:	Good afternoon, Tom. How are you?
Tom:	I am fine. How are you?
Hanako:	I am fine, thank you. Where are you going?
Tom:	I am going to the post office.
	I am sending a letter to (my) grandfather.
Hanako:	Do you write letters to (your) grandfather in Japanese?
Tom:	No, I write in English.
	(My) grandfather does not read Japanese.
	In spring, (my) grandfather is coming to Japan.
Hanako:	Is he coming by airplane?
Tom:	Yes.

Hanako:	Does (your) grandfather speak Japanese?
Tom:	No, he doesn't.
Hanako:	I'll learn English.
	I'll speak English to (your) grandfather.
	See you. Good-bye.
Tom:	Good-bye.

Grammar

Verbs of motion

Verbs of motion have the sentence structure "subject **wa** place **e/kara** **V•masu**".
The particle **wa** follows the subject, the particle **e/kara** follows the place of motion *to/from*.
The verb of motion **V•masu** is placed at the end of the sentence.

go out	demasu
come in, join, get in	hairimasu
go	ikimasu
return	kaerimasu
come	kimasu
get off	orimasu

Note e is translated as **to** in the sense of motion towards a place. It should not be confused with *giving to*, which requires **ni**, as you learned in the Day 13.

Vocabulary - places

Here are some words you can use when talking about places you go.

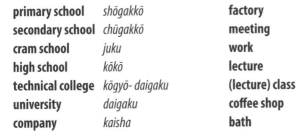

primary school	*shōgakkō*	factory	*kōjō*
secondary school	*chūgakkō*	meeting	*kaigi*
cram school	*juku*	work	*shigoto*
high school	*kōkō*	lecture	*jugyō*
technical college	*kōgyō- daigaku*	(lecture) class	*kurasu*
university	*daigaku*	coffee shop	*kissaten*
company	*kaisha*	bath	*furo*

Here are some typical sentences using verbs of motion:

I go to America with (my) father.
Watashi wa Amerika e otōsan to ikimasu.
Father will come here.
Otōsan wa koko e kimasu.
Father returns from work (company).
Otōsan wa kaisha kara kaerimasu.
Grandmother gets off (from) the bus.
Obāsan wa basu kara orimasu.

Transportation

You can make sentences more complete by saying when, and how, you go somewhere.
In summer, we go to school by bicycle.
Natsu watashi-tachi wa gakkō e jitensha de ikimasu.
In August, Tom will return from America by airplane.
Hachi-gatsu ni Tom-kun wa Amerika kara hikōki de kaerimasu.
(My) father will come here by (his) car at 9 o'clock.
Ku-ji ni otōsan wa koko e kuruma de kimasu.

Vocabulary - Transport

Here are some words you can use when talking about transport.

ship, boat	*fune*	**car**	*kuruma*
airplane	*hikōki*	**motorcycle**	*ōtobai*
automobile	*jidōsha*	**scooter**	*sukūtā*
bicycle	*jitensha*	**taxi**	*takushī*
train	*densha (previously kisha)*	**truck**	*torakku*

Ni

When you are going to an event, and not to a place, ni follows the event and is translated as to. An event should never be followed by e. Using this construction, you can ask someone to go somewhere with you, as in the examples below.
Would you like to come to dinner?
Ban-gohan ni kimasen ka.
I will go to a Japanese lecture.
Watashi wa Nihon-go no jugyō ni ikimasu.
Would you like to go to a movie on Saturday?
Do-yōbi ni eiga ni ikimasen ka.

Ni and *kara*

Instead of saying *take a bath* and *finish a bath*, Japanese uses **furo ni hairimasu**, *come into a bath*, and **furo kara demasu**, *go out from a bath*, since Japanese bathing involves getting into and out of a bathtub.

I take a bath at night.　　　　　　　　**Watashi wa yoru furo ni hairimasu.**
Father finishes (his) bath.　　　　　　**Otosan wa furo kara demasu.**

When you are making an arrangement for a party or a meeting, you'll want to tell the other person when the event will start and end. In this case, you use the expression **A kara B made,** implying *from A to B.* **A kara B made** can also denote locations.

from 9 o'clock till 10 o'clock　　　　**ku-ji kara ju-ji made**
from Osaka to Tokyo　　　　　　　　**Ōsaka kara Tōkyō made**

Exercises

Exercise 1

Your friend is inviting you to various activities. Listen to the phrases on the CD, and write the activities in English.

1 ....
2 ....
3 ....
4 ....
5 ....
6 ....

Exercise 2

Listen to the phrases on the CD and answer the questions in rōmaji.

1 Otōsan wa doko e densha de ikimasu ka..

....

2 Okāsan wa sūpāmāketto e nan de ikimasu ka. ....

....

3 Imōto wa gakkō e basu de ikimasu ka. ....

....

4 Onēsan wa doko e ikimasu ka. ....

....

Exercise 3

Make sentences by matching each phrase on the left with the correct phrase on the right.

1 Ichi-gatsu kara go-gatsu made   •watashi wa densha de ikimasu.

2 Tōkyō kara Ōsaka made   •otōto wa terebi o mimasu.

3 Asa kara yoru made   •otōsan wa gaikoku e ikimasu.

Now translate the complete sentences into English.

1..

2 ....

3 ....

Exercise 4

Translate into English:

1 *Ichi-gatsu ni Betty-san wa Amerika e kaerimasu.* ....

2 *Anata wa doko e densha de ikimasu ka.* ....

3 *Onēsan mo basu kara orimasu.* ....

4 *Otōto mo watashi mo gakkō e kuruma de ikimasen.* ....

5 *Haru ojīsan wa Nihon e fune de kimasu.* ....

Translate into rōmaji:

6 *Father comes out of (goes out from) a bath.* ....

7 *I go to school at 8 o'clock in the morning.* ....

8 *In September, I shall go to America by plane.* ....

9 *Tom will not go back (return) to America in summer.* ....

10 *My younger brother does not enter kindergarten in September.* ....

Writing exercise

Practice the five hiragana characters **ra, ri, ru, re** and **ro.**

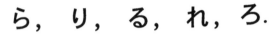

Step by step:

ra   re

ri   ro

ru

Vocabulary

Many foreign words (mostly English) have entered into the Japanese language. In order to make the sounds as close as possible to the original, new syllables such as **ti** have been introduced into Japanese. For more on this, see page 253.

bāsudē	*birthday*	**pātī**	*party*
ranchi	*lunch*		

day:15

Making plans

Day 15 talks about making plans. You will learn the important verb *shimasu* (to do). *Shimasu* can be used in a variety of contexts to mean many things, you you will learn how to say what you enjoy doing, what you do habitually, express a wish, etc.

JAPANESE SPORT

In order to defend themselves against samurai, farmers and tradesmen developed many martial arts such as **karate** *and* **jūdō**. *Deprived of owning weapons, they used simple sticks, mental preparedness and their bodies.* **Sumō** *wrestling is one of the most popular spectator sports in Japan. Two huge men, wearing only loin cloths, push each other in a small ring covered with sand. The rule for winning is very simple. One has to push the opponent out of the ring, or, get any part of his body, except the soles of the feet, to touch the ground.*

Japanese conversation 1: Raishū nani o shimasu ka.

Hanako:	Raishū wa Gōruden-uīku desu. Daigaku wa yasumi desu.
Tom:	(Yasumi wa) itsu kara itsu made desu ka.
Hanako:	(Yasumi wa) getsu-yōbi kara kin-yōbi made desu.
Tom:	Raishū (anata wa) nani o shimasu ka.
Hanako:	(Watashi-tachi wa) ryokō o shimasu.
	(Watashi-tachi wa) ojīsan to obāsan no ie e iki masu.
Tom:	(Anata wa) nani o ojīsan to obāsan no ie de shimasu ka.
Hanako:	Okāsan to obāsan wa ryōri o shimasu.
	Watashi wa tetsudai o shimasu.
Tom:	Anata wa benkyō o shimasu ka.
Hanako:	Iie shimasen.

English conversation 1: What are you doing next week?

Hanako tells Tom about the Golden-Week holiday.

Hanako:	Next week is Golden-Week. Colleges are on holiday.
Tom:	From when to when is it?
Hanako:	From Monday to Friday.
Tom:	What are you doing next week?
Hanako:	We are going to travel.
	We are going to (our) grandfather and grandmother's house.
Tom:	What do you do at (your) grandfather and grandmother's house?
Hanako:	(My) mother and (my) grandmother cook.
	I help (them).
Tom:	Do you study?
Hanako:	No, I don't.

Vocabulary

Gōruden-uīku	*Golden-Week*
yasumi	*holiday*
itsu	*when*

Grammar

Verbs

shimasu **(to do)**
subject wa **direct object** o shimasu

shimasu *(to do)* takes various nouns as direct objects to form a verb which is often expressed by one word in English; such as cook and study.
Ryōri o shimasu ka. Do you cook?
Nihongo o benkyo shimasu. I study Japanese.

Vocabulary

These nouns may be used with shimasu as direct objects, to describe what you, or others, do.

greeting	*aisatsu*	**help**	*tetsudai*
cooking	*ryōri*	**conversation**	*hanashi*
knitting	*amimono*	**driving**	*unten*
laundry	*sentaku*	**shopping**	*kaimono*
study	*benkyō*	**promise**	*yakusoku*
cleaning	*sōji*	**marriage**	*kekkon*
date	*deito*	**travel**	*ryokō*

Nouns with *o shimasu*

Unlike the English language where the verb *do* emphasizes actions (e.g., I *do* greet, I *do* study, etc.), there is no such emphasis with shimasu. Shimasu converts some nouns into single verbs, i.e. "noun + o + shimasu" may be translated as a single verb as follows:

aisatsu o shimasu   means *greet* rather than *do greet*.
benkyō o shimasu   means *study* rather than *do study*.
amimono o shimasu   means *knit* rather than *do knit*.

Okāsan wa amimono o shimasu.   Mother knits.
Otōsan wa ryokō o shimasu.   Father travels.
Anata wa nani o shimasu ka.   What do you do?
Ryōri o shimasen ka.   Would you like to cook?
Otōsan wa aisatsu o sensei ni* shimasu.   The father greets the teacher.
* Note that sensei is an indirect object in the Japanese sentence, so it is followed by ni.

When the direct objects are sports, such as those listed below, shimasu may be translated as *do, play, practice,* etc., according to context.

sports	supōtsu	sumo wrestling	sumō
judo	jūdō	gymnastics	taisō
karate	karate	tennis	tenisu
swimming	suiei	baseball	yakyū

practice karate	karate o shimasu
play tennis	tenisu o shimasu
swim	suiei o shimasu
do not play baseball	yakyū o shimasen

Being more specific: noun + *no* + *o shimasu*

Some nouns may be expanded with no and used with shimasu as shown below.

ryōri	cooking
sakana no ryōri	cooking of fish
sakana no ryōri o shimasu	(I) cook fish

hanashi	talk
Kanada no hanashi	talk about Canada
Kanada no hanashi o shimasu	(I) talk about Canada

Watashi wa Nihon-go no benkyō o shimasu.	I study Japanese.
Anata wa nan no supōtsu o shimasu ka.	What sports do you do?

Noun + shimasu

Some of the nouns that you have learned may be combined directly with shimasu to form single verbs.

ryokō shimasu	to travel
kekkon shimasu	to marry
unten shimasu	to drive
benkyō shimasu	to study
ryōri shimasu	to cook
sentaku shimasu	to do laundry
sōji shimasu	to clean
yakusoku shimasu	to promise

The above nouns + shimasu can also be made more specific with the sentence structure.

subject wa **direct object** o **noun** + shimasu

Watashi wa Nihon-go o benkyo shimasu.
I study Japanese.
Watashi wa seta o sentaku shimasu.
I wash (my) sweater.
Watashi-tachi wa Kyōto o ryokō shimasu.
We travel in Kyoto.
Although *to travel* does not take a direct object in English, ryōko shimasu follows o and should be translated according to context.

Giving more information

The sentence structure _ wa _ o "noun + shimasu" gives more information than the sentence structure _ wa _ o shimasu as can be seen from the examples below.

Watashi wa unten o shimasu.	I drive.
Watashi wa kuruma o unten shimasu.	I drive a car.
Watashi wa ryokō o shimasu.	I travel.
Watashi wa Nihon o ryokō shimasu.	I travel in Japan.

The following sentences have the same meaning. In the examples below, Nihon-go no benkyō, *study of Japanese,* and sētā no sentaku, *laundry of the sweater,* are treated as nouns.

Watashi wa Nihon-go o benkyō shimasu.	I study Japanese
Watashi wa Nihon-go no benkyō o shimasu.	I study Japanese.
Watashi wa sētā o sentaku shimasu.	I wash (my) sweater.
Watashi wa sētā no sentaku o shimasu.	I wash (my) sweater.

Verbs: to date/marry

Although *to date* and *to marry* are transitive verbs in English (we can say *I date Betty* and *I marry Betty* in English), the equivalent deito shimasu *to date* and kekkon shimasu *to marry* are not transitive verbs in Japanese.

You must use expressions equivalent to *I date <u>with</u> Betty* and *I marry <u>with</u> Betty* in Japanese. Therefore, deito shimasu and kekkon shimasu **must follow the particle** to *(together/along with)* and not o.

Watashi wa Betty-san to deito shimasu.	I date Betty.

Exercises

Exercise 1

You will hear some things that Hanako's older sister does on Saturdays.
Answer the questions in rōmaji.

1 Asa hachi-ji ni onēsan wa nani o shimasu ka....

....

2 Asa onēsan wa sentaku to sōji o shimasu ka. ....

....

3 Hiru onēsan wa nani o shimasu ka. ....

....

4 Ban onēsan wa nani o shimasu ka...

....

Exercise 2

Translate into English:

1 *ryokō o shimasu.* ....

2 *sumō o shimasen.* ....

3 *Yoru okāsan wa amimono mo shimasu.* ....

4 *Onīsan wa yakyū o shimasen.*..

Translate into rōmaji:

5 *promise.* ....

6 *do not play tennis.* ....

7 *In August, we travel by car.* ....

8 *What do you do at school?*..

Exercise 3

Rewrite the sentences noun + o + shimasu to become sentences with noun + shimasu.

1 Watashi wa niwa no sōji o shimasu.

Watashi wa niwa o sōji shimasu. ....

2 Ojisan wa torakku no unten o shimasu.

Ojisan wa ....

3 Okāsan wa yasai no ryōri o shimasu.

Okāsan wa...

4 Onēsan wa Eigo no benkyō o shimasu.

Onēsan wa ....

Exercise 4

Translate into English:

1 *Watashi wa kore o ryōri shimasu.* ....

2 *Watashi wa sore o yakusoku shimasu.* ....

3 *Betty-san wa kuruma o unten shimasen.*..

4 *Hachi-gatsu ni watashi-tachi wa kekkon shimasu.*..

Translate into rōmaji:

5 *In fall, I shall travel in America.* ....

6 *I cook steak for lunch..* ....

7 *In spring, I clean the garden.* ....

8 *Does Tom study Japanese?*..

Could you do me a favor? *Onegai shimasu*

When **shimasu** is combined with **onegai**, *appeal/wish,* it can mean many things.
Onegai shimasu, which literally means *do wish* or *do appeal,* is a very useful expression to attract someone's attention and ask a favor; it means *I beg you* or *Please do this.*

Onegai shimasu is used in the following situations:

1 When calling a clerk in a store or a waiter in a restarant for service.
Onegai shimasu.   Excuse me.

2 Ordering food in a restaurant.
Sutēki onegai shimasu.   Steak, please.

3 When you don't understand the amount the salesperson said,
you can ask the person to write it down, by handing over a pencil
and paper and saying:
Onegai shimasu.   Please (write it down).

4 When submitting bills or papers at a bank, a post office or a hospital.
Onegai shimasu.   Please look after this.

5 When you wish to tell the elevator operator your floor.
Go-kai onegai shimasu.   Fifth floor please.

6 When telling a taxi driver your destination.
Eki made* onegai shimasu.   To the train station, please.

7 When you ask for somebody.
Betty-san onegai shimasu.   May I speak to Betty please?

Note *the phrases are used in one-to-one conversations, and the direct objects of the verb* **onegai shimasu**
*(**go-kai**, **eki**, etc.) are not followed by* **o**.

*made = *to (a place)*

Japanese conversation 2: Restoran wa doko ni shimasu ka.

Tom:	(Boku-tachi wa) resutoran wa doko ni shimasu ka.
Hanako:	(Watashi-tachi wa resutoran wa) Edo ni shimasen ka.

***

Tom:	(Anata wa) tabemono wa nani ni shimasu ka.
Hanako:	(Watashi wa tabemono wa) yakisoba ni shimasu.
	Anata wa (tabemono wa nani ni shimasu ka).
Tom:	Boku wa (tabemono wa) tonkatsu ni shimasu.
	(Anata wa) nomimono wa (nani ni shimasu ka).
Hanako:	(Watashi wa nomimono wa) miruku ni shimasu.
	Anata wa (nomimono wa nani ni shimasu ka).
Tom:	Boku wa (nomimono wa) orenji-jūsu ni shimasu.

English conversation 2: Which restaurant should we go to?

Tom and Hanako go to a restaurant.

Tom:	To which restaurant do we go? (Where do we decide on for a restaurant?)
Hanako:	Would you like to go to Edo? (Would you like to decide on Edo?)

Tom and Hanako arrive at Edo restaurant.

Tom:	What will you have for food?
Hanako:	I'll have yakisoba.
	How about you?
Tom:	I'll have a pork cutlet.
	How about the drinks?
Hanako:	I'll have milk.
	How about you?
Tom:	I'll have orange juice.

I choose (Ni shimasu)

If you want to say that one *decides* or *chooses* something, you use the sentence structure
what is chosen ni shimasu, **meaning** *decide on*__.

This is an abbreviation of the sentence structure
subject wa **topic** wa **what is chosen** ni shimasu.

The first wa follows the person making the choice, the second wa follows the topic under discussion and is translated as *as for* or *for,* and ni follows what is chosen.

With this sentence structure, you can talk about very important decisions, like what to eat.

tabemono   food

Sushi ni shimasu.   Decide on sushi.
Are ni shimasu.   Decide on that.

Watashi wa tabemono wa sushi ni shimasu.
I shall have sushi. (I decide on sushi for food.)

Anata wa tabemono wa nani ni shimasu ka.
What will you eat? (What do you decide on for food?)

Exercise 5

Join each question on the left with one of the two correct replies on the right.

Dore ni shimasu ka.   **Koko ni shimasu.**

Doko ni shimasu ka.   **Kore ni shimasu.**

Nan ni shimasu ka.

Exercise 6

Translate into English:

1 *Byōin made onegai shimasu. (in a taxi)* ....

....

2 *Tom-kun onegai shimasu. (on a telephone)* ....

....

3 *(Watashi-tachi wa) kudomono wa nani ni shimasu ka.* ....

....

4 *Doko no (o)tera ni shimasu ka.* ....

....

5 *Dare no ie ni shimasu ka.* ....

....

Translate into rōmaji:

6 *Could you take me to the Tokyo zoo please?* ....

....

7 *May I speak to the English teacher please?* ....

....

8 *What do we decide on for a present for Hanako?* ....

....

9 *On whom do we decide?* ....

....

10 *Where do we decide on for traveling?* ....

....

Exercise 7

You will hear some questions about Dialogue 2. Reply to each question aloud
in Japanese, and check your answers on the CD.

Writing exercise

Practice the three hiragana characters wa, wo and n.

わ， を， ん.

Step by step: wa   wo   n

day:16

Adjectives

Day 16 introduces adjectives. You will learn the Japanese word for cute (*kawaii*), how to describe how you are feeling, as well as people, animals, things, etc. Finally, you will practice writing *katakana*.

ITAI: THAT HURTS!

Here are two adjectives to help you describe how you are feeling. They use the same sentence structure as **suki/kirai** *to describe physical conditions.*

painful	*itai*
itchy	*kayui*
I have a headache.	*Watashi wa atama ga itai desu.*
(As for me, the head is painful.)	
My legs are itchy.	*Watashi wa ashi ga kayui desu.*
(As for me, the legs are itchy.)	

Japanese conversation 1: Kawaii inu desu ne.

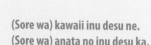

Hanako:	(Sore wa) kawaii inu desu ne.
	(Sore wa) anata no inu desu ka.
Tom:	Hai sō desu.
Hanako:	(Inu no) ashi wa mijikai desu ne.
Tom:	Kono inu wa dakkusufundo desu yo.
	Dakkusufundo no ashi wa mijikai desu yo.
Hanako:	(Inu no) me wa ōkii desu ne. (Inu no) mimi wa nagai desu ne.
	(Inu no) namae wa nan desu ka.
Tom:	(Inu no namae wa) Cute desu.
Hanako:	(Inu no namae wa) kawaii namae desu ne.
Tom:	CUTE wa Nihon-go de KAWAII desu.
Hanako:	(Cute wa) kono inu ni pittari na namae desu ne.

English conversation: He's a cute dog, isn't he?

Hanako meets Tom, walking his dog.

Hanako:	He is a cute dog, isn't he? Is he your dog?
Tom:	Yes, he is.
Hanako:	The legs are short, aren't they?
Tom:	He (This dog) is a dachshund!
	A dachshund's legs are short!
Hanako:	His eyes are big, aren't they? His ears are long, aren't they?
	What is his name?
Tom:	It's Cute.
Hanako:	It's a cute name, isn't it?
Tom:	CUTE is KAWAII in Japanese.
Hanako:	It's a perfectly fit name, isn't it?

Grammar

I-Adjectives

Notice that the adjectives listed below end with _i; these are known as **i-adjectives**.

warm	*atatakai*	cool	*suzushii*
hot (temperature)	*atsui*	cold (temperature)	*samui*
hot (touch)	*atsui*	cold (touch)	*tsumetai*
thick (flat things)	*atsui*	thin (flat things)	*usui*
thick (cylindrical things), fat	*futoi*	thin (cylindrical things)	*hosoi*
spacious	*hiroi*	limited space	*semai*
cute	*kawaii*	ugly	*minikui*
frightful, frightening	*kowai*	gentle	*yasashii*
difficult	*muzukashii*	easy	*yasashii*
long	*nagai*	short (length)	*mijikai*
delicious, tasty	*oishii*	unsavory (taste)	*mazui*
big, large	*ōkii*	small, little	*chiisai*
heavy	*omoi*	light (weight)	*karui*
interesting, amusing	*omoshiroi*	boring	*tsumaranai*
expensive	*takai*	cheap	*yasui*
high, tall	*takai*	low, short (height)	*hikui*
good	*yoi/ii*	bad	*warui*

Japanese adjectives describe nouns, and they precede the nouns they describe, just as in English.

heavy book	**omoi hon**
expensive fruit	**takai kudamono**
small red car	**chiisai akai kuruma**
This is a short pencil.	**Kore wa mijikai enpitsu desu.**
This is a big house.	**Koko wa ōkii ie desu.**
Father buys a big car.	**Otōsan wa ōkii kuruma o kaimasu.**

Negative I-Adjectives

Negative i-adjectives (not big, not delicious, etc.) are formed by changing _i to _ku nai.

ōkii ringo	a big apple
ōkiku nai ringo	not a big apple
oishii ringo	a delicious apple
oishiku nai ringo	not a delicious apple

Ii, good, is an irregular adjective. Ii changes to yoi to conjugate.

ii hon	a good book
yokunai hon	not a good book

I-adjectives that do not have their opposite i-adjectives are listed below. Some colors are also i-adjectives.

Vocabulary

red	*akai*	**dirty**	*kitanai*
blue	*aoi*	**hard (full of**	*kurushii*
brown	*chairoi*	**suffering)**	
yellow	*kiiroi*	**unusual, rare**	*mezurashii*
black	*kuroi*	**lonely**	*sabishii*
white	*shiroi*	**enjoyable**	*tanoshii*
dangerous	*abunai*	**noisy**	*urusai*
busy	*isogashii*		

this and that

day	hi	person	hito

There are many words meaning *this* and *that* in Japanese. Corresponding to the demonstrative adjectives in <u>this</u> book, that station, <u>that</u> person (over there) and <u>Which</u> apple? are kono, sono, ano and dono. As you will expect from what you have learned of kore, sore, are and dore (as well as koko, soko, asoko and doko), the adjective kono describes a thing/person/place near a speaker, sono describes a thing/person/place near a listener, ano describes a thing/person/place away from both a speaker and a listener, and dono is an interrogative adjective meaning *which*. They are placed before the nouns they describe.

this	kono	that	sono
that (over there)	ano	Which?	dono

this book (near the speaker)	kono hon
that pencil (near the listener)	sono enpitsu

that temple (away from the speaker and the listener)	ano (o)tera
Which apple?	dono ringo

If both a demonstrative adjective and an ordinary adjective describe a noun, the ordinary adjective follows the demonstrative adjective.

that big person (over there)	ano ōkii hito
this small dog	kono chiisai inu

This big desk is the teacher's desk.
Kono ōkii tsukue wa sensei no tsukue desu.
That interesting person is my grandfather.
Ano omoshiroi hito wa boku no ojīsan desu.

Note that kore, sore, are and dore (and koko, soko, asoko and doko) are pronouns: they are used instead of nouns and they always stand by themselves. Kono, sono, ano and dono are adjectives: they describe nouns and they are placed before the nouns they describe.

That person is Hanako.	Ano hito wa Hanako-san desu.
That is Hanako.	Are wa Hanako-san desu.
May I have that apple please?	Sono ringo o kudasai.
May I have that please?	Sore o kudasai.
Do you read this book?	Anata wa kono hon o yomimasu ka.
Do you read this?	Anata wa kore o yomimasu ka.
Which book do you read?	Anata wa dono hon o yomimasu ka.
Which do you read?	Anata wa dore o yomimasu ka.

You know now that, when two people are talking, a speaker may ask a listener kore wa nan desu ka, *what is this (near me)?*, meaning something near the speaker. The listener then answers with sore wa pen desu, *that (near you) is a pen*, since the pen is closer to the speaker than to the listener, and whenever they are talking about a thing/place/person away from them both, are/asoko/ano-hito is used.

Note that kore/koko/kono-hito, sore/soko/sono-hito and are/asoko/ano-hito are used not only in the tangible sense, but also in an intangible sense. For example, once a speaker mentions a thing/place/ person, it may be referred to as kore/koko/kono-hito in the rest of his conversation, and it is translated as *it/he/she/*here. The listener refers to it by sore/soko/sono-hito, and it is translated as *it/he/she/there.* Are/asoko/ano-hito can be used to refer to a thing/place/person somehow far away from them both, in an intangible or a temporal sense, but it is also translated as *it/he/she/there.*
In the examples above, ano hito and are, sono ringo and sore, kono hon and kore, and dono hon and dore may be translated as *she, that/it, this/it* and *which* respectively.

Exercises

Exercise 1

You will hear an English adjective. Reply with the corresponding Japanese word. Check your answers on the recording.

Exercise 2

Convert the following phrases to read "not ___."

1 isogashii hito <u>isogashiku nai hito</u>

2 mezurashii tori ....

3 sabishii (o)tera ....

4 urusai inu ....

5 tanoshii hi ....

6 akai ringo ....

Exercise 3

Replace the following two words with a rōmaji word such as kore, koko, etc.

1 kono hito <u>kochira</u>

2 ano tabemono ....

3 ano gakkō ....

4 kono kissaten ....

5 ano kaisha ....

6 sono densha ....

Exercise 4

Translate into English:

1 *aoi me* ....

2 *ōkii sutēki* ....

3 *kono inu* ....

4 *kowaku nai sensei* ....

5 *samuku nai hi* ....

6 *Otōsan wa kaisha e kono kuroi kuruma de ikimasu.* ....

....

7 *Natsu watashi to otōto wa yasashii Nihon-go o naraimasu.* ....

....

8 *Anata wa muzukashii hon o gakkō de yomimasu ka.* ....

....

Translate into rōmaji:

9 *cold water* ....

10 *big person* ....

11 *that (over there) child* ....

12 *not interesting movie* ....

13 *This is a long train.* ....

I-Adjectives as Complements

Look at the following two sentences with the adjective *big*.
1 This is a *big* apple.
2 The apple is *big*.

The *big* in the sentence 1 is an adjective describing the noun *apple*. The *big* in the sentence 2 is an adjective used as the complement of the sentence, which you are going to study now.
I-adjectives can be used as complements, just like English adjectives.

to be red	**akai desu**
to be lonely	**sabishii desu**
to be warm	**atatakai desu**

Sentences that use i-adjectives as complements have the structure

subject wa i-adjective desu.

The apple is red.	**Ringo wa akai desu.**
That dog is frightening.	**Sono inu wa kowai desu.**
This place is dirty.	**Koko wa kitanai desu.**
I am hot.	**Watashi wa atsui desu.**

Negative I-Adjectives as Complements

Look at the following two sentences.

1 This is red.   Kore wa akai desu.
2 This is a book.   Kore wa hon desu.

138

There is no great difference grammatically between the sentences "This is red" and "This is a book" in English. The negative statements are obtained by putting **not** after the verb is for both sentences in English ("this is not red" and "this is not a book"). But the Japanese i-adjectives are very different from English adjectives: they conjugate (change forms), to form negative adjectives.

The negative statement of **subject** wa ___i desu is **subject** wa ___ku nai desu.

To negate the sentence that has an i-adjective as its complement, the i-adjective conjugates while the verb desu remains the same. When the complement is a noun, as in sentence 2 above, the noun remains the same while the verb desu conjugates. The negative statements for sentences 1 and 2 above are as follows.

1 This is not red.   Kore wa akaku nai desu.
(adjective akai conjugates while desu remains unchanged)

2 This is not a book.   Kore wa hon de wa arimasen.
(verb desu conjugates)

The form for the Japanese sentence 1, which has an adjective for its complement, differs from that of the Japanese sentence 2, which has a noun for its complement. The following examples show sentences with adjectives as their complements.

My room is spacious.	Boku no heya wa hiroi desu.
My room is not spacious.	Boku no heya wa hiroku nai desu.
This book is interesting.	Kono hon wa omoshiroi desu.
This book is not interesting.	Kono hon wa omoshiroku nai desu.
An American is unusual.	Amerika-jin wa mezurashii desu.
An American is not unusual.	Amerika-jin wa mezurashiku nai desu.

Exercise 5

You will hear a statement. Reply with the corresponding negative statement.

Check your answers on the recording.

Exercise 6

Translate into English.

1 *Kono natsu wa atsui desu ne.* ....

2 *Betty-san no inu wa kitanai desu.* ....

3 *Kono kudamono wa yasui desu yo.* ....

4 *Umi no mizu wa tsumetai desu ne.* ....

5 *Nihon-jin wa mezurashiku nai desu.* ....

Translate into rōmaji:

6 *Canada is cold.* ....

7 *This is unusual.* ....

8 *Is Britain interesting?.* ....

9 *Is the school enjoyable?* ....

10 *My umbrella is not black.* ....

Exercise 7

Convert the following phrases to read "not ____" and then translate them into English.

1 shinsetsu na hito **shinsetsu de nai hito** *not a kind person*

2 genki na inu ....

....

3 yūmei na (o)tera ....

....

foolish, stupid	*baka na*	**clever**	*rikō na*
convenient	*benri na*	**splendid**	*rippa na*
inconvenient	*fuben na*	**romantic**	*romanchikku na*
healthy, hearty	*genki na*	**kind**	*shinsetsu na*
handsome	*hansamu na*	**quiet, peaceful**	*shizuka na*
strange, suspicious	*hen na*	**precious**	*taisetsu na*
beautiful, clean	*kirei na*	**famous**	*yūmei na*

Na-Adjectives

Another type of adjective is the na-adjective. Na-adjectives end with na.
Na-adjectives precede the nouns and pronouns they describe, just as i-adjectives do.

| kind person | shinsetsu na hito |
| strange person | hen na hito |

Negative Na-Adjectives

Negative na-adjectives (*not* splendid, *not* beautiful, etc.) are formed by changing na to de (wa) nai.

a healthy person	genki na hito
a not healthy person	genki de nai hito
a kind person	shinsetsu na hito
a not kind person	shinsetsu de nai hito

Na-Adjectives as Complements

Na must be dropped when na-adjectives are used as complements.

| He is odd. | Ano hito wa hen desu. |
| I am healthy. | Watashi wa genki desu. |

You may notice that the greeting (o)genki desu ka is the abbreviation and honorific speech for anata wa genki desu ka, meaning *are you healthy?* The reply hai genki desu is the abbreviation of hai watashi wa genki desu, meaning *yes, I am healthy.*

Negative Na-Adjectives as Complements

The negative of "na-adjective (without na) + desu" is obtained by changing desu into de wa arimasen. For na-adjectives, the verb desu conjugates, while the na-adjectives do not.

He is kind.	Ano hito wa shinsetsu desu.
He is not kind.	Ano hito wa shinsetsu de wa arimasen.
This (place) is quiet.	Koko wa shizuka desu.
This (place) is not quiet.	Koko wa shizuka de wa arimasen.

Japanese conversation 2: Yoru Cute wa urusai desu ka.

Tom:	Cute wa rikō desu yo.
	Asa (Cute wa) boku o basu-sutoppu made miokurimasu.
	Gogo (Cute wa) boku no kaeri o basu-sutoppu de machimasu.
	Cute wa boku no taisetsu na inu desu.
Hanako:	Cute wa genki desu ne.
	Yoru Cute wa urusai desu ka.
Tom:	Iie (yoru Cute wa) shizuka desu.

English conversation 1: Is he noisy at night?

Tom and Hanako continue the conversation on Cute.

Tom:	Cute is clever!
	In the morning, he sees me off to the bus stop.
	In the afternoon, he waits for my return at the bus stop.
	Cute is my precious dog.
Hanako:	Cute is energetic, isn't he?
	Is he noisy at night?
Tom:	No, he is quiet.

Exercise 8

Translate into English:

1 *shizuka na (o)tera* ....

2 *hansamu na hito.* ....

3 *Tarō wa genki na neko desu.* ....

....

4 *Kore wa otōsan no taisetsu na hon desu.* ....

....

Translate into rōmaji:

6 *healthy cat.* ....

7 *beautiful eyes* ....

8 *not kind person.* ....

9 *This is a famous picture.* ....

10 *That is a healthy child.* ....

Writing Exercise

Practice the five katakana characters **a**, **i**, **u**, **e**, and **o**

ア，　イ，　ウ，　エ，　オ．

Step by step:　a  e

i  o

u

Vocabulary

dachshund	*dakkusufundo*	**see (a person off)**	*miokurimasu*
perfectly fit	*pittari na*	**return**	*kaeri*

What do you like?

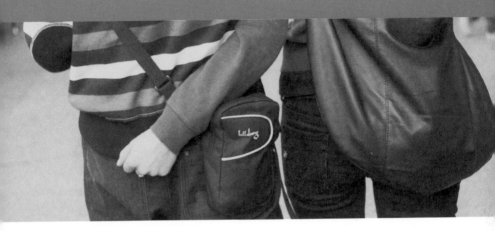

Day 17 is all about what you like and don't like. You will learn how to ask and answer questions, say what you want, and describe people. Take the time to practice what you have learned with the exercise section — you can check your progress using the answer key in the back of the book.

IN THE MOOD FOR...

Watashi wa _ ga suki desu is usually translated as "I like..." However, (watashi wa) anata ga suki desu when spoken to a member of the opposite sex becomes a very strong statement and is interpreted as "I love you" rather than "I like you".

Japanese conversation 1: Non no eiga ga suki desu ka.

Tom:	(Anata wa) eiga ga suki desu ka.
Hanako:	Hai suki desu.
Tom:	(Anata wa) nan no eiga ga suki desu ka.
Hanako:	(Watashi wa) romanchikku na eiga ga suki desu.
Tom:	(Anata wa) tabemono wa nani ga suki desu ka.
Hanako:	(Watashi wa tabemono wa) yakisoba ga suki desu.
Tom:	(Anata wa) nomimono wa nani ga suki desu ka.
Hanako:	(Watashi wa nomimono wa) orenji-jūsu ga suki desu.
Tom:	(Anata wa) dono sensei ga suki desu ka.
Hanako:	(Watashi wa) rekishi no sensei ga suki desu.

English conversation: What kinds of movies do you like?

Tom tries to find out what Hanako likes.

Tom:	Do you like movies?
Hanako:	Yes, I do.
Tom:	What kinds of movies do you like?
Hanako:	I like romantic movies.
Tom:	What foods do you like? (As for food, what do you like?)
Hanako:	I like yakisoba.
Tom:	What drinks do you like? (As for drink, what do you like?)
Hanako:	I like orange juice.
Tom:	Which teacher do you like?
Hanako:	I like the history teacher.

Grammar

I like: adjective + Desu

The sentence structure:

indirect subject wa **grammatical subject** ga "**adjective** + desu" is used to express like, dislike or want and describe skills, physical appearances and conditions.

Wa follows indirect subject ("topic" in Japanese grammar) and is translated as "as for ___", but becomes a subject in English translation.

Ga follows grammatical subject (subject in Japanese grammar but direct object etc. in English translation). The sentence is translated as:
As for (indirect subject) (grammatical subject) *is* (adjective)

Suki Na and *Kirai Na*

The following na-adjectives can help you talk about, and ask others about, likes and dislikes.

object that (I) like   suki na
object that (I) dislike   kirai na

More appropriate English translations for them are *the apple that somebody likes* and *the apple that somebody dislikes.*

The fruit that (I) like is apples.
Suki na kudamono wa ringo desu.
Carrots are vegetables that (I) dislike.
Ninjin wa kirai na yasai desu.

Since the above sentences in Japanese do not state *who* likes apples or who dislikes carrots, it is assumed that the speaker is talking about himself. Hence the above sentences imply *I like apples* and *I dislike carrots.*

Negative Forms

The negative adjectives for suki na and kirai na are obtained just as for other na-adjectives: na is replaced by de (wa) nai.

the food that (I) don't like
the teacher that (I) do not dislike
At night, I read the book that I do not like.

suki de (wa) nai tabemono
kirai de (wa) nai sensei
Yoru watashi wa suki de (wa)
nai hon o yomimasu.

Suki Na and *Kirai Na* as complements

Now consider the adjectives suki na and kirai na as complements. Just as for other na-adjectives, na is dropped—suki desu *to like,* and kirai desu *to dislike*—but they use a different sentence structure from other adjectives you learned.

Suki/kirai na is used as a complement in the sentence structure:
grammatical subject ga suki/kirai desu

Ga follows the grammatical subject and suki/kirai desu is translated as *to like/dislike.*

Ringo ga suki desu. I like apples.
Tenisu ga kirai desu. I dislike tennis.

wa

You have already learned that _wa may be used to express a topic in a sentence and may be translated as *as for _.* Let us put watashi wa in the sentence ringo ga suki desu: watashi wa ringo ga suki desu. The literal translation is *as for me, apples are likable,* but of course, *I like apples* is a more appropriate translation in English.

Here, Suki/kirai desu uses the sentence structure
(English subject) wa **(English object)** ga suki/kirai desu.

Let us consider the sentence watashi wa ringo ga suki desu, *I like apples,* and insert kudamono wa, *as for fruit,* in the sentence. Then, we get watashi wa kudamono wa ringo ga suki desu, *as for fruit, I like apples.*

I like tennis.	Watashi wa tenisu ga suki desu.
I dislike carrots.	Watashi wa ninjin ga kirai desu.
What do you like?	Anata wa nani ga suki desu ka.

The negative of suki/kirai desu is suki/kirai de wa arimasen, just as for other na-adjectives.

Betty does not like apples.
Betty-san wa ringo ga suki de wa arimasen.

-na adjectives II

Here is another set of na-adjectives.

| good (at a particular skill) | jōzu na |
| bad (at a particular skill) | heta na |

Just as for other na-adjectives, negative adjectives are obtained by replacing na with de (wa) nai.

a good picture	jōzu na e
not a good picture	jōzu de (wa) nai e
That good picture is the teacher's picture.	Ano jōzu na e wa sensei no e desu.

When jōzu na and heta na are used as complements, na must be dropped, just as for other na-adjectives: jōzu desu, to be good (at a skill), and heta desu, to be bad (at a skill). Jōzu/heta desu follows the same structure as suki/kirai desu. The negative of jōzu/heta desu is obtained by changing desu into de wa arimasen, just as for other na-adjectives.

Grandfather is good at the Japanese language.
Ojīsan wa Nihon-go ga jōzu desu.
I am not good at tennis.
Boku wa tenisu ga jōzu de wa arimasen.

Hoshii: I want that

desirable	hoshii

Hoshii conjugates like any other i-adjective: the negative of hoshii is hoshiku nai.

the book that (I) want	hoshii hon
the book that (I) don't want	hoshiku nai hon
The fruit that (I) want is strawberries.	Hoshii kudamono wa ichigo desu.

Hoshii desu / *I want* follows the same structure as suki/kirai desu and its negative tense is formed just like any other i-adjective complement: hoshiku nai desu.

I want a red dress.
Watashi wa akai fuku ga hoshii desu.
I don't want breakfast.
Watashi wa asa-gohan ga hoshiku nai desu.
What do you want?
Anata wa nani ga hoshii desu ka.

Exercises

Exercise 1

Write the following sentences in rōmaji using the sentence structure _ wa _ ga _ desu or de wa arimasen.

Write that you like:

1 apple ....

2 tempura ....

Write that you dislike:

3 carrot ....

4 milk ....

Write that you are good at:

5 tennis ....

6 English ....

Write that you are not good at:

7 swimming ....

8 Japanese ....

Write that you want:

9 steak ....

10 TV ....

Exercise 2

You will hear a description of Tom's older brother.

Answer the questions in rōmaji.

1 Onīsan wa nan no supōtsu o shimasu ka. ....
....

2 Onīsan wa jūdō ga jōzu desu ka. Iie ....
....

3 Onīsan wa sumō ga suki desu ka. ....
....

Exercise 3

Translate into English:

1 *suki na hito* ....

2 *hoshii hon* ....

3 *kirai de wa nai sensei* ....

4 *hoshiku nai gohan* ....

5 *Ringo wa suki na kudamono desu.* ....

6 *Watashi wa kirai na hon o gakkō de yomimasu.* ....

....

7 *Ano zō wa anata no banana ga hoshii desu.* ....

....

Translate into rōmaji:

8 *the teacher whom I dislike* ....

9 *bad English* ....

10 *not good Japanese* ....

11 *the drink that I don't want* ....

12 *I like Japanese people.* ....

13 *For dinner, I want a big steak.* ....

....

14 *Whom do you like?* ....

Questions and answers

The replies for _ wa _ ga "adjective + desu" ka are:
hai "adjective + desu"
or
iie negative of "adjective + desu"

Question	Answer
Anata wa ringo ga suki desu ka.	Hai suki desu.
Do you like apples?	Yes, I do.
	Iie suki de wa arimasen.
	No, I don't.
Ananta wa kore ga hoshii desu ka.	Hai hoshii desu.
Do you want this?	Yes, I do.
	Iie hoshiku nai desu.
	No, I don't.

Describing Others with "Adjective + Desu"

These adjectives aren't just for talking about yourself! The same structure as suki/kirai desu can be used to describe other people (and animated subjects), using the following vocabulary.

height, stature	se
quiet (sound, voice)	chiisai
loud (sound, voice)	ōkii

Hanako has big eyes. (As for Hanako, the eyes are big.)
Hanako-san wa me ga ōkii desu.
Americans are tall. (As for Americans, the heights are big.)
Amerika-jin wa se ga takai desu.
Makoto has a quiet voice. (As for Makoto, the voice is quiet.)
Makoto-kun wa koe ga chiisai desu.

The above sentences are equivalent to the following sentences.

Hanako's eyes are big.
Hanako-san no me wa ōkii desu.
Americans are tall. (Americans' heights are big.)
Amerika-jin no se wa takai desu.
Makoto's voice is quiet.
Makoto-kun no koe wa chiisai desu.

Exercise 4

Write in rōmaji that you have pain in the following parts of your body, using the sentence structure _ wa _ ga _ desu.

1 head ....

2 leg ....

3 arm ....

4 eye ....

5 stomach ....

Exercise 5

Translate into English:

1 *Watashi wa onaka ga itai desu.* ....

....

2 *Hanako-san wa me ga kirei desu.* ....

....

3 *Kirin wa kubi ga nagai desu ka.* ....

....

4 *Nihon-jin wa hana ga hikui desu ne.* ....

....

Translate into rōmaji:

5 *My arms are itchy.* ....

....

6 *I have a pain in my leg.* ....

....

7 *My father has big hands.* ....

....

8 *Elephants have long noses.* ....

....

Writing exercise

Practice the five katakana characters ka, ki, ku, ke and ko

カ， キ， ク， ケ， コ.

Step by step:

ka  ke

ki  ko

ku

Out & about

新幹線
Shinkansen

みどりの窓口
Ticket Office
售票处 매표소

きっぷうりば
Tickets
售票处 매표소

Day 18 introduces you to adjectives and adverbs so you can express yourself more comprehensively. You will also learn about Japanese culture and shrine and temple etiquette and you will continue to practice writing Japanese characters.

SHRINES ETIQUETTE

There is a certain etiquette to follow when attending a Japanese shrine. Firstly, modest dress is important. Once you've passed through the torii (gate), you should wash your hands in the stone basin just inside. It is customary to toss a small offering into the cashbox at the foot of the haiden (oratory) before sounding the shaker to attract the attention of the God. Devout worshippers also clap their hands twice, making doubly sure the god is listening.

Japanese conversation 1: Dono aisukurīmu ga ichi-ban suki desu ka.

Tom:	Tōkyō wa totemo atsui desu ne.
Hanako:	(Hai) sō desu ne. Aisukurīmu o tabemasen ka.
Tom:	(Boku wa) aisukurīmu ga suki desu.
Hanako:	(Anata wa) dono aisukurīmu ga ichi-ban suki desu ka.
Tom:	(Boku wa) chokorēto ga ichi-ban suki desu.
Hanako:	Watashi wa banira ga chokorēto yori suki desu.
Tom:	Are wa kirai na sensei desu.
Hanako:	(Anata wa ano sensei ga) naze kirai desu ka.
Tom:	Ano sensei wa Nihon-go no sensei desu.
	Nihon-go wa totemo muzukashii desu.
Hanako:	Anata wa Nihon-go ga jōzu desu yo.

English conversation 1: Which ice cream do you like best?

Tom and Hanko discuss ice cream.

Tom:	Tokyo is very hot, isn't it?
Hanako:	Yes, it is, isn't it? Would you like to eat ice cream?
Tom:	I like ice cream.
Hanako:	Which ice cream do you like best?
Tom:	I like chocolate best.
Hanako:	I like vanilla more than chocolate.
Tom:	Look, that's the teacher I dislike.
Tom:	He is the teacher of the Japanese language.
	Japanese is very difficult.
Hanako:	You're good at Japanese!

Grammar

Adverbs

Adverbs describe adjectives, verbs and adverbs. For example, *very* of a *very delicious apple* describes the adjective *delicious*; *quickly* of *I drive quickly* describes the verb *drive*.

A Japanese adverb is usually placed immediately before the adjective, verb or adverb that it describes.

To form adverbs, convert the final **i** of **i-adjectives** into **ku**.

Adjectives	Adverbs
hayai quick, early, fast	**hayaku** quickly, early, fast
ōkii big	**ōkiku** big
omoshiroi interesting	**omoshiroku** interestingly
osoi late, slow	**osoku** late, slowly
takai expensive, high	**takaku** expensively, highly
tanoshii enjoyable	**tanoshiku** enjoyably
yasui cheap	**yasuku** cheaply
yoi good	**yoku** often, a lot

When you are translating a Japanese word that looks like an adverb ending with **ku**, be careful to check that it is not followed by **nai**: a negative **i-adjective** has the form _**ku nai**.

The adverbs formed from **i-adjectives** by changing **i** into **ku** describe verbs only.

Father goes to America often.
Otōsan wa Amerika e yoku ikimasu.
The younger brother eats meals enjoyably.
Otōto wa gohan o tanoshiku tabemasu.
I shall go to the restaurant late.
Watashi wa resutoran ni osoku ikimasu.
I shall sell you this cheaply.
Watashi wa kore o anata ni yasuku urimasu.

Note that the adverb **yoku**, *well*, has many more meanings than just that of converting **yoi**, *good*, into an adverb.

Totemo (or Taihen)

The adverb **totemo** (or **taihen**) is used to mean *very* when it describes a positive adjective or adverb. The following examples show **totemo** describing adjectives and adverbs respectively.

totemo oishii ringo — a very delicious apple
totemo tanoshii eiga — a very enjoyable movie
Hiroshi-kun wa totemo omoshiroi hito desu. — Hiroshi is a very interesting person.
Ano totemo shizuka na hito wa Kazuko-san desu. — That very quiet person is Kazuko.
Watashi wa kore o totemo takaku urimasu. — I will sell this very expensively.

Amari

The adverb **amari** is used to mean *(not) very* when it describes a negative adjective or adverb describing a negative verb; it is used to mean *(not) a lot* or *(not) much* when it describes a negative verb.

amari oishiku nai sakana — not very delicious fish
Amari takaku nai sakana o kudasai. — May I have (some) not very expensive fish please?
Kono inu wa amari rikō de wa nai desu. — This dog is not very clever.
Watashi wa gakkō e amari hayaku ikimasen. — I don't go to school very early.
Watashi wa tegami o amari kakimasen. — I don't write letters much.

More Adverbs

how, in what way	dō	so, in that way	sō
not yet (used with negative verbs)	mada	soon	sorosoro
again	mata	immediately	sugu
a little	sukoshi	much, many, a lot, plenty	takusan
already	mō	sometimes	tokidoki
more	motto	soon, presently, before long	yagate
why	naze		
a little while ago	sakki	slowly	yukkuri

Would you like to eat more?
Motto tabemasen ka.
Hanako has not come yet.
Hanako-san wa mada kimasen.
Could you (speak) more slowly please?
Motto yukkuri onegai shimasu.
Father buys plenty (of books).
Otōsan wa (hon o) takusan kaimasu.
Why do you go to school this Sunday?
Kono nichi-yōbi ni anata wa gakkō e naze ikimasu ka.

Exercises

Exercise 1

Convert the following adjectives into adverbs.

Adjectives	Adverbs
1 hayai quick early	**hayaku** ....quickly, early
2 nagai long	.... long
3 usui thin	.... thinly
4 yasashii gentle	.... gently
5 tanoshii enjoyable	.... enjoyably

Exercise 2

Write either **totemo** or **amari** in the blanks.

1 ....**oishii ringo**   a very delicious apple

2 ....**oishiku nai ringo**   not a very delicious apple

3 ....**hayai densha**   a very fast train

4 ....**hayakunai densha**   not a very fast train

Japanese conversation 2: Nihon-go de dare to yoku hanashimasu ka.

Makoto:	(Anata wa) Nihon-go de dare to yoku hanashimasu ka.
Tom:	(Boku wa Nihongo de) Hanako-san to (yoku) hanashimasu.
Makoto:	(Anata wa Nihon-go de) Hiroshi-kun to mo yoku hanashimasu ka.
Tom:	(Iie boku wa Hiroshi-kun to) amari hanashimasen.
Makoto:	(Anata wa Hiroshi-kun to) naze (hanashimasen ka).
Tom:	Hiroshi-kun wa (Nihongo o) totemo hayaku ha-nashimasu.
	Hanako-san wa (Nihongo o) totemo yukkuri hanashimasu.

English conversation 2: With whom do you often speak Japanese?

Makoto asks Tom about his Japanese speaking habits.

Makoto:	With whom do you often speak in Japanese?
Tom:	I speak with Hanako.
Makoto:	Do you often speak with Hiroshi too?
Tom:	No, I don't speak much with him.
Makoto:	Why?
Tom:	Hiroshi speaks very quickly.
	Hanako speaks very slowly.

Exercise 3

Write adverbs in the blanks.

1 .... watashi wa soko e ikimasu.

I shall go there immediately.

2 .... anata wa benkyō o shimasu ka.

Why do you study?

3 ....Hanako-san-tachi wa kimasu.

Hanako and the others will come soon.

4 ....mizu o kudasai.

May I have more water please?

Exercise 4

Translate into English:

1 *totemo kirei na doresu* ....

2 *totemo ōkii hito* ....

3 *Watashi wa soko e sugu ikimasu.* ....

....

4 *Anata wa Hanako-san ga naze suki desu ka.* ....

....

5 *Pātī ni sukoshi hayaku ikimasen ka.* ....

....

Translate into rōmaji:

6 *very fast train* ....

7 *not very cute cat* ....

8 *Is a big house very expensive?* ....

....

9 *My younger brother speaks English very slowly.* ....

....

10 *My father will come soon.* ....

....

Comparative and Superlative: More/Most

Japanese adjectives do not have comparative (e.g., *larger*) and superlative (e.g., *largest*) forms. Rather, comparative and superlative are expressed using particles or adverbs, as in the English *beautiful, more beautiful, most beautiful.*

Comparative

The comparative is expressed with the particle **yori** *(more) than.* By inserting **C yori,** *(more) than C,* in the sentence structure **A wa** "adjective + **desu,**" you express the comparative idea: **A wa C yori** "adjective + **desu**" implies *A is _____ -er than C.*

Consider **Tom-kun wa ōkii desu,** *Tom is big.* Inserting **Makoto-kun yori,** *(more) than Makoto,* in the sentence, we get **Tom-kun wa Makoto-kun yori ōkii desu,** *Tom is bigger than Makoto.*

Hanako-san wa kirei desu.	Hanako is pretty.
Hanako-san wa Yōko-san yori kirei desu.	Hanako is prettier than Yoko.

To reinforce the comparison, add the adverb **motto** *more,* before adjectives. **Motto** is most often translated as *much.*

Tom is much bigger than Makoto.	Tom-kun wa Makoto-kun yori motto ōkii desu
Hanako is much prettier than Yoko.	Hanako-san wa Yōko-san yori motto kirei desu.

The sentence **A wa B ga** "adjective + desu" expresses the idea: **A** is **adjective** at **B** (e.g. **Tom-kun wa Nihongo ga jōzu desu,** *Tom is good at English*). You can add **C yori** into this construction in two ways:

A wa C yori B ga "adjective + desu," meaning A is _____-er than C (at B).
A wa B ga C yori "adjective + desu," meaning A is _____-er at B than C.

(My) father is good at English.
Otōsan wa Eigo ga jōzu desu.
(My) father is better than I am at English.
Otōsan wa watashi yori Eigo ga jōzu desu.
This is the case of "A is _____-er than C."

(My) father is good at English.
Otōsan wa Eigo ga jōzu desu.
(My) father is better at English than Japanese.
Otōsan wa Eigo ga Nihon-go yori jōzu desu.
This is the case of "A is _____-er at B than C."

Note that the above sentence **Otōsan wa Eigo ga Nihon-go yori jōzu desu** can also be written as **Otōsan wa Nihon-go yori Eigo ga jōzu desu.** You must determine from the context whether **Nihon-go yori** is compared with **otōsan** or **Eigo.**

Superlative

Superlatives are formed by putting the following adverbs in front of adjectives.

most, best, number one	ichi-ban	most, best	mottomo

Ringo wa yasui kudamono desu.
Ringo wa ichi-ban/mottomo yasui kudamono desu.

Apples are cheap fruits.
Apples are the cheapest fruits.

Watashi wa ichigo ga suki desu.	I like strawberries.
Watashi wa ichigo ga ichi-ban/mottomo suki desu.	I like strawberries most.

Hiroshi-kun wa se ga takai desu.	Hiroshi is tall.
Makoto-kun wa se ga ichi-ban/mottomo takai desu.	Makoto is tallest.

Exercise 5

Convert ordinary statements into comparative statements by inserting _ yori, *more than* _.

1 Kore wa yasui desu. *This is cheap.*

Insert are yori *more than that,* **to get:**

Kore wa are yori yasui desu.

This is cheaper than that.

2 Makoto-kun wa hansamu desu. *Makoto is handsome.*

Insert Hiroshi-kun yori, *more than Hiroshi,* **to get:**

....

Makoto is more handsome than Hiroshi.

3 Ken-kun wa Chūgoku-go ga jōzu desu. *Ken is good at Chinese.*

Insert Nihon-go yori, *more than Japanese,* **to get:**

....

Ken is better at Chinese than Japanese.

4 Watashi wa yakyū ga suki desu. *I like baseball.*

Insert tenisu yori, *more than tennis,* **to get:**

....

I like baseball more than tennis.

Japanese conversation 3: Nozomi

Makoto:	(Anata wa Tōkyō kara Kyōto made) dono kisha de ikimasu ka.
Tom:	(Boku wa) Kodama de ikimasu.
Makoto:	Hikari wa Kodama yori hayai desu yo.
Tom:	Boku wa Hikari de ikimasu.
Makoto:	Nozomi wa mottomo hayai desu yo.
Tom:	Boku wa Nozomi de ikimasu.

English conversation 3: Nozomi

Makoto suggests that Tom go to Kyoto by Nozomi.

Makoto:	By which train do you go (from Tokyo to Kyoto)?
Tom:	I'm going by Kodama.
Makoto:	Hikari is faster than Kodama!
Tom:	I will go by Hikari.
Makoto:	Nozomi is the fastest!
Tom:	I'll go by Nozomi.

Exercise 6

Say the following sentences in Japanese and check your answers on the recording.

1 Hikari is faster than Kodama.

2 Nozomi is faster than Hikari.

3 Kodama is the slowest.

4 Nozomi is the fastest.

Exercise 7

Translate into English:

1 *Nihon no ie wa Kanada no ie yori semai desu.* ....

....

2 *Amerika-jin wa Nihon-jin yori hana ga takai desu.* ....

....

3 *Watashi wa chiri ga rekishi yori motto suki desu.* ....

....

Translate into rōmaji:

4 *The mathematics teacher is kinder than the geography teacher.* ....

....

5 *This dog is bigger than my younger brother.* ....

....

6 *American grapes are much cheaper than Japanese grapes.* ....

....

Writing exercise

Practice the five katakana characters **sa, shi, su, se** and **so.**

サ， シ， ス， セ， ソ.

Step by step: sa 　se

shi 　so

su

Vocabulary

ice cream *aisukurīmu*　　　　**chocolate** *chokorēto*
vanilla *banira*

day:19

At home

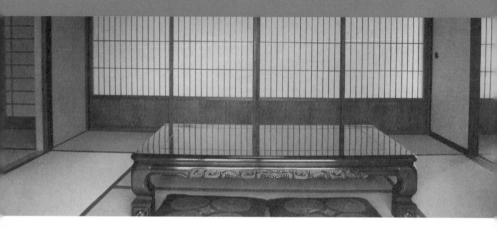

Day 19 talks about your home. You will learn how to say *to be* and *to have* in Japanese and you will be able to reinforce what you have learnt through the exercise section. Finally, you will pick up some country and culture information about traditional Japanese houses.

TRADITIONAL HOUSES

When entering the Japanese houses, there is usually a step before you go on up to the living spaces. At this point you should remove your shoes. This is beacause traditional Japanese houses used to have **tatami** *floors in all the rooms, whereas in modern houses, there are less common. On your arrival, it is polite to say "***Ojamashimasu***" which roughly means "Please excuse the intrusion".*

Japanese conversation 1: Ima (o)uchi ni otōsan ka okāsan ga imasu ka.

Woman:	Ima (o)uchi ni otōsan ka okāsan ga imasu ka.
Tom:	(Ima uchi ni) otōsan mo okāsan mo imasen.
	San-ji made ni (otōsan to okāsan wa) depāto kara kaerimasu.
Woman:	Yo-ji ni (watashi wa) mata kimasu.

English conversation 1: Is Your Father or Mother at Home Now?

A visitor comes to see Tom's parents while they are out shopping.

Woman:	Is (your) father or mother at home now?
Tom:	Neither (my) father nor (my) mother is at home.
	They will be back from the department store by 3 o'clock.
Woman:	I'll come again at 4 o'clock.

Grammar

Verbs: to be

There are four different categories of words and expressions meaning *to be* in Japanese.

1 **Desu** is used to equate one thing with another (*this is* a *book*).
2 To indicate condition, or quality, or characteristics, Japanese uses "adjective + **desu**".
3 The independent verbs **arimasu** and **imasu** may indicate locations/positions.
4 The progressive present tense is expressed by the verb form called **te**-form followed by **imasu** (e.g., **tabete imasu**, *to be eating;* **hanashite imasu**, *to be talking*).

In this lesson, you will learn category 3 above of *to be.*

Position/Location

The following verbs are used to denote position/location.

arimasu	*to be located/to exist* is used to indicate a position/location of a non-living subject.
imasu	*to be located/to exist* is used to indicate a position/location of a living subject.

Arimasu and imasu have the sentence structure.
place ni **subject** ga arimasu/imasu.

The particle ni follows the location of the subject and is translated as *at/in;* the particle ga follows a grammatical subject (a subject in Japanese, but not necessarily a subject in the English translation).

Koko ni inu ga imasu.	Here is a dog. (At this place, a dog is located.)
Soko ni neko ga imasu.	There is a cat. (At that place, a cat is located.)
Niwa ni okāsan ga imasu.	The mother is in the garden.
	(In the garden, the mother is located.)
Koko ni hon ga arimasu.	Here is a book. (At this place, a book is located.)
Niwa ni isu ga arimasu.	A chair is in the garden.
	(In the garden, a chair is located.)
Asoko ni basu-sutoppu ga arimasu.	That (over there) is the bus stop.
	(Over there, the bus stop is located.)

Exercises

Exercise 1

Circle the words that make sense in the blank for the sentence.

Daidokoro ni.........................ga arimasu.

shio   koshō   satō   otōsan   shōyu   onīsan   watashi   neko   koppu

Circle the words that make sense in the blank for the sentence.

Daidokoro ni......................... ga imasu.

kōcha   (o)cha   satō   neko   okāsan   sara

Questions

Interrogatives dare, *who;* doko, *where* and nani, *what,* are used with arimasu and imasu as well.

Here is an apple.	Koko ni ringo ga arimasu.
Where is an apple?	Doko ni ringo ga arimasu ka.
What is here?	Koko ni nani ga arimasu ka.
Father is in the garden.	Niwa ni otōsan ga imasu.
Who is in the garden?	Niwa ni dare ga imasu ka.

Negative Forms

The negatives forms of arimasu and imasu are arimasen (or nai desu) and imasen (or inai desu) respectively. In this book, we use arimasen and imasen.

There isn't salt (there is no salt) in the kitchen.
Daidokoro ni shio ga arimasen.
There isn't a cat in the garden.
Niwa ni neko ga imasen.

The particle mo, which means *also/too*, replaces ga or follows ni.

Here is the salt.
Koko ni shio ga arimasu.
Here is the pepper also (as well as salt).
Koko ni koshō mo arimasu.
Here is a cat.
Koko ni neko ga imasu.
There too is a cat.
Asoko ni mo neko ga imasu.
There is neither salt nor pepper here.
Koko ni shio mo koshō mo arimasen.

Exercise 2

Listen to the descriptions of someone's grocery shopping habits.

Answer the following questions in rōmaji

1 Okāsan wa doko de kaimono o shimasu ka. ....

....

2 Sūpāmāketto ni hito ga ōzei imasu ka. (ōzei-many people) ....

....

3 Sūpāmāketto wa benri desu ka. (Sūpāmāketto wa) fuben desu ka. ....

....

4 Sūpāmāketto ni oishii pan ga arimasu ka. ....

....

5 Doko ni oishii pan ga arimasu ka. ....

....

6 Okāsan wa niku-ya to sakana-ya e mo ikimasu ka. ....

....

Exercise 3

Translate into English:

1 *Asoko ni depāto ga arimasu.* ....
....

2 *Soko ni Makoto-kun ga imasu.* ....
....

3 *Niwa ni ōtosan to okāsan ga imasu..* ....
....

4 *Koko ni shio mo koshō mo arimasu.* ....
....

5 *Daidokoro ni neko ga imasu. Niwa ni mo neko ga imasu.* ....
....

6 *Koko ni nani ga arimasu ka.* ....
....

Translate into rōmaji:

7 *Over there, (there) are father's eyeglasses.* ....
....

8 *At that fruit shop, (there) are very delicious apples and oranges.* ....
....

9 *In the hospital, (there) are medical doctors and nurses.* ....
....

10 *Betty is not in the garden. (In the garden, there is not Betty.)* ....
....

11 *Where is the bank?* ....
....

12 *What is over there?* ....
....

A reply to the question _ ni _ ga arimasu/imasu ka uses the sentence structure hai arimasu/imasu or iie arimasen/imasen.

Question	Answer
Heya ni terebi ga arimasu ka.	Hai arimasu.
Is there a TV in the room?	Yes, there is.
	Iie arimasen.
	No, there isn't.

I have time: _ Wa _ Ga Arimasu

Arimasu is also used to express *to have* where the item possessed is not an animate (living) object. It has the sentence structure

possessor wa **item possessed** ga arimasu.

Wa follows an animate indirect subject (a subject, in English translation).
Ga follows a grammatical subject (an object, in English translation).

Consider the sentence watashi wa tesuto ga arimasu. Watashi wa is translated as *as for me,* and tesuto ga arimasu is translated as *a test exists.* So the literal translation is *as for me, a test exists,* or simply *I have a test.* Here are some words that can come in handy with this sentence structure.

(spare) time jikan	pool pūru
money (o)kane	test tesuto

Do you have (spare) time?	Anata wa jikan ga arimasu ka.
Yes, I do.	Hai arimasu.
I don't have money.	Watashi wa (o)kane ga arimasen.
This cat does not have a name yet.	Kono neko wa namae ga mada arimasen.

The school has a pool: _ Ni _ Ga Arimasu.

If the possessor is inanimate, it is followed by ni, forming the sentence structure _ ni _ ga arimasu. Here arimasu may be translated as *to have* as well as *to be located* or *to exist.*

Department stores have toilets. (At department stores, there are toilets)
Depāto ni toire ga arimasu.
The school has no swimming pool. (At the school, there is not a swimming pool.)
Gakkō ni pūru ga arimasen.

Since both ni and de can mean *at/in* in English, you must be careful about which one you use. De is used when **an action/event** takes place "at/in the place" while ni is used to describe location "*at/in* the place." Start with: Watashi-tachi wa pātī ga arimasu.   We have a party.

Insert **gakkō de** to get:	Watashi-tachi wa gakkō de pātī ga arimasu.	We have a party at the school.	

Change *party* to *test:*	Watashi-tachi wa gakkō de tesuto ga arimasu.	We have a test at the school.
	Watashi-tachi wa gakkō ni pūru ga arimasu.	We have a pool at the school.*

While "a pool" is a thing *located* at the school, "a party" and "a test" are *events that take place* at the school.

* When the subject owns or belong to "place", it sound more natural to use "**no**" instead of "**wa**":
Watashi-tachi no gakkō ni pūru ga arimasu. Our school has a pool.

I have a sister: *imasu*

You may talk of having "living things" by using **imasu**.

Hanako has a younger brother.	Hanako-san wa otōto ga imasu.
(My) aunt does not have a child.	Obasan wa kodomo ga imasen.

Note that, to ask for a fish in a shop, you say (**mise ni**) **sakana ga arimasu ka,** *Do you have fish?* However, you say (**ike ni**) **sakana ga imasu ka,** *Is there a fish (in the pond)?* The fish sold at a shop, whether it is dead or alive, is regarded as an object of food and is treated as inanimate.

Japanese conversation 2: Nani o Hanako-san ni kaimasu ka.

Makoto:	(Boku-tachi wa) nani o Hanako-san ni kaimasu ka.
Tom:	Hon wa dō desu ka.
Makoto:	Hanako-san wa hon o amari yomimasen.
Tom:	Sētā wa dō desu ka.
Makoto:	Sore wa ii aidea desu.
	(Boku-tachi wa sētā wa) ikura no sētā ni shimasu ka.
Tom:	Go-sen-en wa dō desu ka.
Makoto:	Kore wa boku no ni-sen go-hyaku-en desu.
***	
Tom:	Ano sētā wa ikura desu ka.
Clerk:	(Are wa) nana-sen-en desu.
Tom:	(Depāto ni are yori) motto yasui sētā ga arimasu ka.
Clerk:	Kore wa dō desu ka.
Tom:	(Kore wa) suteki desu. (Kore wa) ikura desu ka.
Clerk:	(Kore wa) go-sen-en desu.
Tom:	(Kore wa) totemo yasui desu. (Depāto ni) akai sētā ga arimasu ka.
Clerk:	Hai arimasu.
Tom:	(Boku-tachi wa) kore ni shimasu.

English conversation 2: What should we buy for Hanako?

Makoto and Tom buy a birthday present for Hanako at a department store.

Makoto:	What should we buy for Hanako?
Tom:	How about a book?
Makoto:	Hanako doesn't read books much.
Tom:	How about a sweater?
Makoto:	That's a good idea.
	How much do we want to spend
	(what price of the sweater do we decide on)?
Tom:	How about ¥5,000?
Makoto:	This is my ¥2,500.
***	
Tom:	How much is that sweater?
Clerk:	It's ¥7,000.
Tom:	Do you (the department store) have a cheaper sweater
	(than that)?
Clerk:	How about this?
Tom:	It's lovely. How much?
Clerk:	It's ¥5,000.
Tom:	It's very cheap. Do you (the department store) have
	a red sweater?
Clerk:	Yes, we do.
Tom:	We'll take this one (we shall decide on this).

Exercise 4

You will hear about Hanako's family's plan for tomorrow.

Answer the questions in complete sentences in rōmaji.

1 Ashita Hanako-san wa nani ga arimasu ka. ....

....

2 Ashita onēsan wa daigaku de jugyō ga arimasu ka. ....

....

3 Ashita onēsan wa nani ga arimasu ka. ....

....

4 Imōto wa gakkō ga arimasu ka. ....

....

5 Otōsan wa kaisha de nani ga arimasu ka. ....

....

6 Okāsan wa nani ga arimasu ka. ....

....

Exercise 5

Translate into English:

1 *Ashita no asa watashi-tachi wa Eigo no tesuto ga arimasu.* ....

....

2 *Ashita watashi wa Hanako-san no bāsudē pātī ga arimasu.* ....

....

3 *Anata wa kodomo-san ga imasu ka.* ....

....

4 *Ima watashi wa jikan ga arimasen.* ....

....

Translate into rōmaji:

5 *I have money.* ....

6 *(My) father has a meeting in Tokyo.* ....

....

7 *Do you have a TV in (your) room?* ....

....

8 *Do you have an older brother?* ....

....

Exercise 6

You will hear some questions about Dialogue 2. Listen to the questions and reply to each question aloud in Japanese. Check your answers on the CD.

Writing exercise

Practice the five katakana characters **ta, chi, tsu, te** and **to**.

タ， チ， ツ， テ， ト.

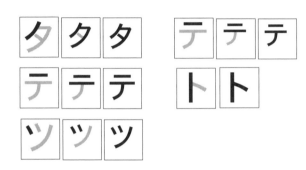

Vocabulary

Notice that the suffix **-ya** is put after nouns to describe shops.

shops	*mise*	**rice bowl**	*(o)chawan*
flower shop	*hana-ya*	**salt**	*shio*
toy shop	*omocha-ya*	**cup**	*koppu*
bookstore	*hon-ya*	**soy sauce**	*shōyu*
bread shop	*pan-ya*	**plate**	*(o)sara*
cake shop	*kēki-ya*	**(English) tea**	*kōcha*
fish shop	*sakana-ya*	**pepper**	*koshō*
fruit shop	*kudamono-ya*	**green tea**	*(o)cha*
liquor store	*sakaya*	**salt**	*shio*
butcher shop	*niku-ya*	**aidea**	*idea*
supermarket	*sūpāmāketto*	**suteki na**	*lovely*
candy shop	*(o)kashi-ya*	**Kore wa dō desu ka.**	*How about this?/How*
vegetable shop	*yaoya*		*do you like this?*

Directions

Day 20 introduces directions to help you find your way around town and the vocabulary you need to do this. You will also learn how to use possessive adjectives to say (my, your, his, etc.). Finally, you can continue to practice your Japanese writing skills.

ENGLISH?

English is taught from the 5th grade of primary school onwards, and students must pass English, mathematics and Japanese in the university entrance exam. Once the student gets into a university, graduation is almost guaranteed, so they spend a good part of their time enjoying themselves or working at part-time jobs.

Japanese conversation 1: Doko ni hon-ya ga arimasu ka.

Tom:	Hanako-san, doko ni hon-ya ga arimasu ka.
Hanako:	(Anata wa) daigaku no mae de basu ni
	norimasu*. (Anata wa) dōbutsuen no mae de basu kara orimasu.
	Soko kara (anata wa) depāto no hōe massugu ikimasu.
	Hidari-gawa ni yūbinkyoku ga arimasu.
	(Anata wa) yūbinkyoku no mae no shingō o hidari e magarimasu.
	Migi-gawa ni hon-ya ga arimasu.

English conversation 1: Where is a bookstore?

Tom asks Hanako for directions to a bookstore..

Tom:	Where is a bookstore, Hanako?
Hanako:	You get (ride) on a bus in front of the college.
	You get off (from) the bus in front of the zoo.
	From there, you go straight toward the direction of the
	department store.
	There is a post office on (your) left side.
	You turn to (your) left at the traffic light in front of the post office.
	On (your) right side, there is the bookstore.

*"A vehicle" + ni norimasu means ride on "a vehicle."

Grammar

Noun No Noun

You may recall that A no B indicates that A is a possessor of B (translated as *A's B*), A is the origin of B or A describes B (translated as *B of/for/in/on A*).

otōsan no hon father's book *(A is a possessor of B)*
Furansu no uta French song *(A is the origin of B)*
getsu-yōbi no asa Monday morning *(A describes B)*
asa no hachi-ji eight o'clock in the morning *(A describes B)*
Nihon-go no hon a book in Japanese *(A describes B)*

Prepositions with No

Look at the following list of nouns of position.

mae	front part, position in front
shita	lower part, space under (something)
yoko	side part, position beside
ue	upper part, space over (something)
ushiro	back part, position behind
tonari	next door, position next to
chikaku	nearby
naka	middle, inside
soto	outside

noun + no + noun of position

produces an adverbial phrase such as *in front of the house, on the table, under the desk,* etc. For example, no mae implies the position in front of, no ue implies the upper part of, no naka implies the inside of, and so on. Hence, ie no mae which is more appropriately *in front of the house.* In the examples below, the appropriate translations are given.

ie no soto	outside the house
tēburu no ue	on the table
heya no naka	in the room
ie no mae	in front of the house
tsukue no shita	under the desk
okāsan no yoko	beside the mother
anata no ushiro	behind you

Betty-san to Robert-kun wa karate o ie no soto de shimasu.
Betty and Robert practice karate outside the house.
Okāsan no ushiro ni otōto ga imasu.
There is (my) younger brother behind (my) mother.
Tsukue no ue ni hon ga arimasu.
There is a book on the desk.
Niwa no tēburu no shita ni neko ga imasu.
There is a cat under the table in the garden.

Prepositions of position

No is also used to connect two nouns in cases where, in English, a preposition of position is used. A preposition of position is just a word placed before another word denoting a position. For example, *at* of *the train at the platform* and *in* of *the chair in the garden* are prepositions of position. They are placed before *the platform* and *the garden* which describe positions of the train and the chair. So, A no B is translated as B in/at A. Note that the particle ni, *in/at,* or any other particle denoting position (such as de, in/on/at) may not be used to connect two nouns.

niwa no isu	the chair in the garden
ike no mizu	pond water (water in the pond)
sora no tori	the bird in the sky
Tōkyō no tatemono	the building in Tokyo
ike	pond
sora	sky
tatemono	building

Exercise 1

Write either **no** or **de** in the blanks.

1 Cute wa kawa.. mizu o nomimasu.

Cute drinks water of the river.

2 Cute wa niwa .... gohan o tabemasu.

Cute eats his meals in the garden.

3 Kisha .... naka de tabemasen ka.

Would you like to eat on the train?

Exercise 2

Say the following phrases using the structure _ no _, and check your
pronunciation on the CD.

1 in the house

2 outside the house

3 near the house

4 beside the house

5 in front of the house

6 behind the house

7 on the desk

8 under the desk

Exercise 3

Look at the picture and write **rōmaji** in the blanks.

1 Tsukue no... **ni hon ga arimasu.**

2 Tsukue no...**ni neko ga imasu.**

3 Tsukue no...**ni isu ga arimasu.**

4 Tsukue no ....**ni enpitsu ga arimasu.**

Exercise 4

Translate into English:

1 *Kono inu wa toire no mizu o nomimasu.* ....

....

2 *Tsukue no ue ni anata no hon ga arimasu yo.* ....

....

3 *Ie no naka ni otōsan to okāsan ga imasu.* ....

....

4 *Watashi no otōto wa manga o basu no naka de yomimasu.* ....

....

5 *Gakkō no mae ni byōin ga arimasu.* ....

....

Translate into rōmaji:

6 *Buildings in New York City (Nyūyōku) are very tall.* ....

....

7 *On the desk, there is a pencil.* ....

....

8 *A big fish is in the sea.* ....

....

9 *The post office is beside that big department store.* ....

....

10 *What is on the table in the kitchen?* ....

....

Before / After

ato   (time) after
mae   (time) before

"Noun" **no mae/ato** is used to express time before/after "noun." This phrase may be followed by **ni**.

Gohan no mae ni watashi wa te o araimasu.
I wash (my) hands before meals.

Ban-gohan no ato ni watashi wa terebi o mimasu.
I watch TV after dinner.

Directions

When you want to mention the point where a turn is to be made (e.g., "turn right at the intersection," "go left at the T-junction") or proceed further ("go straight through the intersection"), the point is followed by **o** as shown below.

**Kōsaten o migi e
ikimasu/ magarimasu.**
Go/turn (to) right at the
intersection.

**Tsukiatari o hidari e
magarimasu/ ikimasu.**
Turn/go (to) left at the
T-junction.

**Kōsaten o massugu
ikimasu.**
Go straight through (at) the
intersection.

Direction words

Arimasu is used to ask a direction. Here is a list of words which are associated with directions.

hō	direction (of travel/motion)
hōkō	direction(s)
kōsaten	intersection
tsukiatari	T-junction
dōro	road, way, highway
michi	road, path, way
shingō	traffic light
hantai	opposite
hidari	left
migi	right
magarimasu	turn
norimasu	ride (on)
massugu	straight through
-gawa	- side

Exercise 5

Look at the map. You are driving a car, going from southwest to northeast.

Write and say aloud what you can see at each exit, using the sentence

structure _ ni _ ga arimasu. Check your answers and your pronunciation on the CD.

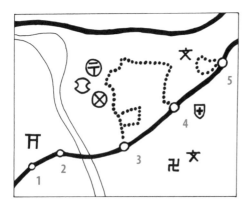

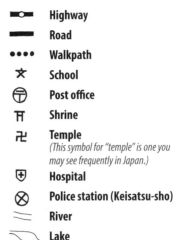

▬◗▬	Highway
▬▬	Road
••••	Walkpath
🏫	School
〒	Post office
卉	Shrine
卍	Temple *(This symbol for "temple" is one you may see frequently in Japan.)*
✚	Hospital
⊗	Police station (Keisatsu-sho)
≈	River
◡	Lake
฿	Bank

1 ....

2 ....

3 Hidari-gawa ni ....

  Migi-gawa ni ....

  Ushiro ni ....

4 ....

5 ....

Exercise 6

Say the following sentences in Japanese, and check your answers on the CD.

1 Turn right at the intersection

2 Turn left at the intersection

3 Go straight through the intersection

4 Turn right at the T-junction

5 Turn left at the T-junction

Exercise 7

Translate into English:

1 *Watashi wa kono michi o massugu ikimasu.* ....

....

2 *Basu wa shingō o migi e magarimasu.* ....

....

3 *(Anata wa) ano tsukiatari o hidari e magarimasu.* ....

....

4 *San-ban no basu wa Higashi-kōen e ikimasu.* ....

....

5 *Watashi wa (o)tera no hantai-gawa de kuruma o tomemasu.* ....

....

Translate into rōmaji:

6 *(You) go straight through that traffic light.* ....
....

7 *(You) turn right at the T-junction.* ....
....

8 *This bus will go in the direction of Mt. Atago.* ....
....

9 *There is a bread shop at the opposite side of the station* ....
....

10 *(You) turn left before that hotel.* ....
....

Writing Exercise

Practice the five katakana characters **na, ni, nu, ne** and **no.**

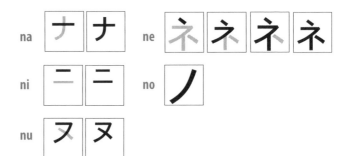

The weather

Day 21 talks about the weather. You will learn transitive and intransitive verbs as well as the active and passive voice. Finally, you will have a summary of what you have already learned about *wa* and *ga* and how to use them.

TAXI

A Japanese taxi driver wears a suit with white gloves. Unlike in the West, a taxi driver in Japan will not come out and open the door for you; instead he will use a lever at his seat to open and close the back door (on the left side only). So, stand out of the way and don't touch the door. It is not common to tip taxi drivers in Japan.

Japanese conversation: Heya ga arimasu ka.

Tom:	Konnichiwa. (Yūsuhosuteru ni) heya ga arimasu ka.
Clerk:	Hai arimasu.
Tom:	(Heya wa) ikura desu ka.
Clerk:	(Heya wa) go-sen-en desu. Asa-gohan to ban-go- han ga tsukimasu.
Tom:	(Yūsuhosuteru ni) furo ga arimasu ka.
Clerk:	Hai arimasu. (Furoba wa) ik-kai* desu.
Tom:	Kyō boku wa (yūsuhosuteru ni) tomarimasu.
	Ashita ame ga furimasu ka.
Clerk:	Hai furimasu.

English conversation: Do you have a room?

Tom visits a youth hostel.

Tom:	Good afternoon. Do you (the youth hostel) have a room?
Clerk:	Yes, we do.
Tom:	How much is it?
Clerk:	It's ¥5,000. Breakfast and dinner is included.
Tom:	Do you (the youth hostel) have a bath?
Clerk:	Yes, we do. It's on the first floor.
Tom:	I'll stay tonight (today).
	Will it rain tomorrow?
Clerk:	Yes, it will.

*ichi + kai, one + floor, has undergone a phonetic change and became ik-kai, first floor.

Grammar

Intransitive Verbs

Intransitive V•masu-verbs (V•masu-verbs which do not have direct objects) have the following sentence structure: **subject** wa/ga V•masu.

Wa follows a subject responsible for the action.
Ga follows a subject where action is presented as natural occurrence.

You have learned so far that subjects for the verbs of motion are followed by wa while the subject for arimasu/imasu is followed by ga. This lesson will introduce some more subtle distinctions between wa and ga that determine which particle should be used.

Let's consider watashi wa yama e ikimasu, *I go to the mountain.* In this sentence, "going to the mountain" is an action performed by *I*. Because watashi, *I*, is responsible for the action, it is followed by wa.

Now consider basu ga kimasu, *the bus is coming or the bus comes.* "The bus coming" is a natural occurrence and hence the subject basu, *bus,* is followed by ga.

Let's consider niwa ni otōsan ga imasu, *father is (located) in the garden.* Because imasu means *to be located or to exist,* there is no action performed by father: "father" is merely located or exists in the garden. Hence otōsan, father, is followed by ga. The subject may be followed by wa only if the subject is responsible for being there. For instance, koko ni watashi wa imasu, *I'll be here,* implies a decision of the speaker——watashi is responsible for being here and therefore it is followed by wa.

Transitive and intransitive Verbs

The translation of an English verb into a Japanese verb or vice versa may sometimes be confusing.

I stop a car. *("stop" is a transitive verb in this case)*
A car stops. *("stop" is an intransitive verb in this case)*

In English, the verb stop may be both transitive and intransitive. For the sentence with the transitive verb, the direct object of the verb (a car) is stated; for the sentence with the intransitive verb, the sentence is complete without a direct object. The sentence with a **transitive verb** always states **the person responsible for the action,** while the action is stated as a **natural occurrence** in the sentence with an **intransitive verb.**

In Japanese, transitive and intransitive verbs are almost always two different words. The only exception is owarimasu which is both transitive, meaning *finish/end (something),* and intransitive, meaning *be finished;* the intransitive verb owarimasu also has a transitive counterpart oemasu, *finish (something).* The following example shows that tomemasu, *stop (something),* is a transitive verb while tomarimasu, *stop,* is an intransitive verb; but both would be translated as *stop* in English.

Watashi wa kuruma o tomemasu.	I stop a car.
Kuruma ga tomarimasu.	A car stops.

Verbs

Here are some more examples of words that have two translations in Japanese, although in English they are the same word.

Verbs (Intransitive)		Verbs (Transitive)	
hajimarimasu	begin	hajimemasu	begin (something)
kowaremasu	break	kowashimasu	break (something)
tomarimasu	stop	tomemasu	stop (something)
ugokimasu	move	ugokashimasu	move (something)

Jugyo ga hajimarimasu.	The lesson will start.
Watashi wa benkyō o hajimemasu.	I will start (my) study.

Koppu ga kowaremasu.	The cup will break.
Watashi wa koppu o kowashimasu.	I will break a cup.

Basu ga ugokimasu.	The bus will move.
Watashi wa tsukue o ugokashimasu.	I will move a desk.

Intransitive Verbs

aimasu	*meet*	**oyogimasu**	*swim*
arukimasu	*walk*	**tomarimasu**	*stay (overnight)*
hatarakimasu	*work*	**furimasu**	*fall (rain, snow)*
nakimasu	*cry*	**tokemasu**	*melt*
nemasu	*sleep*	**yamimasu**	*stop (rain, snow)*
okimasu	*wake up*		

Note that *meet* is usually transitive in English, but the Japanese equivalent aimasu is intransitive and follows *ni*.

Watashi wa Robert-kun ni hon-ya de aimasu.	I meet Robert at the bookstore.
Watashi wa eki made arukimasu.	I'll walk to the station.

Exercises

Exercise 1

Write wa or ga in the blanks and then translate the sentences into English.

1 Isu ga kowaremasu yo. <u>The chair will break!</u>

2 Sorosoro basu.................... kimasu yo...

....

3 Sugu eiga .... hajimarimasu...

....

4 Kono natsu watashi ....Eigo no benkyō o

hajimemasu. ....

5 Densha............................ugokimasu yo ....

Exercise 2

Listen to the phrases on the CD about a father's day at work. Answer the
questions in rōmaji.

1 Otōsan wa nan-ji ni okimasu ka. ....

....

2 Otōsan wa kaisha e basu de ikimasu ka. ....

....

3 Otōsan wa doko de hatarakimasu ka..

....

4 Otōsan wa nan-ji ni uchi e kaerimasu ka...

....

Exercise 3

Translate into English:

1 *Ashita yuki ga furimasu.* ....

....

2 *Roku-gatsu ni onīsan no ie ga dekimasu.*..

....

3 *Otōto wa tomodachi to pūru de oyogimasu.* ....

....

4 *Kuruma ga ie no mae de tomarimasu.* ....

....

5 *Otōsan wa kuruma no kōjō de hatarakimasu.* ....

....

6 *Akachan wa okāsan no ude no naka de nakimasen.* ....

....

7 *Nan-ji ni Nihon no eiga ga hajimarimasu ka.* ....

....

Translate into rōmaji:

8 *The rain will stop soon.* ....

....

9 *When does that mountain snow (snow on the mountain) melt?* ....

....

10 *The mother's voice is heard from the house next door.* ....

....

11 *In summer, I'll swim in the sea.* ....

....

12 *The mountain is visible..* ....

....

13 *In the spring, I'll meet my uncle in Canada.* ....

Active and Passive Verbs

Consider this sentence with a transitive verb: *I eat the apple.* The verb *eat* is called an active verb because the subject, I, performs the action, *eating.* If you change the sentence to *The apple is eaten by me,* the verb is *eaten* is called a passive verb because the subject, *the apple,* is described as experiencing rather than performing the action. Notice that *apple,* the direct object of the active verb, is now the subject of the passive verb. Any sentence with an active transitive verb (any sentence with a direct object) may be made into a sentence with a passive verb in English.

Sentences with intransitive verbs cannot be made into passive forms since they do not have direct objects. In some cases, however, Japanese intransitive verbs are translated as passive verbs in English. Here are some examples:

dekimasu	be made, be possible	umaremasu	be born
tsukimasu	be accompanied,	kikoemasu	be heard
	be included	miemasu	be visible
kimarimasu	be decided	okuremasu	be late
		wakarimasu	be understandable

Pan ga dekimasu.	The bread is made.
Ongaku ga niwa de kikoemasu.	The music is heard in the garden.
Watashi wa deito ni okuremasu.	I will be late for a date.

Wa or Ga?

Here is a summary of what you have learned so far about wa and ga.

Desu is an intransitive verb and is used in the sentence structure _ wa _ desu. In this structure, the subject is always followed by wa. Most of the "adjective + desu" constructs have the sentence structure _ wa "adjective + desu"; the subject is also always followed by wa. Some of the adjectives (suki na, kirai na, jōzu na, heta na, itai, kayui, hoshii, etc.) have the sentence structure _ wa _ ga "adjective + desu". Wa follows what is the subject in the English translation (the topic or indirect subject in Japanese) and ga follows the object or something else in the English translation (the grammatical subject in Japanese). Intransitive verbs wakarimasu and dekimasu (to be discussed in the following section) have the sentence structure _ wa _ ga wakarimasu/dekimasu. Wa follows what is the subject in the English translation (the topic or indirect subject in Japanese) and ga follows what is the object in the English translation (the grammatical subject in Japanese).

The verbs of motion, arimasu and imasu, and some of those listed in the vocabulary in this lesson, are intransitive verbs (they do not have direct objects). They use the sentence structure _ ga/wa V·masu. Wa follows the subject when the subject is responsible for the action, while ga follows the subject when the action occurs naturally.

Ojisan wa Amerika kara kimasu.	(My) uncle comes from America.
Kisha ga kimasu.	The train comes.

Transitive verbs have the sentence structure _ wa _ o V•masu. All the transitive verbs are action verbs with their subjects being responsible for the actions; therefore, the subjects are followed by wa.

I understand: *Dekimasu/Wakarimasu*

Dekimasu, *be made/produced/possible,* and wakarimasu, *be understandable,* may be translated as follows.

Pan ga dekimasu.	The bread is made.
Wain ga dekimasu.	The wine is produced.
Eigo ga wakarimasu.	The English language is understandable.

Dekimasu/wakarimasu may be used to express abilities with the sentence structure

indirect subject wa **grammatical subject** ga dekimasu/wakarimasu.

Wa follows the indirect subject (subject in the English) and ga follows the grammatical subject (object in the English).

Consider watashi wa Nihon-go ga dekimasu. It may be translated as *as for me, Japanese is possible.* Of course, *I can speak Japanese* is a more appropriate translation in English. Hence dekimasu may be thought of as *can (do)* in English and should be translated according to context.

Watashi wa Nihon-go ga dekimasu.	I can speak Japanese (I can do Japanese).
Watashi wa ryōri ga dekimasu.	I can cook (I can do cooking).

Note how dekimasu, *can do,* is different from the verb shimasu, *do.*

Watashi wa tenisu o shimasu.	I play tennis.
Watashi wa tenisu ga dekimasu.	I can play tennis.
Watashi wa suiei o shimasu.	I swim.
Watashi wa suiei ga dekimasu.	I can swim.

You may use the following adverb, as well as those learned before, to express abilities in detail.

zenzen	not at all, entirely (used with negative verbs)
Watashi wa Nihon-go ga sukoshi dekimasu.	I can speak Japanese a little.
Okāsan wa suiei ga zenzen dekimasen.	Mother cannot swim at all.
Anata wa Nihon-go ga yoku wakarimasu ne.	You understand Japanese well, don't you?

A direct answer to a question _ wa _ ga dekimasu/wakarimasu ka has the form hai dekimasu/wakarimasu or iie dekimasen/wakarimasen, just as does suki/kirai desu.

Exercise 4

Listen as Tom talks about his family's ability with the Japanese language.

Write **rōmaji** in the blanks.

1 ....wa Nihon-go ga mottomo dekimasen.

2 .... wa Nihon-go ga sukoshi dekimasu.

3 .... wa onīsan yori Nihon-go ga dekimasu.

4 ....wa Nihon-go ga ichiban dekimasu.

Exercise 5

Translate into English:

1 *Anata wa kono e ga wakarimasu ka.* ....

....

2 *Watashi wa Nihon-go ga sukoshi wakarimasu.*.................................

....

3 *Anata wa nan no supōtsu ga dekimasu ka.* ....

....

4 *Otōto wa kuruma no unten ga dekimasen.* ....

....

5 *Ano hito wa Nihon-go ga zenzen dekimasen yo..* ....

....

Translate into **rōmaji**:

6 *I don't understand Hanako at all.* ....

....

7 *My younger brother can do judo.*...

....

8 *I cannot study at home.* ....

....

9 *Mother cannot speak English at all.* ....

....

....

10 *Do you understand Hanako's English?* ....

....

....

Writing exercise

Practice the five katakana characters **ha, hi, fu, he** and **ho.**

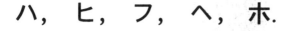

ハ， ヒ， フ， ヘ， ホ.

Step by step: ha  he

hi   ho

fu

Vocabulary

ame	**rain**	Haru yama no yuki
kumo	**cloud**	**In spring, mountain**
tenki	**weather**	ga tokemasu.
kumori	**cloudy weather**	**snow melts.**
niji	**rainbow**	Gogo ame ga yamimasu.
hare	**fine weather**	**(The) rain will stop in the afternoon.**
yuki	**snow**	yūsuhosuteru
matawa	**or**	**youth hostel**

Leisure time

Day 22 is all about leisure activities and how to talk about what you do. You will learn how to talk about things in the present tense, as well as in the perfect (past) tense. Finally, you will further build your vocabulary.

SPORT

*Although **baseball** has long been an athletic obsession in Japan, **sumo** remains the official national sport. This is fitting, partly because of its history, which dates back to the 3rd century, and also for its quasi-religious ritualism — but mostly because, in Japan, it's a more exciting sport.*
*If you ever wondered how the **sumo** wrestlers bulk up, look no further than **chankonabe**, a stew of meat, fish, tofu, noodles and vegetables in broth.*

Japanese conversation 1: Kinō anata wa nani o shimashita ka.

Hanako:	Kinō anata wa nani o shimashita ka.
Tom:	Asa (boku wa) daigaku e ikimashita.
	Hiru (boku wa) daigaku kara kaerimashita.
	Sorekara (boku wa) yakyū o Hiroshi-kun-tachi to shimashita.
	Sorekara (boku wa) ban-gohan o tabemashita.
	Yoru (boku wa) terebi o mimashita.
Hanako:	Itsu (anata wa) benkyō o shimashita ka.
Tom:	Kinō (boku wa) benkyō o shimasen deshita.
	Ototoi (boku-tachi wa) sūgaku no tesuto ga arimashita ne. Boku wa hyaku-ten o torimashita.
	Dakara kinō (boku wa) asobimashita.
Hanako:	Watashi wa totemo warui ten o torimashita.
	Dakara kinō (watashi wa) sūgaku no benkyō o shimashita.
	Korekara (watashi wa) mata benkyō o shimasu.

English conversation 1: What Did You Do Yesterday?

Tom and Hanako talk about what they did yesterday.

Hanako:	What did you do yesterday?
Tom:	In the morning, I went to a class (college).
	In the afternoon, I returned (home) from school. After that, I played baseball with Hiroshi and the guys.
	After that, I ate dinner.
	At night, I watched television.
Hanako:	When did you study?
Tom:	Yesterday, I did not study.
	The day before yesterday, we had the math test, didn't we? I scored 100.
	So, yesterday, I played.
Hanako:	I got a very bad grade. So, I studied math yesterday. Now, I'll study again.

Grammar

Tense

There are two basic tenses in Japanese: present tense and past tense. Japanese uses the same **V·masu**-verb for the present and future tenses, but the rest of the sentence makes the tense clear with a word or phrase such as tomorrow, now, or next year.

kinō	yesterday	kyonen	last year
kyō	today	kotoshi	this year
ashita	tomorrow	rainen	next year
itsuka	someday		

sen-shū	last week	sen-getsu	last month
kon-shū	this week	kon-getsu	this month
rai-shū	next week	rai-getsu	next month

mai-asa	every morning	ototoi	the day before yesterday
mai-ban	every evening	asatte	the day after tomorrow
mai-toshi	every year	kesa	this morning
mai-nichi	every day	konban	this evening
mai-shū	every week		

You may have noticed the following prefixes:

kon-	this *(-getsu, -shū)*
mai-	every *(-asa, -ban, -toshi, -nichi, -shū)*
rai-	next *(-getsu, -nen, -shū)*
sen-	last *(-getsu, -shū)*

Perfect tense

Form the perfect (past) tense by converting:

1 **desu** into **deshita**
2 **de wa arimasen** into **de wa arimasen deshita**
3 **V·masu** into **V·mashita**
4 **V·masen** into **V·masen deshita**
5 **_i desu** into **_katta desu**
6 **_ku nai desu** into **_ku nakatta desu**

1 Koko wa hon-ya desu.	This is a bookstore.
Koko wa hon-ya deshita.	This was a bookstore.
2 Ano hito wa Betty-san de wa arimasen.	She is not Betty.
Ano hito wa Betty-san de wa arimasen deshita.	She was not Betty.
3 Watashi wa pan o tsukurimasu.	I make bread.
Watashi wa pan o tsukurimashita.	I made bread.
Watashi wa gakkō e ikimasu.	I go to school.
Watashi wa gakkō e ikimashita.	I went to school.
Koko ni hon ga arimasu.	Here is a book.
Koko ni hon ga arimashita.	Here was a book.
Ame ga furimasu.	It rains. (Rain falls.)
Ame ga furimashita.	It rained. (Rain fell.)
4 Kyō otōsan wa shigoto o shimasen.	Today, father does not work.
Kinō otōsan wa shigoto o shimasen deshita.	Yesterday, father did not work.
Kyō watashi wa gakkō e ikimasen.	Today, I do not go to school.
Kinō watashi wa gakkō e ikimasen deshita.	Yesterday, I did not go to school.

For the "i-adjective + desu," form the past tense by replacing _i desu with _katta desu. The negative past tense is formed by replacing _ku nai desu with _ku nakatta desu.

5 Kono ki wa chiisai desu.	This tree is small.
Kono ki wa chiisakatta desu.	This tree was small.
6 Kono bideo wa omoshiroku nai desu.	This video is not interesting.
Kono bideo wa omoshiroku nakatta desu.	This video was not interesting.

The past "na-adjective (without na) + desu" is formed by replacing desu with deshita. The negative past tense is formed by replacing de wa arimasen with de wa arimasen deshita. In other words, desu of the "na-adjective (without na) + desu" conjugates while na-adjective (without na) remains unchanged.

7 (O)tera wa shizuka desu.	The temple is quiet.
(O)tera wa shizuka deshita.	The temple was quiet.
8 Ano hito wa rikō de wa arimasen.	He is not clever.
Ano hito wa rikō de wa arimasen deshita.	He was not clever.

Relative Time

The times listed in the vocabulary on page 195, (except those starting with mai-) are called "**relative times,**" that is, the time depends on when "now" is. Sen-getsu, *last month,* is a relative time because it means April if it is May now, but it means July if it is August now. When you refer to a relative time, you do not put ni after it.

Sen-getsu watashi wa Amerika e ikimashita.
Watashi wa sen-getsu Amerika e ikimashita.

Last month, I went to America.
I went to America last month.

Exercises

Exercise 1

Convert the rōmaji sentences from present tense into past tense by filling in the blanks, then translate them into English.

1 Kyō wa yoi (o)tenki desu ne.

Kinō wa yoi (o)tenki deshita ne.

The weather was good yesterday, wasn't it?

2 Kyō no tesuto wa yasashii desu yo.

Kinō no tesuto wa ....

....

3 Watashi wa Hanako-san ga suki desu.

Kyonen watashi wa Hanako-san ga ....

....

4 Kyō wa sui-yōbi de wa arimasen yo.

Kinō wa ....

....

5 Kyō wa samuku nai desu ne.

Kinō wa ....

....

Exercise 2

Listen to Tom's essay about his summer vacation.

Answer the following questions in rōmaji.

1. Kyonen no natsu Tom-kun wa doko e ikimashita ka.

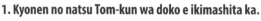

....

2 Tom-kun wa doko ni tomarimashita ka.

....

3 Tom-kun wa Amerika o ryokō shimashita ka.

....

4 Tom-kun wa doko ga ichiban suki deshita ka.

....

5 Mai-nichi Tom-kun wa nani o shimashita ka.

....

6 Tom-kun wa nani-go o Amerika de hanashimashita ka.

....

7 Amerika wa suzushikatta desu ka.

....

8 Tom-kun no natsu-yasumi wa tanoshii natsu-yasumi deshita ka, (Tom-kun no natsu-yasumi wa) tsumaranai natsu-yasumi deshita ka.

....

Exercise 3

Translate into English:

1 *Ano hito wa Makoto-kun no onīsan deshita.* ....

....

2 *Kinō Furansu-go no uta ga yūsuhosuteru de kikoemashita.* ....

....

3 *Kyonen no natsu koko ni ōkii ki ga arimashita.* ....

....

4 *Sen-getsu watashi-tachi wa kaimono o Amerika de shimashita.* ....

....

5 *Kinō boku wa isu o otōsan to tsukurimashita.* ....

....

6 *Kinō anata wa nani o ranchi ni tabemashita ka.* ....

....

Translate into rōmaji:

7 *That was a temple.* ....

....

8 *Last year, I went to America by airplane.* ....

....

9 *Yesterday, there was a newspaper on the desk.* ....

....

10 *The long travelling has finished.* ....

....

11 *Last night, I did not eat dinner.* ....

....

12 *I did not play tennis with Makoto yesterday.* ....

....

Writing exercise

Practice the five katakana characters ma, mi, mu, me and mo.

マ， ミ， ム， メ， モ．

Step by step: ma ［マ マ］ me ［メ メ］

mi ［ミ ミ ミ］ mo ［モ モ モ］

mu ［ム ム］

Vocabulary

korekara	*from now on*	**isogashii**	*busy*
dakara	*so, therefore*	**kitanai**	*dirty*
ten	*mark, grade*	**kurushii**	*hard (full of suffering)*
sorekara	*after that, and then*	**mezurashii**	*unusual, rare*
torimasu	*score*	**sabishii**	*lonely*
asobimasu	*play, amuse, enjoy*	**tanoshii**	*enjoyable*
-ten	*grade*	**urusai**	*noisy*
abunai	*dangerous*		

The future

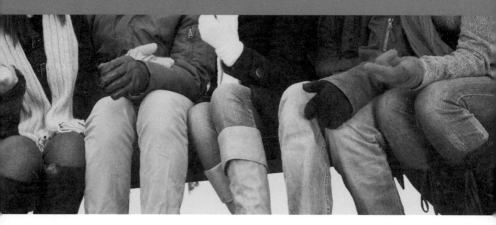

Day 23 introduces the future tense. You will also learn about Japanese festivities and religious beliefs and be able to further practice your *katakana* writing skills.

CHRISTMAS AND NEW YEAR'S DAY

Most Japanese people do not celebrate Christmas but they do celebrate New Year's. On New Year's Eve, people eat soba (Japanese thin buckwheat noodles) either with a dipping sauce or in a hot broth. You are expected to slurp it down your throat loudly. It signifies that the coming year will go smoothly, just as the noodles go through the throat. New Year celebrations can last from three to seven days.

Japanese religious beliefs

Concepts of religion among Japanese people are very different from those of Westerners. The Shinto religion is an ancient native Japanese religion, well established before the introduction of Buddhism in the sixth century. In this religion, people believe that when one dies, his spirit becomes a god who stays somewhere near his descendants. So, people worship ancestors, and every household has a miniature shrine on a small shelf near the ceiling for worshipping the dead. The sun, mountains, wind, rain, trees, rocks and other natural phenomena are believed to be inhabited by individual gods. If worshipped, a god would be benevolent towards people, but, if neglected, a god would be provoked to wrath and might cause a calamity. Shinto has many rituals which have become second nature to all Japanese people, irrespective of their religion. Shinto offers no philosophical teaching or moral code, but places great emphasis on fertility and ritual purity.

Buddhism is the major religion in Japan. Buddhism has moral codes and a complex philosophical system of thought centering on the principles of mercy and humanity. It condemns killing and emphasizes the links among all things. Buddhism stresses the achievement of enlightenment, which may be obtained through faith and good behavior. When one finally reaches the state of enlightenment, one is called a buddha. However, if one behaves badly, one may be reborn as a lower-ranking creature. Buddhism has its origins in India and it came to Japan through China and Korea, where it was transformed by the local religions, and then was also influenced by Shintoism. There are many sects in Japanese Buddhism, and some of them have even adopted the Shinto belief that the dead become buddhas instantly, just as the dead become gods in Shinto.

Daily life in Japan has little connection with religion, except for funeral ceremonies, which are usually Buddhist with deep religious significance. An interesting characteristic of Japanese religions is that they are not mutually exclusive: almost all Japanese families consider themselves as belonging to one of many Buddhist sects, yet you will find some homes with Shinto shrines as well as Buddhist altars. Many Shinto and Buddhist beliefs and practices have merged over the years. In Japan, a person might be a Buddhist, but practice Shinto rituals, might be married at a Shinto or Christian ceremony and he/she might have a Buddhist funeral. Christianity was introduced to Japan in 1549, but less than one percent of the population is Christian.

Japanese conversation 1: Kyō wa samui desu ne.

Tom:	Kyō wa samui desu ne.
Hanako:	Gogo (wa) atatakaku narimasu yo.
	Hachi-gatsu wa totemo atsuku narimasu yo.
Tom:	Ku-gatsu wa (hachi-gatsu yori) suzushiku narimasu ka.
Hanako:	Hai (ku-gatsu wa) hachi-gatsu yori suzushiku narimasu.

English conversation 1: It's cold today!

Tom and Hanako talk about temperature.

Tom:	It is cold today, isn't it?
Hanako:	It will be warm in the afternoon!
	It will be very hot in August!
Tom:	Will it be cooler in September?
Hanako:	Yes, it will be cooler than in August.

Grammar

Future Tense

The present and future tenses for V•masu-verbs have the same form in Japanese, but there is rarely any confusion between tenses, because the context provides clues.

Rainen watashi-tachi wa Amerika e ikimasu.	Next year, we will go to America.
Ashita watashi wa Eigo no benkyō o shimasu.	Tomorrow, I will study English.
Korekara watashi wa ongaku o kikimasu.	From now (on), I will listen to music.
Korekara okāsan wa gohan o tsukurimasu.	From now (on), (my) mother will make a meal.
Ashita watashi wa e o kakimasen.	Tomorrow, I will not draw a picture.
Ashita ame ga furimasu.	It will rain tomorrow. (Tomorrow, rain will fall.)
Rai-shū gakkō ga hajimarimasu.	Schools will start next week.

In the examples above, you may have noticed that words specifying the future (such as *tomorrow, next year,* etc.) are included in each sentence. In a conversation, once a speaker establishes the time frame, it is not necessary to mention it again, as we saw in the dialogue.

Someday: *ni narimasu*

Unlike **V•masu**-verbs, the verb **desu** does not express the future tense unless the subjects indicate the future, as shown in the examples below.

Ashita wa atatakai desu yo.	Tomorrow will be warm!
Ashita no tesuto wa muzukashiku nai desu.	Tomorrow's test will not be difficult.

The idea of the future tense for **desu** is expressed by using **narimasu**, *to become*, in the future tense. The future tense for _ wa _ **desu** is

subject wa **complement** ni narimasu where wa follows a subject and ni follows a complement.

Watashi wa sensei desu.	I am a teacher.
Raigetsu watashi wa sensei ni narimasu.	Next month, I will be a teacher.

The future tense for _ wa "i-adjective + desu" is

subject wa _ku narimasu.

The future tense for _ wa "na-adjective (without na) + desu" is

subject wa "na-adjective (without na)" ni narimasu.

The future tense for _ wa _ ga "na-adjective (without na) + desu" is

indirect subject wa **grammatical subject** ga "na-adjective (without na)" ni narimasu.

Kono inu wa ōkii desu.	This dog is big.
Kono inu wa sugu ōkiku narimasu.	This dog will be big soon.
Yoru gakkō wa shizuka desu.	At night, school is quiet.
Yoru gakkō wa shizuka ni narimasu.	At night, school will be quiet.
Anata wa tenisu ga jōzu desu.	You are good at tennis.
Itsuka anata wa tenisu ga jōzu ni narimasu.	Someday, you will be good at tennis.

The negative future tense may be obtained by changing **narimasu** into **narimasen**.

Hanako-san wa sensei ni narimasen.	Hanako will not be a teacher.
Ashita wa atsuku narimasen.	It will not be hot tomorrow.
Koko wa benri ni narimasen yo.	This place will not be convenient!
Ano hito wa taisō ga jōzu ni narimasen.	He will not be good at gymnastics.

Exercises

Exercise 1

Circle the words associated with the future tense.

ashita   rainen   senshū   raishū   sengetsu   ototoi   asatte

korekara   kinō   kyonen   raigetsu

Circle the words associated with the past tense.

ashita   rainen   senshū   raishū   sengetsu   ototoi   asatte

korekara   kinō   kyonen   raigetsu

Exercise 2

Translate into English:

1 *Asatte wa getsu-yōbi desu.* ....

....

2 *Ashita otōsan to okāsan wa Igirisu kara kaerimasu.* ....

....

3 *Rai-shū onīsan no ie ga dekimasu.* ....

....

4 *Assatte watashi wa ban-gohan o Betty-san no ie de tabemasu.* ....

....

5 *Ashita no eiga wa omoshiroku nai desu yo.* ....

....

6 *Ashita watashi wa anata o eki de machimasu ne.* ....

....

7 *Rai-shū kono hon o anata ni kaeshimasu.* ....

....

8 *Ashita watashi wa tenisu o shimasen.* ....

....

9 *Rai-shū no sui-yōbi ni gakkō ga hajimarimasu.* ....

....

10 *Rai-shū kaimono ni ikimasen ka.* ....

....

Translate into rōmaji:

11 *Tomorrow will be Sunday.* ....

....

12 *Someday, I will study French.*

....

13 *Tomorrow, (my) younger brother and I will go to the temple.* ....

....

14 *What will you do tomorrow?* ....

....

15 *Tomorrow morning, I'll draw a picture of the mountain.* ....

....

16 *Next year, will your grandfather come to Japan?* ....

....

17 *Tomorrow, I will not watch television.* ....

....

18 *Next year, I will buy an expensive blue coat.* ....

....

19 *Next month, a baby will be born to (my) aunt.* ....

....

20 *Tomorrow, I'll put on this dress.* ....

....

Exercise 3

You will hear sentences telling you what people want to be when they grow up.
Match the person with what he/she wants to be.

Tom	a judo instructor
Mari	a nurse
Makoto	an office worker
Hanako	a school teacher
Ken	a medical doctor

Exercise 4

Complete the table below.

Adjective	Meaning	"Adjective + desu"	Meaning	Future Tense
nagai	long	nagai desu	to be long	nagaku narimasu
hoshii	desirous			
muzukashii				
benri na				
rippa na				

Exercise 5

You will hear some questions about the Dialogue. Reply to each question aloud in Japanese, and write your answers below. Check your pronunciation on the CD.

1 ....

2 ....

3 ....

4 ....

Exercise 6

Translate into English:

1 *Raigetsu Akiko-obasan wa okāsan ni narimasu.* ....

....

2 *Nihon-go no benkyō wa muzukashiku narimasu ka.* ....

....

3 *Itsuka ano hito wa yūmei ni narimasu yo.* ....

....

4 *Pātī no ato daidokoro wa kitanaku narimasu.* ....

....

5 *Anata wa Nihon no rekishi ga suki ni narimasu yo.* ....

....

Translate into rōmaji:

6 *Someday, you will be good at tennis.* ....

....

7 *Will you become a medical doctor someday?* ....

....

8 *Next year, skirts will be short!* ....

....

9 *This tree will not be big.* ....

....

10 *You will like Japanese food.* ....

....

Writing exercise

Practice the three **katakana** characters **ya**, **yu**, and **yo**.

Step by step: ya    yo

yu

day:24

A visit to Kyoto

Day 24 takes you to Kyoto. You will learn about Japanese trains and delve further into the future tense. You will also learn how to form the imperative to give commands and you will further increase your vocabulary.

BULLET TRAINS

*Japanese bullet trains, known as **Shinkansen**, are world-famous for their speed, safety and comfort. There are six **Shinkansen lines** and each has two or three different types of trains (faster ones making fewer stops). For instance, for the line between Tokyo and Hakata, there are three types of Shinkansen: they are called **Nozomi**, **Hikari** and **Kodama**, in decreasing order of their speeds.*

Shinkansen

Each Shinkansen has three types of cars: gurinsha (first class with reserved seats), shiteiseki (reserved seats) and jiyūseki (non-reserved seats). Gurinsha and shiteiseki cost extra. You need two tickets to board a Shinkansen, one for the basic fare (the charge for the distance; it may be used for any other types of trains) and another one for the supplementary fare (the charge for the speed of a particular type of Shinkansen train, and a seat for a particular car).

There are other types of trains for traveling shorter distances. There are as many as four types of trains for each line. They are tokkyū (super express), kyūkō (express), kaisoku (limited express or rapid) and futsū (ordinary). Faster trains make fewer stops than slower ones. Whether one uses a tokkyū, kyūkō, kaisoku or futsū, the fare is usually the same (the basic fare); some of them have reserved seats, for which there is an additional charge.

Except for the reserved seats, all the tickets may be bought from jidō-hanbaiki (ticket vending machines) as well as at kippu uriba (ticket selling counters).

Japanese conversation 1: Kyōto

Hanako:	Ashita Kyōto e ikimasen ka.
Tom:	Hai (Boku wa Kyōto e) ikimasu.
Hanako:	Kyōto ni (o)tera to jinja ga takusan arimasu yo.
Tom:	(Boku-tachi wa Kyōto e) nan de ikimasu ka.
Hanako:	Shinkansen de ikimashō.
Tom:	Nan-ji ni (boku-tachi wa Kyōto e) ikimasu ka.
Hanako:	Jikokuhyō o mimashō.
Tom:	Shichi-ji sanjūgo-fun no Kodama de ikimashō.
	(Boku-tachi wa Kyōto ni) jūichi-ji nijūgo-fun ni tsukimasu.
Hanako:	Shichi-ji gojūrop-pun no Nozomi wa jū-ji
	jūip-pun ni (Kyōto ni) tsukimasu.
	(Kyōto e) Nozomi de ikimashō.
Tom:	Nozomi wa totemo hayai desu ne.
Hanako:	Nozomi wa tokkyū desu.

English conversation 1: Kyoto

Tom and Hanako plan to go to Kyoto.

Hanako:	Would you like to go to Kyoto tomorrow?
Tom:	Yes, I would.
Hanako:	There are a lot of temples and shrines in Kyoto!
Tom:	How (With what) are we going to Kyoto?
Hanako:	Let's go by Shinkansen.
Tom:	What time do we leave (go)?
Hanako:	Let's look the timetable.
Tom:	Let's go by a Kodama at 7:35. We'll arrive at 11:25.
Hanako:	The Nozomi at 7:56 will arrive (at Kyoto) at 10:11. Let's go by Nozomi.
Tom:	The Nozomi is very fast, isn't it?
Hanako:	The Nozomi is a super express.

Exercises

Exercise 1

The speaker will suggest things to do together.

Write what they are in English.

1 Let's listen to Japanese music.

2 ....

3 ....

4 ....

5 ....

6 ....

7 ....

Grammar

Future Tense

By dropping the subject, and converting **V·masu** into **V·mashō**, you can produce a polite imperative sentence that may be translated as *Let's* __ .

Watashi wa hon o yomimasu.	I read a book.
Hon o yomimashō.	Let's read a book.
Yama e ikimashō.	Let's go to the mountain.
Nihon-go no benkyō o shimashō.	Let's study Japanese.
Nemashō.	Let's sleep.
Pūru de oyogimashō.	Let's swim in the pool.

Exercise 2

Translate into English:

1 *Ashita no hachi-ji ni depāto no mae de aimashō.* ....

....

2 *Kono ringo o ojīsan ni agemashō.* ....

....

3 *Ashita tomodachi o hiru-gohan ni manekimashō.* ....

....

4 *Kore o kaimashō.* ....

....

5 *Natsu umi de oyogimashō.* ....

....

6 *Korekara benkyō o shimashō.* ....

....

Translate into rōmaji:

7 *Let's watch TV tonight.* ....

....

8 *Let's study Japanese next year.* ....

....

9 *Let's put on warm sweaters.* ....

....

10 *Let's eat (our) dinner.* ....

....

11 *Tomorrow morning, let's go to the department store by bus.* ....

....

12 *Let's play.* ....

....

Imperatives

You may form an imperative (that is, give an order or instruction) by converting V·masu into V·nasai.

(subject) wa **direct object** o V·nasai
subject wa V·nasai

This form of a sentence is most commonly used by a mother to a child or by a teacher to a student. Since the order or instruction is made by an older person to a younger person, -san and -kun are often dropped. The subject is usually followed by wa.

(Robert wa) hon o yominasai.	Read the book, Robert!
(Betty wa) benkyō o shinasai.	Study, Betty!
(Tom wa) nenasai.	Go to bed (Sleep), Tom!
(Anata wa) koko ni inasai.	Stay here (Be here)!
Koko e kinasai.	Come here!

Japanese conversation 2: Kibun ga warui desu.

Tom: Sumimasen. (Boku wa) atama ga itai desu.
Nurse: Kono byōin wa hajimete desu ka.
Tom: Hai.
Nurse: (Anata wa) hokenshō ga arimasu ka.
Tom: Hai. Kore (wa boku no hokenshō) desu.
Nurse: (Anata wa) kao (no) iro ga yoku nai desu ne. Netsu o hakarimashō.
***
Doctor: (Anata wa) dō shimashita ka.
Tom: (Boku wa) atama ga itai desu. (Boku wa) netsu ga arimasu.
          (Boku wa) kibun ga warui desu.
Doctor: Taionkei o kudasai. (Anata wa) netsu ga san-jū hachi-do arimasu.
          Kore wa kaze desu. Kyō daigaku o yasuminasai.
          Ie de nenasai. Mizu o takusan nominasai. Furo wa dame desu.
          Kyō to ashita kono kusuri o nominasai.
Tom: Dōmo arigatō gozaimashita. Sayōnara.

English conversation 2: I don't feel well.

Tom visits a doctor.
Tom: Excuse me. I have a headache.
Nurse: Is this (your) first time in this hospital?
Tom: Yes.
Nurse: Do you have a health insurance card?
Tom: Yes. This is it.
Nurse: You don't look well, do you?
          Let's take (measure) (your) temperature.
***
Doctor: What's wrong?
Tom: I have a headache. I have a fever.
          I feel bad (I have bad feeling).
Doctor: May I have the thermometer please? You have a temperature of
          38 degrees Celsius. This is a cold. Stay home (be absent) from
          college today! Sleep at home! Drink plenty of water!
          Don't take a bath (a bath is not good).
          Take this medicine today and tomorrow!
Tom: Thank you very much. Good-bye.

Exercise 3

You will hear some commands. Write what they are in English.

1   **Get well fast!**

2 ....

3 ....

4 ....

5 ....

6 ....

Exercise 4

You will hear some questions about Dialogue 2. Reply to each question aloud in Japanese, and write down your answers. Check your pronunciation on the CD.

1 ....

2 ....

3 ....

4 ....

Exercise 5

Translate into English:

1 *(Amy wa) tegami o heya de kakinasai.* ....

....

2 *(Robert wa) gyūnyū o neko ni agenasai.* ....

....

3 *Ashita Kimi to Betty wa gakkō e basu de ikinasai.* ....

....

4 *(Tom wa) soto de asobinasai.* ....

....

5 *Betty wa Furansu-go no benkyō o shinasai.* ....

....

Translate into rōmaji:

6 *Betty, clean your room!* ....

....

7 *Go to school, Makoto!.* ....

....

8 *Eat the tomato, Robert!.* ....

....

9 *Kimi, come here!* ....

....

10 *Before a meal, wash your hands, Tom!* ....

....

Writing exercise

Practice the five katakana characters **ra, ri, ru, re**, and **ro**.

ラ， リ， ル， レ， ロ.

Step by step:　ra　ラ ラ　　re　レ

ri　リ リ　　ro　ロ ロ ロ

ru　ル ル

Vocabulary

jikokuhyō	timetable	taionkei	clinical thermometer
tsukimasu	arrive	hakarimasu	measure, weigh
tokkyū	super express	hajimete	for the first time
dame na	not good	nomimasu	take (medicine)
-do	degree	yasumimasu	be absent from, rest from, take time off from
iro	color		
kaze	a cold	(Anata wa) dō shimasu ka.	What will you do (about it)?
kibun	feeling		
kusuri	medicine	(Anata wa) dō shimashita ka.	What's wrong/happened/ the matter (with you)?
hokenshō	health insurance card		
netsu	body temperature, fever		

Quantities

Day 25 talks about quantities. You will also continue to practice writing in Japanese and you will learn more about Japanese superstition and culture. Finally, you will continue to learn and practice writing *katakana*.

QUANTITIES

Goods in Japan tend to be sold in small quantities/portions. For example, vegetables are usually sold per piece or in pre-packaged bags containing a specific number within it rather than by weight. This is mainly down to the fact that certain numbers are considered to be bad luck!

Japanese conversation 1: Nani ka tabemasen ka.

Makoto:	Nani ka tabemasen ka.
Hanako:	(Watashi wa) nan demo tabemasu yo.
Tom:	Boku wa nani mo tabemasen.
	(Boku wa) onaka ga ippai desu.
	Sakki (boku wa) hiru-gohan o tabemashita.
	(Boku wa yakisoba o) ippai tabemashita.
Makoto:	Korekara nani ka minna de shimasen ka.
Hanako:	(Watashi wa) nan demo shimasu yo.
Tom:	Boku wa nani mo shimasen.
	Korekara boku wa uchi e kaerimasu.
	Dareka boku no uchi e kimasu.
Makoto:	Ashita dokoka e minna de ikimasen ka.
Hanako:	(Watashi wa) doko e demo ikimasu.
	Atago-yama wa dō desu ka.
Tom:	Boku wa doko e mo ikimasen.
	Ashita (boku wa) isogashii desu.

English conversation 1: Would you like to eat something?

Makoto suggests activities to Hanako and Tom. Hanako is very agreeable while Tom is not.

Makoto:	Would you like to eat something?
Hanako:	I'll eat anything!
Tom:	I won't eat anything. I'm full. A little while ago, I ate (my) lunch. I ate plenty.
Makoto:	Would you like to do something (from) now, with all of us?
Hanako:	I'll do anything!
Tom:	I won't (do anything).
	I'll go back to (my) house (from) now.
	Somebody's coming to my house.
Makoto:	Would you like to go somewhere tomorrow, with all of us?
Hanako:	I'll go anywhere. How about Mt. Atago?
Tom:	I won't go anywhere. I'm busy tomorrow.

Grammar

Interrogatives

Since interrogatives are the starting point of this lesson, let's review the interrogatives you have learned so far. Remember that **nan** is used before a word starting with **n/t/d**; **nani** is used in all other cases.

dare	who	dore	which one
itsu	when	doko	where
nan/nani	what	dono	which "thing/person"

The Particles Ka, Demo, and Mo

Some: Interrogative + **KA** + Positive Verb
"Interrogatives + **ka** + positive verbs" form the following expressions:

dareka	somebody	doreka	something
itsuka	someday	dokoka	somewhere
dono	some "thing/person"		
nanika	something		

Any: Interrogative + **DEMO** + Positive Verb
"Interrogatives + **demo** + positive verbs" form the following expressions:

dare demo	anyone, everyone	dore demo	anything
itsu demo	anytime	doko demo	anywhere
dono "noun" demo	any "noun" everywhere		
nan demo	anything, everything		

(Not) Any: Interrogative + **MO** + Negative Verb
"Interrogatives + **mo** + negative verbs" form the following expressions:

dare mo	(not) anyone	dore mo	(not) any of them
itsu mo	(not) anytime	doko mo	(not) anywhere
dono "noun" mo	(not) any "noun"		
nani mo	(not) anything		

Forming sentences with Some and Any

As with other question words, to form sentences *some* and *any*, start with a "basic statement" and find the word that will be replaced by *some* or *any*.

Consider a basic statement **Watashi wa ringo o tabemasu,** I eat an apple.
We want to change *I eat an apple* into *I eat something, I eat anything* and *I do not eat anything.* **Ringo** is the word to be replaced with the expressions *something, anything* and *(not) anything*. Because **ringo** is a "thing," **nani/nan** is the interrogative word we need. Hence, to replace **ringo,** we have expressions **nanika,** *something;* **nan demo,** *anything* and **nani mo,** *(not) anything*. Since **ringo** is followed by **o, o** must be omitted from the new sentences with the expressions (rule 1).

Putting it all together, we get:

Watashi wa ringo o tabemasu.	I eat an apple.
Watashi wa nanika tabemasu.	I eat something.
Watashi wa nan demo tabemasu.	I eat anything.
Watashi wa nani mo tabemasen.	I do not eat anything.

Note that **nani mo** must be followed by a negative verb to mean *(not) anything*.

As shown in the example above, check the particle following the word, and follow the rules below.
Rules
1 If the word you are replacing is followed by the particle **wa/ga/o,** the particle must be dropped.

2 If the word you are replacing is followed by the particle **ni/e** and if the expression you are replacing it with ends with **demo/mo,** the particle **ni/e** must be put in between the interrogative word and **demo/mo** of the expression.

3 If the word you are replacing is followed by the particle **ni/e** and if the expression ends with **ka, ni/e** follows the **ka** of the expression.

The above rules sound complicated. It is much easier to see what they mean by going through the following examples. Let's start with "basic statements".

Let's do the same thing with another sentence, **Watashi wa eki e ikimasu,** *I will go to the station.* We want to change *I will go to the station* into *I will go somewhere, I will go anywhere* and *I will not go anywhere*. **Eki** is the word to be replaced. Because **eki** is a "place," **doko** is the interrogative word to be used. Hence we have expressions **dokoka,** *somewhere;* **doko demo,** *anywhere,* and **doko mo,** *(not) anywhere* to replace **eki.**

Consider the expression **dokoka**, *somewhere*, first. Since **eki** is followed by **e** and the expression ends with **ka**, **e** must follow **ka** (rule 3). Hence we get: **Watashi wa dokoka e ikimasu**, *I will go somewhere*. Now consider the expression **doko demo**, *anywhere*. Using rule 2, **e** must be put in between **doko** and demo in the new sentence. Hence we get: **Watashi wa doko e demo ikimasu**, *I will go anywhere*.

Now consider the expression **doko mo**, *(not) anywhere*. Using rule 2, **e** must be put in between **doko** and **mo**. Changing the positive verb into the negative verb, we get:
Watashi wa doko e mo ikimasen, *I will not go anywhere*.

Exercises

Exercise 1

Say the following words aloud in Japanese, and check your pronunciation on the CD.

1 somebody

2 somewhere

3 someday

4 anyone

5 anywhere

6 anytime

7 (not) anyone

8 (not) anywhere

9 (not) anytime

Exercise 2

Translate into rōmaji:

1 *I will read these books.* <u>*Watashi wa kono hon o yomimasu.*</u>

I will read some books ....

I will read any book ....

I will not read any book. ....

2 *I will buy this.*   <u>*Watashi wa kore o kaimasu.*</u>

I will buy something. ....

I will buy anything. ....

I will not buy anything. ....

3 *I will give this to you.* <u>*Watashi wa kore o anata ni agemasu.*</u>

I will give this to somebody....

I will give this to anybody...

I will not give this to anybody. ....

Exercise 3

Translate into English:

1 *Watashi wa nani mo hoshiku nai desu.*..

....

2 *Watashi wa dore mo kaimasen.* ....

....

3 *Nanika nomimasen ka.* ....

....

4 *Watashi wa nanika yomimasu.* ....

....

5 *Dareka kono video o mimasen ka.*...

....

6 *Dare mo yama e ikimasen deshita.* ....

....

7 *Itsu demo watashi wa tenisu o shimasu yo!*..

....

Translate into rōmaji:

8 *This dog eats anything.* ....

....

9 *I won't buy any fruit.* ....

....

10 *Would you like to go somewhere?* ....

....

11 *I did not see anything.* ....

....

12 *I will not buy any dress.* ....

....

13 *Makoto does not come to a party ever (any time).* ....

....

14 *Would you like to go to a mountain someday?* ....

....

Writing Exercise

Practice the three katakana characters **wa**, **wo** and **n**.

ワ， ヲ， ン．

Step by step: wa    n

wo

Note: This stroke is drawn from
the lower end to the higher end.

day:26

A daytrip

Day 26 takes you on a daytrip to the mountains. You will learn how to say what *you want* (and *do not want* to do), and how to form the past tense of the latter. Finally, you will discover some facts about Japan's most famous peak, Mount Fuji.

MOUNT FUJI

Mount Fuji (Fujisan), located on Honshu Island, is the highest mountain in Japan at 3,776.24 m (12,389 ft). An active stratovolcano that last erupted in 1707–08, Mount Fuji lies about 100 kilometres (60 miles) south-west of Tokyo, and can be seen from there on a clear day. In 2013, it was registered on the World Heritage List. Every year, it opens to the public on July 1 for two months.

Japanese conversation 1: Yama

Hanako:	Ashita yama e ikimasen ka.
Tom:	(Boku wa yama e) ikitai desu.
	(Boku wa) yama de e ga kakitai desu.
Hanako:	Watashi wa hana ga mitai desu.
	(Watashi wa) tori no koe mo* kikitai desu.
	Nan-ji ni (watashi-tachi wa) ikimasu ka.
Tom:	Asa-gohan no ato wa dō desu ka.
Hanako:	Nan-ji ni (anata wa) asa-gohan o tabemasu ka.
Tom:	Shichi-ji ni (boku wa asa-gohan o) tabemasu.
Hanako:	Hachi-ji ni ie o demashō .
	Watashi wa (watashi-tachi no)
	(o)bentō o tsukurimasu.
Tom:	(Boku-tachi wa) dono yama e ikimasu ka.
Hanako:	Atago-yama wa dō desu ka.
Tom:	(Sore wa) ii desu ne.
Hanako:	Korekara watashi wa (o)bentō o tsukurimasu.
	Dewa mata ashita.

***

Tom:	Yama wa kirei desu ne.
	(Boku-tachi wa) yoku arukimashita ne.
	(Anata wa) tsukaremashita ka.
Hanako:	Iie (Watashi wa tsukaremasen deshita).
	(Watashi wa) onaka ga sukimashita.
	(Watashi wa) (o)bentō ga tabetai desu.
Tom:	(O)bentō o tabemashō.

* When mo, *also/too,* refers to the word followed by ga, ga is ommitted.

English conversation 1: Mountain

Hanako and Tom go on a trip to a mountain.

Hanako:	Would you like to go to a mountain tomorrow?
Tom:	I'd like to.
	I want to draw a picture on the mountain.
Hanako:	I want to see flowers. I want to listen to the cries of birds too. What time will (do) we go?
Tom:	How about after breakfast?
Hanako:	What time do you eat (your) breakfast?
Tom:	I eat at 7 o'clock.
Hanako:	Let's leave (our) houses at 8 o'clock. I will make our lunch (in boxes).
Tom:	To which mountain are we going?
Hanako:	How about Mt. Atago?
Tom:	That's good, isn't it?
Hanako:	Right now (from now) I will make our lunch (in boxes). See you tomorrow.

***

Tom:	The mountain is beautiful, isn't it? We walked a lot, didn't we? Did you get tired?
Hanako:	No, I didn't. I'm hungry.
Tom:	I want to eat lunch. Let's eat.

Grammar

Transitive Verbs - I want to: *V·tai desu*

Sentences with transitive verbs, _ wa _ o V·masu, may be transformed to express wishes by changing o into ga and V·masu into V·tai desu.

subject wa **direct object** ga V·tai desu

Sentences with intransitive verbs, _ wa/ga V·masu, may be transformed to express wishes by changing ga into wa and V·masu into V·tai desu.

subject wa V·tai desu

Japanese verbs V·tai desu may be translated as *want to _*.
For example:

Watashi wa hon o yomimasu.	I read a book.
Watashi wa hon ga yomitai desu.	I want to read a book.
Okāsan wa ryokō o shimasu.	Mother travels.
Okāsan wa ryokō ga shitai desu.	Mother wants to travel.
Watashi wa nemasu.	I sleep.
Watashi wa netai desu.	I want to sleep.
Koko ni neko ga imasu.	A cat is here.
Koko ni watashi wa itai desu.	I want to be here.

In the above example, *I want to be here* expresses "my desire". Therefore, the subject is not followed by ga, which follows a subject when the action is stated as a natural occurrence.
For example:

Anata wa nani ga nomitai desu ka.	What do you want to drink?
Anata wa nani ga shitai desu ka.	What do you want to do?
Anata wa dono hon ga yomitai desu ka.	Which book do you want to read?
Anata wa doko e ikitai desu ka.	Where do you want to go?

When an expression "interrogative + ka/demo/mo (e.g. dareka, dokoka, doreka, etc.)" is used, the rules you learned last chapter about particles apply.
For example:

Anata wa nanika tabetai desu ka.	Do you want to eat something?
Anata wa dokoka e ikitai desu ka.	Do you want to go somewhere?
Watashi wa doko e demo ikitai desu.	I want to go anywhere.
Dareka nanika tabetai desu ka.	Does somebody want to eat something?

I don't want to: *V•taku nai desu*

subject wa **direct object** ga/o V•taku nai desu

You may make negative statements by converting V•tai desu into either V•taku arimasen or V•taku nai desu. We will use V•taku nai desu in this book. The direct object may be followed by either ga or o.

Watashi wa hon ga/o yomitaku nai desu.	I do not want to read the book.
Watashi wa Eigo ga/o naraitaku nai desu.	I do not want to learn English.
Tarō-kun wa sumō ga/o shitaku nai desu.	Taro does not want to do sumo.
Otōto wa arukitaku nai desu.	The younger brother does not want to walk.

A direct answer to a question _ wa _ ga _tai desu ka is either hai _tai desu or iie _taku nai desu.

Exercises

Exercise 1

Complete the table below.

V.masu	Meaning	Want to	Don't Want to
naraimasu	learn	naraitai desu	naraitaku nai desu
okurimasu			
shimasu			
aimasu			
kimasu			

Exercise 2

You will hear what someone wants to do. Write what it is in English.

1 ....

2 ....

3 ....

4 ....

5 ....

Exercise 3

Translate into English:

1 *Anata wa dono zasshi ga yomitai desu ka.* ....

....

2 *Ima watashi wa nakitai desu.* ....

....

3 *Onīsan wa kawa de oyogitai desu.* ....

....

4 *Kyō watashi wa ban-gohan ga/o tabetaku nai desu.* ....

....

5 *Watashi wa benkyō ga/o shitaku nai desu.* ....

....

Translate into rōmaji:

6 *I want to watch a video tonight.* ....

....

7 *I want to eat steak for dinner.* ....

....

8 *I want to walk.* ....

....

9 *That cat wants to go out from the room.* ....

....

10 *Mother wants to buy an Italian handbag* ....

....

I wanted to: _takatta Desu

You can convert to the past tense by changing _tai desu into _takatta desu.

Watashi wa hon ga yomitakatta desu.	I wanted to read a book.
Watashi wa Amerika e ikitakatta desu.	I wanted to go to America.
Watashi wa ryokō ga shitakatta desu.	I wanted to travel.
Amerika ni watashi wa itakatta desu.	I wanted to be in America.
Anata wa nani ga nomitakatta desu ka.	What did you want to drink?
Anata wa nani ga shitakatta desu ka.	What did you want to do?
Anata wa dokoka e ikitakatta desu ka.	Did you want to go somewhere?

I didn't want to: _taku Nakatta Desu

You can form the negative past tense by changing _taku nai desu into _taku nakatta desu (or by changing _taku arimasen into _taku arimasen deshita). The direct object may be followed by either ga or o.

Kinō watashi wa benkyō ga/o shitaku nakatta desu.	Yesterday, I did not want to study.
Imōto wa ban-gohan ga/o tabetaku nakatta desu.	The younger sister did not want to eat an evening meal.
Watashi wa Amerika kara kaeritaku nakatta desu.	I did not want to return from America.
Onīsan wa daigaku e ikitaku nakatta desu.	The elder brother did not want to go to the university.
Robert-kun wa kekkon shitaku nakatta desu.	Robert did not want to get married.

Exercise 4

Listen to the phrases on the CD. Convert the sentences into negative statements, write them in rōmaji, and say them aloud. Check your pronunciation on the CD.

1 ....

2 ....

3 ....

4 ....

5 ....

Exercise 5

Translate into English:

1 *Watashi wa yama no e ga kakitakatta desu.* ....

....

2 *Kyonen ojīsan wa Amerika e kaeritakatta desu.* ....

....

3 *Natsu-yasumi ni onēsan wa hatarakitakatta desu.* ....

....

4 *Watashi wa machi de kaimono ga shitakatta desu.* ....

....

Translate into rōmaji:

5 *I wanted to go to England last year.* ....

....

6 *My mother wanted to buy a very expensive dress.* ....

....

7 *I wanted to drive a car.* ....

....

8 *I wanted to drink coffee.* ....

....

Exercise 6

Listen to the phrases on the CD. Convert the sentences into the past tense and write them below.

1 ....
2 ....
3 ....
4 ....
5 ....

Exercise 7

Translate into English:

1 *Kyonen watashi wa Nihon e kitaku nakatta desu.* ....
....

2 *Watashi wa densha kara oritaku nakatta desu.* ....
....

3 *Otōto wa Furansu-go ga/o naraitaku nakatta desu.* ....
....

4 *Otōsan wa kono kuruma ga/o kaitaku nakatta desu.* ....
....

Translate into rōmaji:

5 *I did not want to go to Germany.* ....
....

6 *I did not want to invite Robert to my birthday party.* ....
....

7 *I did not want to meet you.* ....
....

8 *Yesterday, my younger sister did not want to study math.* ....
....

Adjectives

Day 27 discusses adjectives and how to form negatives in the past tense. You will also learn about the tense of adjectives. Finally, you will pick up some more country and culture information about sushi.

SUSHI

Sushi consists of cooked vinegared rice combined with other ingredients, usually raw fish or or other seafood. Ingredients and forms of *sushi* presentation vary widely. Originating in the 4th century B.C. in Southeast Asia, initially the vinegared rice was only for the purpose of preserving fish (i.e. the rice wasn't to be eaten with fish and was thrown away). However, as it reached Japan it developed into what is today known as *sushi*, successfully combining the rice and fish.

Japanese conversation: Tom to Hanako wa ranchi wo tabemasu.

Hanako:	(Anata wa) tomato to kyūri no sandoicchi ga tabetai desu ka. (Anata wa) tamago no sandoicchi ga tabetai desu ka.
Tom:	(Boku wa) tamago (no sandoicchi) ga tabetai desu.
Hanako:	(Anata wa) mizu ga nomitai desu ka. (Anata wa) jūsu ga nomitai desu ka.
Tom:	(Boku wa) jūsu ga nomitai desu.

***

Tom:	Asoko ni mezurashii tori ga imasu. Kyonen boku wa Nihon e kitaku nakatta desu. Boku wa Nihon ga kirai deshita. Ima boku wa Nihon ga dai-suki desu.

English conversation: Hanako and Tom have lunch

Tom and Hanako are about to eat the boxed lunches.

Hanako:	Do you want to eat a tomato and cucumber sandwich, or (do you want to eat) an egg sandwich?
Tom:	I want to eat egg.
Hanako:	Do you want to drink water or juice?
Tom:	I want to drink juice.

***

Tom:	There is a rare bird over there. Last year, I did not want to come to Japan. I disliked Japan. Now, I like Japan very much.

Grammar

Adjective clauses

-tai can act as an adjective clause by itself and it precedes the word it describes. It is translated as *which/when/where/that (somebody) wants to __*. The subject of the adjective clause is the same as that of the main clause.

koto	thing (abstract)	mono	thing (article)
keshō	make-up	toki	time, moment
mukashi	long time ago	tokoro/ basho	place

tabetai okashi	the candy which (somebody) wants to eat
shitai koto	the thing that (somebody) wants to do
ikitai toki	the moment when (somebody) wants to go
ikitai tokoro	the place where (somebody) wants to go

Tabetai, shitai and ikitai, above, describe the nouns okashi, koto, toki and tokoro, and they may be translated as *that/when/where somebody wants to eat/do/go*. Notice that the translation for the adjective clauses starts with *that*, *when* and *where* according to the nouns they describe.

Forming sentences with adjective clauses

The easiest way to make a sentence with an adjective clause is to first make a sentence without the adjective clause, and then insert the adjective clause in front of the noun it describes.
Let's make the sentence *I buy the fruit that I want to eat*.
First, consider *I buy the fruit*: Watashi wa kudamono o kaimasu.
Insert tabetai, *that I want to eat*, in front of kudamono to get:
Watashi wa tabetai kudamono o kaimasu, *I buy the fruit that I want to eat*.

The following examples show adjective clauses in sentences:
Watashi wa tabetai mono o kaimasu.
I buy what I want to eat. (I buy the things that I want to eat.)
Watashi wa ikitai tokoro e ikimasu.
I go where I want. (I go to the place where I want to go.)
Ikitai toki ni ikinasai.
Go when you want. (Go at the moment when you want to go.)
Kaitai fuku wa takai desu.
The dress that I want to buy is expensive.
Watashi wa yomitai hon o yomimasu.
I read the book that I want to read.
Miki wa yomitai hon o yominasai.
Miki, read the book that you want to read.

Miki-san wa yomitai hon o yomimasu.
Miki reads the book that she wants to read.

Notice that the subjects of the adjective clauses are the same as those of the main clauses. For example, in the last three sentences, **yomitai hon** is translated as *the book that I want to read, the book that you want to read* and *the book that she wants to read,* respectively, because the subjects of the main clauses are **watashi, Miki** (implying *you*) and **Miki-san** (implying *she*), respectively.

Negatives and Past Tense

_**taku nai**, _**takatta** and _**taku nakatta** are adjective clauses for the negative present, past and negative past, respectively.

yomitai hon	the book that (somebody) wants to read
yomitaku nai hon	the book that (somebody) does not want to read
yomitakatta hon	the book that (somebody) wanted to read
yomitaku nakatta hon	the book that (somebody) did not want to read

Kaitai kutsu wa totemo takai desu.
The shoes that I want to buy are very expensive.
Kinō onīsan wa ikitakatta Amerika e ikimashita.
Yesterday, (my) older brother went to America, where he wanted to go.
Watashi wa kaitaku nakatta takai kutsu o kaimashita.
I bought the expensive shoes, which I did not want to buy.

Exercises

Exercise 1

Say the following phrases aloud in Japanese and write them below.

Check your answers on the CD.

1 **when (I) want to go** ....

2 **when (I) do not want to go** ....

3 **when (I) wanted to go** ....

4 **when (I) did not want to go** ....

5 **the person (I) want to meet** ....

6 **the person (I) do not want to meet** ....

7 **the person (I) wanted to meet** ....

8 **the person (I) did not want to meet** ....

Exercise 2

You will hear some adjective clauses in Japanese. Match the phrase you hear with the correct English translation.

1 ....a. the thing that I want to eat

2 ....b. the thing that I do not want to eat

3 ....c. the thing that I wanted to eat

4 .... d. the thing that I did not want to eat

5 ....e. the place I want to go

6 ....f. the place I do not want to go

7 ....g. the place I wanted to go

8 ....h. the place I did not want to go

Exercise 3

Translate into English:

1 *Watashi wa shitai koto ga arimasen.*

....

2 *Koko wa kitakatta tokoro desu.*

....

3 *Aitakatta hito wa Amerika e ikimashita.*

....

4 *Kore wa tabetakatta kudamono desu*

....

5 *Noritakatta basu ga ikimashita.*

....

6 *Kyō watashi wa kinō tabetakunakatta kudamono o tabemasu.*

....

Translate into **rōmaji**:

7 *At this shop, there isn't a thing that I want to buy.*

....

8 *I don't do things that I don't want to do.*

....

9 *Yesterday, I saw the movie that I wanted to see.*

....

10 *This is the book that I wanted to read.*

....

11 *My elder brother went to a party to which he did not want to go.*

....

12 *Right now (from now), I am going to read the book that I did not want to read yesterday.*

....

Japanese adjectives have tenses

You know that every adjective can be written as an adjective clause. The adjective *big* of *I eat a big apple* may be replaced by an adjective clause to form *I eat an apple that is big*.

For **i**-adjectives, form past and negative past adjectives by changing _i with _katta and _ku nakatta, respectively.

omoshiroi hon	the book that is interesting (the interesting book)
omoshiroku nai hon	the book that is not interesting (the uninteresting book)
omoshirokatta hon	the book that was interesting
omoshiroku nakatta hon	the book that was not interesting

Ano omoshirokatta hito wa Tarō-kun no ojīsan desu.
That person who was interesting is Taro's grandfather.
Watashi wa kono karēraisu o kinō no oishiku nakatta niku de tsukurimashita.
I made this curry with yesterday's meat, which was not delicious.

Tense of *na*-adjectives

For *na*-adjectives, you may obtain past and negative past adjectives by replacing **na** with **datta** and **de (wa) nakatta** respectively.

suki na hito	the person (somebody) likes
suki de (wa) nai hito	the person (somebody) does not like
suki datta hito	the person (somebody) liked
suki de (wa) nakatta hito	the person (somebody) did not like

Ima boku wa mukashi kirai datta Nihon ga suki desu.
Now I like Japan, which I disliked a long time ago.
Mukashi kirei de nakatta Hanako-san wa ima kirei ni narimashita.
Hanako, who was not pretty a long time ago, has become pretty now.

Exercise 4

Complete the adjective table below.

Meaning	Present	Negative Present	Past	Negative Past
big	ōkii	ōkiku nai	ōkikatta	ōkiku nakatta
	akai			
	isogashii			
	genki na			
	benri na			
	suki na	suki de (wa) nai	suki datta	suki de (wa) nakatta

Exercise 5

Translate into English:

1 *Otōto wa karai karēraisu ga kirai desu.* ....

....

2 *Kinō watashi-tachi wa omoshiroku nai eiga o gakkō de mimashita.* ....

....

....

3 *Hon-ya ni hoshikatta hon ga arimasen deshita.* ....

....

4 *Watashi wa tanoshiku nakatta toki no koto o kakimashita.* ....

....

5 *Watashi wa rippa na isha ni naritai desu.* ....

....

6 *Benri de nai apāto wa yasui desu.* ....

....

7 *Shinsetsu datta hito wa Hanako-san no onēsan deshita.* ....

....

8 *Hanako-san wa mukashi jōzu de nakatta tenisu ga totemo jōzu ni narimashita.* ....

....

....

Translate into rōmaji:

9 *The long holiday has finished.* ....

....

10 *Let's go to the place that is not dangerous.* ....

....

11 *That isn't the dog that was noisy.* ....

....

12 *I bought the dress that was not too expensive.* ....

....

13 *I did a stupid thing yesterday.* ....

....

14 *We took (our) residence at a not very convenient place (sumimasu—to live, reside, take up*

residence). ....

....

15 *The person whom I liked got married.* ....

....

day:28

Hiragana

Day 28 is all about *hirigana* and writing Japanese. Take the time to study the tables and to practice writing the characters. Finally, you will also learn how to read Japanese.

WHICH CHARACTERS?

Japanese was a spoken language only until the fifth century when the Chinese method of writing was introduced to Japan. Many systems were devised over the years, but it was **Manyōgana** *that became prominent. Here, the Japanese syllable was written using the Chinese character of the same sound. Around 1,000 Chinese characters were used to represent 100 Japanese syllables, which became the basis for* **hiragana** *and* **katakana.** *In the mid-ninth century, hiragana developed from* **Manyōgana** *to represent Japanese sounds.*

Grammar

Writing Japanese

When you write a sentence in Japanese, you can write it entirely in hiragana. However, if you do know kanji for any word, you should use it, and if a word is an imported word (i.e. from another language such as your name!), write it in katakana.

Below you can see the same word watashi, *I,* in the four variations.

わたし	ワタシ	私	watashi
Hiragana	**Katakana**	**Kanji**	**Rō maji**

The sentences below are perceived as being written by an educated person as a mixture of kanji, katakana and hiragana have been used.

Watashi	wa	Tom	desu.	I am Tom.
私	は	トム	です。	
Kanji	**Hiragana**	**Katakana**	**Hiragana**	

Koko	wa	gakkō	desu.	Here is a school.
ここ	は	学校	です。	
Hiragana	**Hiragana**	**Kanji**	**Hiragana**	

The sentences below are perceived as being written by a less educated person as all the characters are in hiragana.

Watashi	wa	Tom	desu.	I am Tom.
わたし	は	とむ	です。	

All the characters are in **hiragana.**

Koko	wa	gakkō	desu.	Here is a school.
ここ	は	がっこう	です。	

All the characters are in **hiragana.**

Hiragana

The table shows the **hiragana** for each **rōmaji** syllable.

Vowels

a あ	i い	u う	e え	o お

Basic syllables

ka か	ki き	ku く	ke け	ko こ
sa さ	shi し	su す	se せ	so そ
ta た	chi ち	tsu つ	te て	to と
na な	ni に	nu ぬ	ne ね	no の
ha は	hi ひ	fu ふ	he へ	ho ほ
ma ま	mi み	mu む	me め	mo も
ya や		yu ゆ		yo よ
ra ら	ri り	ru る	re れ	ro ろ
wa わ				wo を
n ん				

Second third: Modified syllables

ga が	gi ぎ	gu ぐ	ge げ	go ご
za ざ	ji じ	zu ず	ze ぜ	zo ぞ
da だ	ji ぢ	zu づ	de で	do ど
ba ば	bi び	bu ぶ	be べ	bo ぼ
pa ぱ	pi ぴ	pu ぷ	pe ぺ	po ぽ

Third third: Ya, Yu, Yo syllables

kya きゃ	kyu きゅ	kyo きょ
sha しゃ	shu しゅ	sho しょ
cha ちゃ	chu ちゅ	cho ちょ
nya にゃ	nyu にゅ	nyo にょ

hya ひゃ	hyu ひゅ	hyo ひょ
mya みゃ	myu みゅ	myo みょ
rya りゃ	ryu りゅ	ryo りょ
gya ぎゃ	gyu ぎゅ	gyo ぎょ
ja じゃ	ju じゅ	jo じょ
bya びゃ	byu びゅ	byo びょ
pya ぴゃ	pyu ぴゅ	pyo ぴょ

Remember that both rō maji and hiragana are phonetic symbols (associated with speech sounds) and that a syllable in hiragana may be represented by a syllable in rō maji.

わ	wa
た	ta
わたし	watashi

Modified syllables and *ya, yu, yo*

The hiragana in the second third, called modified syllables, are obtained by adding ゜ or ゜ to each character in rows 2, 3, 4 and 6. Note that there are two different hiragana for ji and for zu: both じ and ぢ are pronounced as ji, and both ず and づ are pronounced as zu.

The third third contains contracted syllables (or Ya, Yu, Yo syllables), because two syllables are contracted to obtain a single syllable. Consider the syllable kya. When you pronounce kya, the syllable starts out as ki and ends with ya. When the two syllables are pronounced as one syllable, you hear kya. When it is written in hiragana the second letter is written smaller.

き	ki	+	や	ya	→	きゃ	kya
み	mi	+	よ	yo	→	みょ	myo
き	ki	+	ゆ	yu	→	きゅ	kyu

Small characters

Whether a character is small or standard size makes a great difference to its meaning. For example, いしや ishiya, means *a stonemason* while いしゃ isha, means *a medical doctor*.

Exercises

Exercise 1

Write the following hiragana words in rōmaji, (refer to the table on page 246 if necessary), and then translate them into English.

1 こんにちわ..

2 ただいま ....

3 すみません..

4 みかん...

5 りんご...

6 やさい...

7 くだもの ....

8 せんせい ....

9 いぬ...

Exercise 2

You will hear a word in Japanese; write it below in hiragana.

1 .... 6 ....

2 ....7 ....

3 ....8 ....

4 ....9 ....

5 ....10..

Long vowels and double consonants

Converting rō maji into hiragana, and vice versa, is fairly straightforward, except when the words include long vowels or double consonants. Here are the rules for converting long vowels and double consonants.

Long vowels

Look at the romanized syllables in the hiragana table.

a appears in the first column in a, ka, sa, ta, na, etc. Hence the long vowel aˉ may occur in āˉ, kaˉ, saˉ, taˉ, naˉ, etc. These are pronounced as a/a, ka/a, sa/a, ta/a, na/a, and they are written as ああ, かあ, さあ, たあ, なあ, in hiragana. For example, okā san is written as おかあさん.

Look at i in the hiragana table.

i appears in the second column in i, ki, shi, chi, ni, etc. Hence the long vowel ī may occur in ī, kī, shī, chī, nī, etc. These are pronounced as i/i, ki/i, shi/i, chi/i, ni/i, and they are written as いい, きい, しい, ちい, にい. For example, onī san is written as おにいさん.
The long vowel ū occurs in the third column in ū, kū, sū, tsū, nū, etc.
These are pronounced as u/u, ku/u, su/u, tsu/u, etc., and they are written as うう, くう, すう, つう, etc. For example, senpū ki is written as せんぷうき.

The long vowel ē may occur in the fourth column in ē, kē, sē, tē, nē, etc.

These are pronounced as e/e, ke/e, se/e, te/e, ne/e, etc., and written as えい, けい, せい, てい, ねい, etc. An exception to this rule is onē san, which is written as おねえさん. Most often ē occurs in words written in katakana.

The long vowel ō may occur in the fifth column in ō, kō, sō, tō, nō, etc.

These are pronounced as o/o, ko/o, so/o, to/o, no/o, etc., and written as おう, こう, そう, とう, のう. Otō san is written as おとうさん. There are some exceptions to this rule. The most important, and the only one encountered in this book, is that of ō kii, which is written as おおきい.

obā san	おばあさん	arigatō	ありがとう
ojisan	おじいさん	dō zo	どうぞ
yū binkyoku	ゆうびんきょく	Tō kyō	とうきょう
otō to	おとうと		

In summary い and う each have two different pronunciations.

い is pronounced as i except for some long vowels, in which it is pronounced as e.
う is pronounced as u except for some long vowels, in which it is pronounced as o.

When you see い or う, the only way to correctly pronounce it is to know the pronunciation of the word which contains it.

Double Consonants (kk, pp, tt, ss)

A word with a double consonant in **rō maji** is written in **hiragana** by replacing the "(small pause)" with a small つ.

Nippon is pronounced as **Ni**/(small pause)/**po/n,** and written as にっぽん.

Similarly, **kitte, kippu** and **zasshi** are written as きって, きっぷ and ざっし.

Exercise 3

Write the pronunciations **a, i, u, e** or **o** for the following underlined **hiragana**.

1 う̲し	cow	....
2 どう̲ぞ	Please	....
3 おかあ̲さん	mother	....
4 こう̲えん	park	....
5 よう̲ちえん	kindergarten	....
6 ありがとう̲	Thank you	....
7 おはよう̲ございます	Good morning	....
8 お̲かえりなさい	Welcome home	....
9 ゆう̲びんきょく	post office	....
10 いもう̲と	younger sister	....

Exercise 4

You will hear a word in Japanese; write it below in **hiragana**.

1..	6	....
2..	7	....
3..	8	....
4	9	....
5..	10	....

Reading Japanese

There are no capital letters in Japanese. The small や, ゆ, よ and つ are written about a quarter of the size of the other characters. There is no question mark used in Japanese because the particle ka, at the end of a sentence, indicates that it is a question. The end of a sentence is denoted by 。.
When the sounds wa, e and o are particles, they must be written as は, へ and を.

Watashi wa Hanako desu. The first wa is a part of a word, and so it is written as わ. The second wa is a particle, and so it is written as は.

Watashi wa eki e ikimasu. The first e is a part of a word, and so it is written as え. The second e is a particle, and so it is written as へ.

Otō san wa ringo o tabemasu. The first o is a part of a word, and so it is written as お. The second o is a particle, and so it is written as を.

Japanese sentences are traditionally written without spaces between words. Punctuation marks, "、", which are comparable to English commas, are inserted as in English. Although there are no spaces between words in written Japanese, in this book we will insert a small space after each adverb, adjective and particle to make learning easier. If there is more than one particle, one after another, a small space will be inserted after the second particle. This is a common practice used to avoid confusion when Japanese children are taught to read and write.

Japanese sentences are written either horizontally or vertically. Books on mathematics, science, music and foreign languages are usually written horizontally to accommodate Arabic numerals, scientific symbols, musical notes and foreign words.

Novels, and other books that contain only words, are written vertically. To do this, you proceed from top to bottom and from right to left. The periods 。 and punctuation marks 、 are both placed at the same location as small characters, that is, at the top right half of the square when the sentence is written vertically, and at the bottom left half of the square when the sentence is written horizontally.

Exercise 5

Convert the following sentences into rōmaji and then translate them into English.

1 ここは　えきです。...

....

....

2 これは　わたしの　いぬです。...

....

....

3 あなたは　すしを　たべますか。..

....

4 あした、　わたしたちは　やまへ　いきます。.........................

....

....

5 これから、　あなたは　なにを　しますか。.............................

....

....

6 あそこに　くだものやが　あります。...

....

....

7 わたしは　はなこです。..

....

....

Katakana

Day 29 talks about *katakana* and how foreign words have evolved in the Japanese language. You will learn how to write *katakana* and you will learn how English words have been Japanized!

SOUNDS LIKE ENGLISH...

Japanese contains many Japanized English words such as aisukurīmu (ice cream), **conpyūtā** *(computer) and* **banana** *(banana). Other patterns include:*

1 *new words from sets of English words:* **wan-man-basu** *(one-man-bus), meaning a bus in which the driver collects the fares*

2 *new words from the first two or three syllables of English words:* **apāto** *(apartment),* **biru** *(building),* **infure** *(inflation).*

3 *New words from initials:* **ōeru** *(office lady).*

4 *New words from abbreviating compound words:* **wāpuro** *(word processor).*

5 *New words combining Japanese and Japanized English words:* **ha** *with* **burashi** *(brush), creates* **haburashi**, *toothbrush.*

Grammar

Katakana

Katakana is used in the following situations:

1 Words of foreign origin, other than Chinese, which have become Japanese. Foreign words which did not exist in Japanese were modified to fit into the Japanese phonetic system, and written in katakana.

Banana became banana バナナ.
Radio became rajio ラジオ.

2 Foreign personal names, places and other proper nouns. These are written as closely as possible to the way they are pronounced.

Smith is Sumisu スミス.
Ann is An アン.
America is Amerika アメリカ.

3 Describing the sounds around us, like the meowing of a cat or barking of a dog.

Wanwan ワンワン for woof woof.
Nyā ニャー for meow.

Syllables in Katakana

On the next page is the table of katakana. Unlike hiragana, which is made up of cursive lines, katakana is made up of simpler straight and curved lines.

Vowels

a ア	i イ	u ウ	e エ	o オ

First third

ka カ	ki キ	ku ク	ke ケ	ko コ
sa サ	shi シ	su ス	se セ	so ソ
ta タ	chi チ	tsu ツ	te テ	to ト
na ナ	ni ニ	nu ヌ	ne ネ	no ノ
ha ハ	hi ヒ	fu フ	he ヘ	ho ホ

ma マ	mi ミ	mu ム	me メ	mo モ
ya ヤ		yu ユ		yo ヨ
ra ラ	ri リ	ru ル	re レ	ro ロ
wa ワ				wo ヲ
n ン				

Second third: Modified syllables

ga ガ	gi ギ	gu グ	ge ゲ	go ゴ
za ザ	ji ジ	zu ズ	ze ゼ	zo ゾ
da ダ	ji ヂ	zu ヅ	de デ	do ド
ba バ	bi ビ	bu ブ	be ベ	bo ボ
pa パ	pi ピ	pu プ	pe ペ	po ポ

Third third: Ya, Yu, Yo, syllables

kya キャ	kyu キュ	kyo キョ
sha シャ	shu シュ	sho ショ
cha チャ	chu チュ	cho チョ
nya ニャ	nyu ニュ	nyo ニョ
hya ヒャ	hyu ヒュ	hyo ヒョ
mya ミャ	myu ミュ	myo ミョ
rya リャ	ryu リュ	ryo リョ
gya ギャ	gyu ギュ	gyo ギョ
ja ジャ	ju ジュ	jo ジョ
bya ビャ	byu ビュ	byo ビョ
pya ピャ	pyu ピュ	pyo ピョ

Hiragana and Katakana: Similarities

Just like in hiragana, modified syllables in katakana are formed by adding ゜or ゜to characters in rows 2, 3, 4, and 6. Ya, yu and yo syllables are formed by adding ヤ, ユ and ヨ.

1 When hiragana has ゜or ゜, so does katakana.

hiragana
ga (が) is ka (か) + ゜.
pa (ぱ) is ha (は) + ゜.

katakana
ga (ガ) is ka (カ) + ゜.
pa (パ) is ha (ハ) + ゜.

2 When hiragana is followed by a small や, ゆ or よ, so is katakana.

hiragana
kya (きゃ) is ki (き) + ya (や)
gyu (ぎゅ) is gi (ぎ) + yu (ゆ)

katakana
kya (キャ) is ki (キ) + ya (ャ)
gyu (ギュ) is gi (ギ) + yu (ュ)

Since katakana symbols are syllabic, one syllable in katakana may be represented by one syllable in rō maji, just as in hiragana.

te ⇆ テ　　　su ⇆ ス　　　　　　　　tesuto ⇆ テスト

Some words are written in a combination of katakana and hiragana. Amerika-jin literally means *America-person,* hence Amerika is written in katakana and jin is written in hiragana: アメリカじん.

Exercises

Exercise 1

You will hear a word in Japanese; write it below in katakana.

1.. 6 ....

2.. 7 ....

3.. 8 ....

4 .... 9 ....

5.. 10 ....

Exercise 2

. Convert the following katakana into rōmaji and then translate them into English.

1 オレンジ ....

....

2 トイレ ....

....

3 ラジオ ....

....

4 バナナ ....

....

5 ペン ....

....

6 プレゼント...

....

Katakana : long vowels and double consonants

When converting **rōmaji** words into **katakana,** all long vowels are indicated by using horizontal lines " ー ," when you write horizontally.

bō ru	ボ ー ル
kō hī	コ ー ヒ ー
uē tā	ウ エ ー タ ー

When writing **katakana** vertically, a vertical line "**l**" is used for long vowels.

ウ	コ	ボ
エ	｜	｜
｜	ヒ	ル
タ	｜	
｜		

Double consonants

For double consonants, the same rule applies as in **hiragana:** "(short pause)" is replaced by small ツ. **koppu** is pronounced as **ko**/(short pause)/**pu** and written as コップ.

Exercise 3

You will hear a word in Japanese; write it below in **katakana**.

1.. 6 ....

2.. 7 ....

3.. 8 ....

4 .... 9 ....

5.. 10 ....

Exercise 4

Translate the following sentences into rōmaji and English.

1 わたしの　おかあさんは　アメリカじんです。

....

....

2 おとうさんは　ラジオを　にわで　ききます。

....

....

3 まことくんは　テレビを　みません。

....

4 スミスさんは　コーヒーを　のみます。

....

....

5 わたしたちは　ステーキを　たべました。

....

....

6 トイレは　どこですか。

....

....

Kanji

Congratulations, you've reached the end of this course. Day 30 talks about *kanji* and how to develop your Japanese even more. By now you should be confident understanding, reading and speaking Japanese and you should have a good vocabulary. Well done!

KANJI

*The kanji of the year (Kotoshi no Kanji) is a Japanese character chosen by the **Japanese Kanji Proficiency Society** through a national ballot in Japan, starting in 1995. The character with the most votes is announced in a ceremony on December 12 (**Kanji Day**) at Kiyomizu Temple. A kanji is selected to represent the events of that year. For example, in 1995, the year when the Great Hanshin-Awaji earthquake occurred, 震 (**shin** meaning "quake") got the most votes and in 2010, 暑 (**sho** meaning "hot") won as the record heatwaves affected both people's livelihoods and the natural environment.*

Writing Japanese

Kanji, which originated between 4,000 and 5,000 years ago in China, were originally simple pictures of objects in daily life, e.g. 日 月 山. More complicated kanji characters, composed of combinations of simple kanji characters, were developed with time.

木 signifies *tree*.

| 木＋木 → | 林 | | *wood* (few trees make a wood) |
| 木＋木＋木 | | → 森 | *forest* (many trees make a forest) |

日 signifies *sun*.
月 signifies *moon*.

日＋月 →　　　明　　*bright* (sun and moon together makes things very bright)

As the writing system developed, characters were needed to express even more complicated words, and two or more kanji characters were combined to make one word.

The characters 山 *mountain* and 林 *wood* were combined to make the word related to both:
山林　sanrin *wood* in the *mountain (forest on a mountain)*

Pronouncing Kanji

Each kanji character may be pronounced in more than one way depending on the other kanji character(s) it is combined with to make another word. So, when you are learning to pronounce kanji, you must remember the whole word (a combination of one or more characters) and not just one particular character, as may be seen in the examples below.

日 and 山 have several different pronunciations, shown below (the pronunciations of 日 and 山 are underlined).

Since the character 日 was derived from *sun*, it was combined with other kanji characters to make words related to either *sun* or *day*.

日	hi	sun, daytime, day
月曜日	getsuyo ̄ bi*	Monday
六日	muika	sixth day of a month, six days
元日	ganjitsu	first day of a year
一日	ichi-nichi	one day

Since the character 山 was derived from *mountain,* it was used to make words related to *mountain.*

山	yama	mountain
山林	sanrin	wood in the mountain
火山	kazan*	volcano (fire and mountain makes volcano)

*bi is the phonetic transformation of hi.
*zan is the phnetic transformation of san.

Numbers

Although prices in train stations, supermarkets, department stores, etc. are listed in Arabic numerals, many restaurants, especially the traditional ones, list prices vertically in **kanji.**

〇	zero	0
一	ichi	1
二	ni	2
三	san	3
四	yon/shi	4
五	go	5
六	roku	6
七	nana/shichi	7
八	hachi	8
九	kyū/ku	9
十	jū	10
百	hyaku	100
千	sen	1,000
万	man	10,000

Exercise 1

Imagine yourself in Japan. From the options given below, choose the signs you must follow to get to the following places:

1 You want to buy a train ticket. ....

2 You want to go to a washroom. ....

3 You want to take a bus. ....

4 You want to take a taxi. ....

5 You want to check in your luggage. ....

6 You want to make a phone call. ....

7 You want to reserve a seat on a Shinkansen. ....

8 You want to get on the Shinkansen. ....

a. ↑ お手洗   b. ← タクシー

c. 新幹線のりば →   d. きっぷうりば →

e. 荷物一時預り所 →   f. ← みどりの窓口

g. ← バス   h. ↑ 電話

Vocabulary

案内所	annaijo	Information
荷物一時預り所	nimotsu-ichiji-azukarisho	Luggage Check-in
コインロッカー	koin-rokkā	Coin Lockers
精算所	seisansho	Fare Adjustment
きっぷうりば	kippu-uriba	Ticket Office
新幹線のりば	Shinkansen-noriba	Shinkansen Tracks
JR線のりば	JR-sen-noriba	JR Line Tracks
電話	denwa	Telephone
国際電話	kokusai-denwa	International Telephone
自動きっぷうりば	jidō -kippu-uriba	Automatic Ticket Dispenser (Machines)
お手洗	otearai	Washrooms
みどりの窓口	midori-no-madoguchi*	Train Reservation Office (for Shinkansen tickets)
バス	basu	bus
タクシー	takushī	taxi
バスの停留所	basu no teiryū jo	bus stop
地下鉄	chikatetsu	underground, subway

Key to Exercises

Day 1

Exercise 1: 1. mo 2. ri 3. te 4. ku 5. su 6. na 7. hi 8. ya 9. no 10. ga 11. bi 12. kyu 13. sha 14. cho 15. a 16. ā 17. o 18. ō 19. i 20. ī

Exercise 2: 1. o/ya/su/mi/na/sa/i 2. ta/da/i/ma 3. ko/n/ba/n/wa

Exercise 3: 1. a 2. d 3. h 4. c 5. f 6. i 7. e 8. g 9. b

Exercise 4: 1. ha/ji/me/ma/shi/te 2. o/ka/e/ri/na/sa/i 3. ko/n/ni/chi/wa 4. su/mi/ma/se/n 5. o/to/o/sa/n 6. o/ka/a/sa/n 7. ko/(small pause)/pu 8. ki/(small pause)/te

Day 2

Exercise 1: 1. Okaerinasai 2. Hajimemashite 3. Konnichiwa 4. Konbanwa 5. Ohayōgozaimasu 6. Sayōnara 7. Dō itashimashite 8. Oyasuminasai

Exercise 2: 1. d 2. b 3. c 4. e 5. a 6. h 7. g 8. f

Day 3

Exercise 1: 1. d 2. h 3. a 4. g 5. f 6. e 7. b 8. c

Exercise 2: 1. May I have a banana please? 2. May I have sushi please? 3. steak and bread 4. May I have steak and bread please? 5. a coffee or a juice 6. May I have a coffee or a juice please? 7. May I have an apple, a tangerine and a banana please? 8. Ringo o kudasai. 9. Karēraisu o kudasai. 10. banana ka orenj 11. Banana ka orenji o kudasai. 12. tenpura to soba 13. Tenpura to soba o kudasai. 14. Tonkatsu to pan to kōhī o kudasai.

Exercise 3: called ex 2 on CD: 1. Hanbāgā o kudasai. 2. Jūsu o kudasai. 3. Sarada o kudasai. 4. Sutēki o kudasai. 5. Kōhī to sandoicchi o kudasai.

Day 4

Exercise 1: 1. Nihon-jin, gakusei 2. Tom, Amerika-jin, gakusei

Exercise 2: 1. sensei 2. kun 3. chan 4. sensei

Exercise 3: 1. father 2. mother 3. Ken

Exercise 4: 1. kaishain 2. okāsan, sensei 3. okāsan, Kanada-jin 4. Tom, Ken 5. onīsan

Exercise 5: 1. lion, tiger 2. bear 3. giraffe, elephant

Exercise 6: 1. kore 2. koko 3. sore 4. soko 5. are 6. asoko

Exercise 7: 1. I am Hanako. 2. This is Amy. 3. This is a cat. 4. Those (over there) are (my) younger sister and (my) younger brother. 5. That (over there) is (our) teacher. 6. Watashi wa Betty desu. 7. Watashi-tachi wa gakusei desu. 8. Kore wa okāsan desu. 9. Kore wa buta to ushi desu. 10. Betty wa imōto desu.

Exercise 8: 1.Kore wa imōto desu. 2. Sore wa onēsan desu. 3. Are wa otōsan desu. 4. Kore wa neko desu. 5. Are wa tori desu. 6. Koko wa ginkō desu. 7. Asoko wa yama desu.

Day 5

Exercise 1: 1. Kore wa usagi desu ka. Is this a rabbit? 2. Anata wa (o)isha-san desu ka. Are you a medical doctor? 3. Koko wa ima desu ka. Is this a family room? 4. Asoko wa byōin desu ka. Is that (place far away) a hospital? 5. Sore wa suika desu ka. Is that a watermelon?

Exercise 2: 1. Kore wa usagi de wa arimasen. 2. Anata wa (o)isha-san de wa arimasen. 3. Koko wa ima de wa arimasen. 4. Asoko wa byōin de wa arimasen. 5. Sore wa suika de wa arimasen.

Exercise 3: 1. Excuse me. Is this (place) a post-office? No, this (place) is not a post office. This (place) is a bank. 2. Is Tom French? No, Tom is not French. Tom is American. 3. Anata wa Amy-san desu ka. Iie watashi wa Amy de wa arimasen. Watashi wa Betty desu. 4. Anata wa Amerika-jin desu ka. Iie watashi wa Amerika-jin de wa arimasen. Watashi wa Doitsu-jin desu.

Exercise 4: 1. Iie kore wa onēsan de wa arimasen. Kore wa obāsan desu. 2. Iie kore wa jagaimo de wa arimasen. Kore wa ninjin desu. 3. Iie koko wa gakkō de wa arimasen. Koko wa kōen desu.

Exercise 5: 1. (a) obāsan (b) obāsan (c) dare 2. (a) ninjin (b) ninjin (c) nan 3. (a) kōen (b) kōen (c) doko

Exercise 6: 1. Anata wa Imaeda Kazuko-san/sensei desu. 2. Hai anata wa sensei desu. 3. Iie anata wa Amerika-jin de wa arimasen 4. Hai anata wa otona desu.

Exercise 7: 1.Kore wa nan desu ka. 2. Sore wa nan desu ka. 3. Are wa nan desu ka. 4.Kore wa dare desu ka. 5. Sore wa dare desu ka. 6. Are wa dare desu ka. 7. Koko wa doko desu ka. 8. Soko wa doko desu ka. 9. Asoko wa doko desu ka.

Exercise 8: 1. What is that (over there)? That is a book. 2. Where is this (place)? This (place) is a park. 3. Where is the house? 4. Achira wa dare desu ka. Achira wa sensei desu. 5. Koko wa doko desu ka. Koko wa depāto desu. 6. Anata wa dare desu ka. Watashi wa Peter desu.

Exercise 9: 1. Purezento wa sakuranbo desu. 2. Hai onēsan wa gakusei desu. 3.Mari-san wa imōto desu. 4.Koko wa kōen desu.

Day 6

Exercise 1: 1. watashi no hon 2. anata no hon 3. otōto no hon 4. watashi no otōsan 5. anata no otōsan 6. Tom-kun no otōsan

Exercise 2: 2. Tom's book 3. (my) younger brother's briefcase 4. my eyeglasses 5. your handbag 6. a friend's umbrella

Exercise 3: 2. watashi-tachi no tēburu 3. Tom-kun no kuni 4. Igirisu no shuto 5. Eigo no zasshi 6. tabe-mono no hon

Exercise 4: 2. mother's 3. older brother's 4. older sister's 5. mine

Exercise 5: 1. wa 2. wa, Is this a school? 3. wa, no, Is this your school? 4. wa, to, no, Is this your and your older sister's school? 5. o, May I have a pen please? 6. to, o 7. ka, o

Exercise 6: 1. doko 2. dare 3. nan

Exercise 7: 1. teacher's chair 2. mother's purse 3. Hanako's father 4. This is my mother. 5. That is our dog. 6. Which country is this (place)? This is Italy. 7. Watashi no tomodachi 8. Anata no kazoku 9. Kore wa okāsan no kasa desu. 10. Watashi no nōto o kudasai. 11. Watashi wa Eigo no seito desu. 12. Kore wa nan no kudamono desu ka. Kore wa suika desu.

Day 7

Exercise 1: 1. Watashi wa sakana o tabemasu. 2. Watashi wa gyūnyū o nomimasu. 3. Watashi wa Eigo o hanashimasu. 4. Watashi wa shinbun o yomimasu. 5. Watashi wa okashi o kaimasu. 6. Watashi wa ongaku o kikimasu. 7. Watashi wa Nihon-go o naraimasu.

Exercise 2: 1. Father reads newspapers. 2. Mother makes bread. 3. The older brother speaks Japanese. 4. I eat meat. 5. The older sister writes a letter. 6. The younger sister drinks milk. 7. The younger brother watches TV.

Exercise 3: 1. nan 2. nani, What language do you speak? 3. nani, What do you drink?

Exercise 4: 1. I watch TV. 2. I and my younger brother learn Japanese. 3. My father reads newspapers and magazines. 4. We listen to the music. 5. Do you speak Japanese? 6. What do you eat? 7. What (kinds of) books do you read? 8. What do you buy? 9. What do you make? 10. Watashi-tachi wa Nihon-go no hon o yomimasu. 11. Watashi-tachi wa Eigo o naraimasu. 12. Watashi wa Nihon no ongaku o kikimasu. 13. Anata no otōsan wa sake o nomimasu ka. 14. Anata wa nani-go o hanashimasu ka. 15. Anata wa nani o nomimasu ka. 16. Anata wa nan no kudamono o tabemasu ka. 17. Anata wa nan no hon o yomimasu ka. 18. Anata wa nan no eiga o mimasu ka.

Day 8

Exercise 1:

Meaning	Positive verb	Negative verb
read	yomimasu	yomimasen
take	torimasu	torimasen
sell	urimasu	urimasen
send	okurimasu	okurimasen
drink	nomimasu	nomimasen

Exercise 2: 1. Hai nomimasu. 2. Iie nomimasen. 3. Iie yomimasen. 4. Hai naraimasu. 5. Hai mimasu. 6. Iie hanashimasen.

Exercise 3: 1. I do not wash a dog. 2. (My) older sister does not eat meat. 3. (My) mother does not buy fruit. 4. (My) younger sister does not make bread. 5. (My) younger brother does not read (my) father's books. 6. I do not speak English. 7. Do you learn German? No, I don't. 8. Watashi wa tegami o kakimasen. 9. Okāsan wa gyūnyū o nomimasen. 10. Makoto-kun wa udon o tabemasen. 11. Tom-kun wa shinbun o yomimasen. 12. Watashi wa ongaku o kikimasen. 13. Watashi wa Nihon-go o hanashimasen. 14. Anata wa kore o kaimasu ka. Iie kaimasen.

Exercise 4: 1. watch TV 2. drink wine 3. buy that 4. read a magazine 5. eat steak

Exercise 5: 1. Nomimasen ka. 2. Mimasenka 3. Kaimasen ka. 4. Nihon-go o naraimasen ka. 5. Yakisoba o tabemasen ka.

Exercise 6: 1. Would you like to see (watch) this? 2. Would you like to learn French? 3. Would you like to listen to the music? 4. Would you like to speak Japanese? 5. Would you like to eat sushi? Yes, thank you. 6. Would you like to drink water? No, thank you. 7. Eigo o hanashimasen ka. 8. E o kakimasen ka. 9. Nihon no ongaku o kikimasen ka. 10. Doitsu-go o naraimasen ka. 11. (O)cha o nomimasen ka. Hai itadakimasu.

Day 9

Exercise 1: 1. eye 2. ear 3. stomach 4. nose 5. hair 6. mouth 7. leg 8. finger 9. arm 10. shoulder 11. head 12. face 13. hand

Exercise 2: 1. Watashi wa tegami o te de kakimasu. 2. Watashi wa tegami o niwa de kakimasu. 3. Watashi wa tegami o pen de kakimasu. 4. Watashi wa tegami o Eigo de kakimasu. 5. Watashi wa sutēki o daidokoro de tabemasu. 6. Watashi wa sutēki o naifu to hōku de tabemasu.

Exercise 3: 1. I eat udon with chopsticks. 2. (My) older sister listens to the English songs on radio. 3. With what do you write letters? 4. (My) father reads books in the room. 5. We learn English at school. 6. (My) mother does not grow fruit in the garden. 7. Where does the grandfather buy bread? 8. Hanako-san wa neko o mizu de araimasu. 9. Watashi-tachi wa niku o naifu to hōku de tabemasu. 10. Obāsan wa hon o megane de yomimasu. 11. Zō wa banana o hana de tabemasu. 12. Watashi wa tegami o Nihon-go de kakimasu. 13. Anata wa ongaku o gakkō de naraimasu ka. 14. Watashi wa Nihon-go o ie de hanashimasen.

Exercise 4: 1. What is this in Japanese? 2. What is this in English?

Exercise 5: 1. water 2. leg 3. cat 4. inu 5. hon

Exercise 6: 1. Ashi wa Eigo de leg desu. 2. Mimi wa Eigo de ear desu. 3. Face wa Nihon-go de kao desu. 4. Mouth wa Nihon-go de kuchi desu.

Day 10

Exercise 1: 1. Are wa Hanako-san no onēsan desu ne. 2. Koko wa (o)tera desu ne. 3. Mimi wa Eigo de ear desu ne. 4. Watashi wa kore o tabemasu ne. 5. Watashi wa inu o araimasu ne.

Exercise 2: 1. Watashi wa kōhī o tomodachi to nomimasu. 2. Watashi wa terebi o kazoku to mimasu. 3. Watashi wa Nihon-go o onīsan to hanashimasu. 4. Watashi wa Nihon-go o otōto to naraimasu. 5. Watashi wa ongaku o okāsan to kikimasu.

Exercise 3: 1. I listen to the music with Makoto. 2. Would you like to eat sukiyaki with us? 3. With whom do you speak English? 4. You are Hanako, aren't you? 5. That is our bus! 6. Anata wa nani o Makoto-kun to tsukurimasu ka. 7. Bideo o watashi to mimasen ka. 8. Watashi wa Hanako-san to hanashimasen. 9. Soko wa byōin desu ne. 10. Kore wa watashi no desu yo.

Exercise 4: 1. Nihon-go to Eigo o Tom-kun wa hanashimasu yo.
2. Watashi wa ranchi o Hanako-san to tabemasu, Hanako-san to watashi wa ranchi o tabemasu, Hanako-san to ranchi o watashi wa tabemasu, Ranchi o watashi wa Hanako-san to tabemasu, Ranchi o Hanako-san to watashi wa tabemasu. 3. none

Day 11

Exercise 1: ichi, ni, san, yon/shi, go, roku, nana/shichi, hachi, kyu/ku, jū, hyaku, sen, man

Exercise 2: 2. 086-255-2100 3. 056-362-2561

Exercise 3: 1. 2,732 2. 34,568 3. 4,981 4. nana-hyaku sanjū go 5. go-sen ni-hyaku yon-jū ichi 6. kyū-sen nana-hyaku ni-jū roku

Exercise 4: 1. 530 2. 7,450 3. 14,300 4. 25,700

Exercise 5: 1. July 5th 2. November 10th 3. March 28th 4. February 13th 5. October 4th

Exercise 6: 2. San-gatsu mikka wa Hinamatsuri desu. 3. Go-gatsu itsuka wa Kodomo no hi desu. 4. Shichi-gatsu nanoka wa Tanabata desu. 5. Jūni-gatsu nijūgo-nichi wa Kurisumasu desu. 6. Jūni-gatsu sanjūichi-nichi wa Ōmisoka desu.

Exercise 7: 1. Wednesday 5th March 2002. 2. Monday 25th June 2000. 3. Saturday 2nd March 1981. 4. Sunday 19th August 1726. 5. Ni-sen yo-nen* ni-gatsu jūyokka doyōbi.
(Note that yon-nen has undergone phonetic transformation and has become yo-nen. Note also that shi is not used with nen.) 6. Sen go-hyaku nana-jū kyū/ku-nen jū-gatsu nijūhachi-nichi sui-yōbi. 7. Sen yon-hyaku-nen shichi-gatsu itsuka nichi-yōbi. 8. Ni-sen ichi-nen ichi-gatsu tsuitachi getsu-yōbi.

Day 12

Exercise 1: 1. 2 o'clock 2. 5:30 3. 7:45 4. 4:50 5. after 3 6. 11:10
Exercise 2: 1. ni-ji jūgo-fun 2. yo-ji sanjup-pun 3. roku-ji 4. hachi-ji yonjup-pun 5. jū-ji nijup-pun 6. jūni-ji
Exercise 3: 1. 11:25 2. 17 minutes to 9 3. 6:30 P.M. 4. 5:30 5. gogo ichi-ji jūgo-fun 6. gogo jūni-ji sanjup-pun/han 7. gozen roku-ji yonjūgo-fun 8. gogo shichi-ji nijūsan-pun

Day 13

Exercise 1: 1. mo, mo 2. mo, mo
Exercise 2: 1. ni 2. ni (My) father does not eat dinner at six o' clock. 3. (ni) In the evening, we watch TV. 4. (ni) In summer, (my) father will sell the house.
Exercise 3: 1. Shichi-ji han ni Tom-kun wa asa-gohan o tabemasu. 2. Roku-ji ni Tom-kun wa ban-gohan o tabemasu. 3. Tom-kun wa pan o asa-gohan ni tabemasu. 4. Hai mimasu.
Exercise 4: 1. I drink water. (My) younger sister also drinks water. 2. Both (my) mother and (my) father read books in the room. 3. Would you also like to watch a video with us tomorrow? 4. At night, we write letters to (our) friends. 5. The British eat lunch at 1 o'clock. 6. Hanako-san wa Furansu-go no hon o yomimasen. Makoto-kun mo Furansu-go no hon o yomimasen. 7. Jūni-gatsu ni watashi-tachi wa purezento o ojīsan to obāsan ni okurimasu. 8. Watashi wa Eigo mo Nihon-go mo hanashimasu. 9. Otōsan mo okāsan mo Eigo o hanashimasen. 10. Jūni-ji ni watashi-tachi wa Nihon no ongaku o rajio de kikimasu.
Exercise 5: 1. Watashi mo tomodachi o ranchi ni manekimasu. 2. Watashi mo basu o koko de machimasu. 3. Watashi mo tegami o kōkūbin de okurimasu. 4. Watashi mo shashin o sensei ni misemasu.
Exercise 6: 1. I will borrow this. 2. In spring, the teacher resigns from the school. 3. In summer, (my) mother will invite (my) grandmother to Japan. 4. Where does the father stop the car? 5. Do you wear a hat in winter? 6. Otōto to watashi wa Robert-kun o (watashi-tachi no) ie ni manekimasu. 7. Onēsan wa bōshi o atsumemasu. 8. Watashi wa anata o wasuremasen. 9. Fuyu anata wa kōto o kimasu ka. 10. Watashi wa e o otōsan ni misemasen.

Day 14

Exercise 1: 1. Would you like to go to Kyoto next week by train? 2. Would you like to come to my house for lunch tomorrow? 3. Would you like to get off the bus here? 4. Would you like to go out from the station? 5. Would you like to go to Japanese language class? 6. Would you like to go to a coffee shop?
Exercise 2: 1. Otōsan wa kaisha e densha de ikimasu. 2. Okāsan wa sūpāmāketto e kuruma de ikimasu. 3. Iie ikimasen. 4. Onēsan wa daigaku e ikimasu.
Exercise 3: 1. Ichi-gatsu kara go-gatsu made otōsan wa gaikoku e ikimasu. From January to May, (my)

father will go abroad. 2. Tōkyō kara Ōsaka made watashi wa densha de ikimasu. I will go to Tokyo to Osaka by train. 3. Asa kara yoru made otōto wa terebi o mimasu. From morning to night, (my) younger brother watches TV.

Exercise 4: 1. In January, Betty will return to America. 2. Where do you go by train? 3. (My) older sister also gets off the bus. 4. Neither (my) younger brother nor I go to school by car. 5. In spring, (my) grandfather will come to Japan by boat. 6. Otōsan wa furo kara demasu. 7. Asa no hachi-ji ni watashi wa gakkō e ikimasu. 8. Ku-gatsu ni watashi wa Amerika e hikōki de ikimasu. 9. Natsu Tom-kun wa Amerika e kaerimasen. 10. Ku-gatsu ni otōto wa yōchien ni* hairimasen. (*ni is used since "entering a kindergarten" does not mean a motion of going into a kindergarten, but an event.)

Day 15

Exercise 1: 1. Asa hachi-ji ni onēsan wa kao o araimasu. 2. Hai shimasu. 3. Hiru onēsan wa (okāsan to) kaimono o shimasu. 4. Ban onēsan wa deito o shimasu.

Exercise 2: 1. travel 2. do not play sumo wrestling 3. At night, (my) mother knits also. 4. (My) older brother does not play baseball. 5. yakusoku o shimasu 6. tenisu o shimasen 7. Hachi-gatsu ni watashi-tachi wa ryokō o kuruma de shimasu. 8. Anata wa nani o gakkō de shimasu ka.

Exercise 3: 2. torakku o unten shimasu 3. yasai ya ryōri shimasu 4. Eigo o benkyō shimasu

Exercise 4: 1. I will cook this. 2. I will promise that. 3. Betty does not drive a car. 4. In August, we will get married (we will marry). 5. Aki watashi wa Amerika o ryokō shimasu. 6. Watashi wa sutēki o hiru-gohan ni ryōri shimasu. 7. Haru watashi wa niwa o sōji shimasu. 8. Tom-kun wa Nihon-go o benkyō shimasu ka.

Exercise 5: Dore ni shimasu ka. – Kore ni shimasu.; Doko ni shimasu ka. – Koko ni shimasu.; Nan ni shimasu ka. – Kore ni shimasu.

Exercise 6: 1. Could you take me to a hospital please? 2. May I speak to Tom please? 3. Which fruit do we decide on? 4. Which temple do we decide on? 5. Who's house do we decide on? 6. Tōkyō (no)* dōbutsuen onegai shimasu. (Tōkyō dōbutsuen is a personal pronoun meaning Tokyo Zoo while Tōkyō no dōbutsuen means Zoo in Tokyo.) 7. Eigo no sensei onegai shimasu. 8. Hanako-san ni purezento wa nan ni shimasu ka. 9. Dare ni shimasu ka. 10. Ryokō wa doko ni shimasu ka.

Exercise 7: 1. Tom-kun to Hanako-san wa Edo e ikimasu. 2. Tom-kun wa tonkatsu o tabemasu. 3. Hanako-san wa yakisoba o tabemasu. 4. Hanako-san wa gyūnyū o nomimasu.

Day 16

Exercise 1: 1. abunai 2. mezurashii 3. tanoshii 4. urusai 5. isogashii 6. akai 7. aoi

Exercise 2: 2. mezurashiku nai tori 3. sabishiku nai (o)tera 4. urusaku nai inu 5. tanoshiku nai hi 6. akaku nai ringo

Exercise 3: 2. are 3. asoko 4. koko 5. asoko 6. sore

Exercise 4: 1. blue eye 2. large steak 3. this dog 4. not a frightful teacher (teacher who is not frightening) 5. not a cold day 6. (My) father goes to his work (company) in this black car. 7. In summer, I and (my) younger brother learn easy Japanese. 8. Do you read a difficult book at school?
9. tsumetai mizu 10. ōkii hito 11. ano kodomo 12. omoshiroku nai eiga 13. Kore wa nagai kisha desu.

Exercise 5: 1. Ano inu wa kowaku nai desu. 2. Kono ringo wa oishiku nai desu. 3. Mari-chan wa kawaiku nai desu. 4. Kono hon wa omoshiroku nai desu. 5. Kore wa muzukashiku nai desu.

Exercise 6: 1. This summer is hot, isn't it? 2. Betty's dog is dirty. 3. This fruit is cheap! 4. The sea water is cold, isn't it? 5. A Japanese person is not rare. 6. Kanada wa samui desu. 7. Kore wa mezurashii desu. 8. Igirisu wa omoshiroi desu ka. 9. Gakkō wa tanoshii desu ka. 10. Watashi no kasa wa kuroku nai desu.

Exercise 7: 2. genki de nai inu, not an energetic (healthy) dog 3. yūmei de nai (o)tera, not a famous temple

Exercise 8: 1. a quiet temple 2. a handsome man (person) 3. Taro is an energetic (healthy) cat. 4. This is my father's precious book. 5. genki na neko 6. kirei na me 7. shinsetsu de nai hito 8. Kore wa yūmei na e desu. 9. Sore wa genki na kodomo desu.

Day 17

Exercise 1: 1. Watashi wa ringo ga suki desu. 2. Watashi wa tenpura ga suki desu. 3. Watashi wa ninjin ga kirai desu. 4. Watashi wa gyūnyū ga kirai desu. 5. Watashi wa tenisu ga jōzu desu. 6. Watashi wa Eigo ga jōzu desu. 7. Watashi wa suiei ga heta desu. 8. Watashi wa Nihon-go ga heta desu. 9. Watashi wa sutēki ga hoshii desu. 10. Watashi wa terebi ga hoshi desu.

Exercise 2: 1. Onīsan wa suiei to tenisu to jūdō to taisō o shimasu. 2. jōzu de wa arimasen. 3. Iie suki de wa arimasen.

Exercise 3: 1. the person whom somebody likes 2. the book that somebody wants 3. the teacher whom somebody does not dislike 4. the meal that somebody does not want 5. The apples are the fruit that I like. 6. I read the book I dislike at school. (I read the dislikeable book at school.) 7. That elephant wants your banana. 8. kirai na sensei 9. heta na Eigo 10. jōzu de nai Nihon-go 11. hoshiku nai nomimono 12. Watashi wa Nihon-jin ga suki desu. 13. Watashi wa ōkii sutēki ga ban-gohan ni hoshii desu. 14. Anata wa dare ga suki desu ka.

Exercise 4: 1. Watashi wa atama ga itai desu. 2. Watashi wa ashi ga itai desu. 3. Watashi wa ude ga itai desu. 4. Watashi wa me ga itai desu. 5. Watashi wa onaka ga itai desu.

Exercise 5: 1. I have a pain in my stomach. (As for me, the stomach is painful.) 2. Hanako has beautiful eyes. (As for Hanako, the eyes are beautiful.) 3. Do giraffes have long necks? (As for giraffes, are the necks long?) 4. Japanese have short noses, don't they? (As for Japanese, the noses are short, aren't they?) 5. Watashi wa ude ga kayui desu. 6. Watashi wa ashi ga itai desu. 7. Otōsan wa te ga ōkii desu. 8. Zō wa hana ga nagai desu.

Day 18

Exercise 1: 2. nagaku 3. usuku 4. yasashiku 5. tanoshiku

Exercise 2: 1. totemo 2. amari 3. totemo 4. amari

Exercise 3: 1. Sugu 2. Naze 3. Yagate/Sorosoro 4. Motto

Exercise 4: 1. a very beautiful dress 2. a very large person 3. I will go there immediately 4. Why do you like Hanako? 5. Would you like to go to the party a bit early? 6. totemo hayai densha 7. amari kawaiku nai neko 8. Ōkii ie wa totemo takai desu ka. 9. Otōto wa Eigo o totemo yukkuri hanashimasu. 10. Yagate/Sorosoro otōsan wa kimasu.

Exercise 5: 2. Makoto-kun wa Hiroshi-kun yori hansamu desu. 3. Ken-kun wa Chūgoku-go ga Nihon-go yori jōzu desu. 4. Watashi wa yakyū ga tenisu yori suki desu. (Hiroshi-kun yori, Nihon-go yori and tenisu yori may be inserted before/after _ wa or before "adjective + desu.")

Exercise 6: 1. Hikari wa Kodama yori hayai desu. 2. Nozomi wa Hikari yori hayai desu. 3. Kodama wa mottomo osoi desu. 4. Nozomi wa mottomo hayai desu.

Exercise 7: 1. Japanese houses are less spacious than Canadian houses. 2. Americans have longer noses than Japanese have. 3. I like geography much more than I like history. 4. Sūgaku no sensei wa chiri no sensei yori shinsetsu desu. 5. Kono inu wa (watashi no) otōto yori ōkii desu. 6. Amerika no budō wa Nihon no budō yori motto yasui desu.

Day 19

Exercise 1: 1. shio, koshō, satō, shōyu, koppu 2. neko, okāsan

Exercise 2: 1. Okāsan wa sūpāmāketto de kaimono o shimasu. 2. Hai imasu. 3. Sūpāmāketto wa totemo benri desu. 4. Iie arimasen. 5. Kēki-ya ni oishii pan ga arimasu. 6. Iie ikimasen.

Exercise 3: 1. Over there, (there) is the department store. 2. There is Makoto. 3. (My) father and (my) mother are in the garden. 4. There is also salt and pepper here. 5. There is a cat in the kitchen. There is a cat in the garden also. 6. What is here? 7. Asoko ni otōsan no megane ga arimasu. 8. Ano kudamono-ya ni totemo oishii ringo to orenji ga arimasu. 9. Byōin ni (o)isha-san to kangofu-san ga imasu. 10. Niwa ni Betty-san ga imasen. 11. Doko ni ginkō ga arimasu ka. 12. Asoko ni nani ga arimasu ka.

Exercise 4: 1. Ashita Hanako-san wa (Eigo no) tesuto ga arimasu. 2. Hai arimasu. 3. Yoru onēsan wa deito ga arimasu. 4. Iie arimasen. 5. Otōsan wa kaigi ga arimasu. 6. Okāsan wa pātī ga arimasu.

Exercise 5: 1. We have an English test tomorrow morning. 2. I have Hanako's birthday party tomorrow. 3. Do you have (any) children? 4. I don't have any time now. 5. Watashi wa (o)kane ga arimasu. 6. Otōsan wa kaigi ga Tōkyō de* arimasu. (*Note that meeting is an action/event taking place in Tokyo, and hence Tōkyō is followed by de and not ni.) 7. Anata no heya ni terebi ga arimasu ka. 8. Anata wa onīsan ga imasu ka.

Exercise 6: 1. Iie yomimasen. 2. Tom-kun to Makoto-kun wa sētā o Hanako-san ni kaimasu. 3. Sētā wa akai desu. 4. Sētā wa go-sen-en desu.

Day 20

Exercise 1: 1. no 2. de 3. no

Exercise 2: 1. ie no naka 2. ie no soto 3. ie no chikaku 4. ie no yoko 5. ie no mae 6. ie no ushiro 7. tsukue no ue 8. tsukue no shita

Exercise 3: 1. ue 2. yoko 3. mae 4. shita

Exercise 4: 1. This dog drinks toilet water (water in a toilet). 2. Your book is on the desk! 3. (My) father and (my) mother are in the house. 4. My younger brother reads cartoons in the bus. 5. There is a hospital in front of the school. 6. Nyūyōku no tatemono wa totemo takai desu. 7. Tsukue no ue ni enpitsu ga arimasu. 8. Umi no naka ni ōkii sakana ga imasu. 9. Ano ōkii depāto no yoko ni yūbinkyoku ga arimasu. 10. Daidokoro no tēburu no ue ni nani ga arimasu ka.

Exercise 5: 1. Hidari-gawa ni jinja ga arimasu. 2. Mae ni kawa ga arimasu. 3. Hidari-gawa ni ginkō to yūbinkyoku to keisatsu-sho ga arimasu. Migi-gawa ni (o)tera to gakkō ga arimasu. Ushiro ni kawa ga arimasu. 4. Migi-gawa ni byōin ga arimasu. 5. Hidari-gawa ni gakkō ga arimasu.

Exercise 6: 1. Kōsaten o migi e magarimasu. 2. Kōsaten o hidari e magarimasu. 3. Kōsaten o massugu ikimasu. 4. Tsukiatari o migi e magarimasu. 5. Tsukiatari o hidari e magarimasu.

Exercise 7: 1. I will go straight along this road. 2. The bus will turn right at the traffic light. 3. Turn left at that T-junction. 4. The number three bus will go to Higashi Park. 5. I will stop the car at the opposite side of the temple. 6. Ano shingō o massugu ikimasu. 7. Tsukiatari o migi e magarimasu. 8. Kono basu wa Atago-yama no hō e ikimasu. 9. Eki no hantai-gawa ni pan-ya ga arimasu. 10. Ano hoteru no mae o hidari e magarimasu.

Day 21

Exercise 1: 2. ga, The bus will come soon. 3. ga, The movie will start immediately. 4. wa, This summer, I will start a study of English. 5. ga, The train will move!

Exercise 2: 1. Otōsan wa roku-ji han ni okimasu. 2. Iie ikimasen. 3. Otōsan wa kuruma no kaisha de hatarakimasu. 4. Yoru shichi-ji ni otōsan wa uchi e kaerimasu.

Exercise 3: 1. It will snow tomorrow. 2. In June, (my) older brother's house will be completed. (house will be made) 3. My younger brother swims in the pool with (his) friend. 4. A car stops in front of the house. 5. (My) father works at a car factory. 6. A baby does not cry in its mother's arms. 7. What time does the Japanese movie start? 8. Yagate/Sorosoro ame ga yamimasu. 9. Itsu ano yama no yuki ga tokemasu ka. 10. Okāsan no koe ga tonari no ie kara kikoemasu. 11. Natsu watashi wa umi de oyogimasu. 12. Yama ga miemasu. 13. Haru watashi wa ojisan ni Kanada de aimasu.

Exercise 4: 1. okāsan 2. otōsan 3. Tom-kun 4. Tom-kun

Exercise 5: 1. Do you understand this picture (painting)? 2. I understand Japanese a little. 3. What (kind of) sports can you do? 4. (My) younger brother cannot drive a car. 5. He (That person) cannot speak (do) Japanese at all! 6. Watashi wa Hanako-san ga zenzen wakarimasen. 7. (Watashi no) otōto wa jūdō ga dekimasu. 8. Watashi wa benkyō ga ie de dekimasen. 9. Okāsan wa Eigo ga zenzen dekimasen. 10. Anata wa Hanako-san no Eigo ga wakarimasu ka.

Day 22

Exercise1: 2. yasashikatta desu yo, Yesterday's test was easy! 3. suki deshita, I liked Hanako last year. 4. sui-yōbi de wa arimasen deshita yo, Yesterday wasn't a Wednesday! 5. samuku nakatta desu ne, Yesterday wasn't cold, was it?

Exercise 2: 1. Tom-kun wa Amerika e ikimashita. 2. Tom-kun wa obasan to ojisan no ie ni tomarimashita. 3. Hai shimashita. 4. Tom-kun wa kariforunia ga ichiban suki deshita. 5. Tom-kun wa terebi o mimashita. 6. Tom-kun wa Eigo o hanashimashita. 7. Hai suzushikatta desu. 8. Tom-kun no natsu-yasumi wa tanoshii natsu-yasumi deshita.

Exercise 3: 1. He (That person) was Makoto's older brother. 2. Yesterday, I heard French songs (French songs were heard) at the youth hostel. 3. Last summer, there was a big tree here. 4. Last month, we did shopping in America. 5. Yesterday, I made a chair with (my) father. 6. What did you eat for lunch yesterday? 7. Are wa (o)tera deshita. 8. Kyonen watashi wa Amerika e hikōki de ikimashita. 9. Kinō tsukue no ue ni shinbun ga arimashita. 10. Nagai ryokō ga owarimashita. 11. Kinō no ban watashi wa ban-gohan o tabemasen deshita. 12. Kinō watashi wa tenisu o Makoto-kun to shimasen deshita.

Day 23

Exercise 1: 1. ashita, rainen, rai-shū, asatte, korekara, rai-getsu 2. sen-shū, sen-getsu, ototoi, kinō, kyonen

Exercise 2: 1. The day after tomorrow will be a Monday. 2. Tomorrow, (my) father and (my) mother will return from Britain. 3. Next week, (my) older brother's house will be completed (made). 4. The day after tomorrow, I will eat dinner at Betty's house. 5. Tomorrow's movie will not be interesting! 6. Tomorrow, I will wait for you at the station, will I? 7. Next week, I will return this book to you. 8. Tomorrow, I will not play tennis. 9. The school will start next Wednesday (Wednesday of next week). 10. Would you like to go shopping next week? 11. Ashita wa nichi-yōbi desu. 12. Itsuka watashi wa Furansu-go o naraimasu (benkyō shimasu). 13. Ashita otōto to watashi wa (o)tera e ikimasu. 14. Ashita anata wa nani o shimasu ka. 15. Ashita no asa watashi wa yama no e o kakimasu. 16. Rainen anata no ojisan wa Nihon e kimasu ka. 17. Ashita watashi wa terebi o mimasen. 18. Rai-nen watashi wa aoi takai kōto o kaimasu. 19. Rai-getsu akachan ga obasan ni umaremasu. 20. Ashita watashi wa kono doresu o kimasu.

Exercise 3: 1. Tom – a medical doctor, Mari – a nurse, Makoto – a judo instructor, Hanako – a school teacher, Ken – an office worker

Exercise 4:

Adjective	Meaning	Adjective + desu	Meaning	Future Tense
Nagai	Long	Nagai desu	To be long	Nagaku narimasu

Hoshii	Desirous	Hoshii desu	To be desirous	Hoshiku narimasu
Muzukashii	Difficult	Muzukashii desu	To be difficult	Muzukashiku narimasu
Benri na	Convenient	Benri desu	To be convenient	Benri ni narimasu
Rippa na	Splendid	Rippa desu	To be splendid	Rippa ni narimasu

Exercise 5: 1. Kyō wa samui desu. 2. Gogo wa atatakaku narimasu. 3. Hachi-gatsu wa totemo atsuku narimasu. 4. Ku-gatsu wa hachi-gatsu yori suzushii desu.

Exercise 6: 1. Next month, (my) aunt Akiko will become a mother. 2. Will the study of Japanese language be difficult? 3. Someday, he (that person) will be famous! 4. After a party, the kitchen will be dirty. 5. You will like Japanese history! 6. Itsuka anata wa tenisu ga jōzu ni narimasu. 7. Itsuka anata wa (o)isha-san ni narimasu ka. 8. Rainen sukāto wa mijikaku narimasu yo. 9. Kono ki wa ōkiku narimasen. 10. Anata wa Nihon no tabemono ga suki ni narimasu.

Day 24

Exercise 1: 2. Let's buy this sweater. 3. Let's wait for Hanako until three o'clock here. 4. Let's show this to (our) teacher tomorrow. 5. Let's trurn right at that traffic light. 6. Let's walk to the mountain. 7. Let's move (our) father's desk.

Exercise 2: 1. Let's meet in front of the department store at eight o'clock tomorrow. 2. Let's give this apple to (our) grandpa. 3. Let's invite a friend for lunch tomorrow. 4. Let's buy this. 5. Let's swim in the sea in summer. 6. Let's study (from) now. 7. Kyō no yoru terebi o mimashō. 8. Rainen Nihon-go o naraimashō (benkyō shimashō). 9. Atatakai sētāo kimashō. 10. Ban-gohan o tabemashō. 11. Ashita no asa depāto e basu de ikimashō. 12. Asobimashō.

Exercise 3: 2. Drink plenty of water! 3. Speak Japanese at home! 4. Return that to Mari! 5. Go to school! 6. Put on a much longer skirt!

Exercise 4: 1. Tom-kun wa atama ga itai desu. 2. Hai ikimashita. 3. Hai agemashita. 4. Kyōto ashita Tom-kun wa kusuri o nomimasu.

Exercise 5: 1. Amy, write your letter in (your) room! 2. Robert, give milk to the cat! 3. Kimi and Betty, go to the school by bus tomorrow! 4. Tom, play outside! 5. Betty, study French! 6. (Betty wa) heya no sōji o shinasai (heya o sōji shinasai). 7. (Makoto wa) gakkō e ikinasai. 8. (Robert wa) tomato o tabenasai. 9. (Kimi wa) koko e kinasai. 10. Gohan no mae ni (Tom wa) te o arainasai.

Day 25

Exercise 1: 1. dareka 2. dokoka 3. itsuka 4. dare demo 5. doko demo 6. itsu demo 7. dare mo 8. doko mo 9. itsu mo

Exercise 2: 1. Watashi wa dono hon ka yomimasu; Watashi wa dono hon demo yomimasu; Watashi wa dono hon mo yomimasen. 2. Watashi wa nanika kaimasu; Watashi wa nan demo kaimasu; Watashi wa nani mo kaimasen. 3. Watashi wa kore o dareka ni agemasu; Watashi wa kore o dare ni demo agemasu; Watashi wa kore o dare ni mo agemasen.

Exercise 3: 1. I don't want anything. 2. I will not buy any of them. 3. Would you like to drink something? 4. I will read something. 5. Would someone like to watch this video? 6. Nobody went to the mountain. 7. I will play tennis anytime! 8. Kono inu wa nan demo tabemasu. 9. Watashi wa dono kudamono mo kaimasen. 10. Dokoka e ikimasen ka. 11. Watashi wa nani mo mimasen deshita. 12. Watashi wa dono doresu mo kaimasen. 13. Makoto-kun wa itsu mo pātī ni kimasen. 14. Itsuka yama e ikimasen ka.

Day 26

Exercise 1:

V.masu	Meaning	"Want to" Form	"Don't Want to" Form
naraimasu	learn	naraitai desu	naraitaku nai desu
okurimasu	send	okuritai desu	okuritaku nai desu
shimasu	do	shitai desu	shitaku nai desu
aimasu	meet	aitai desu	aitaku nai desu
kimasu	come	kitai desu	kitaku nai desu

Exercise 2: 1. I want to eat a watermelon. 2. I want to go to the Christmas party. 3. I want to get up early in the morning. 4. I want to stay (be) here. 5. I want to go somewhere.

Exercise 3: 1. Which magazine do you want to read? 2. I want to cry now. 3. (My) older brother wants to swim in the river. 4. I don't want to eat (my) dinner today. 5. I don't want to study. 6. Kyō no yoru watashi wa bideo ga mitai desu. 7. Watashi wa sutēki ga ban-gohan ni tabetai desu. 8. Watashi wa arukitai desu. 9. Ano neko wa heya kara detai desu. 10. Okāsan wa Itaria no handobaggu ga kaitai desu.

Exercise 4: 1. Watashi wa suika ga tabetakunai desu. 2. Watashi wa Kurisumasu pātī ni ikitakunai desu. 3. Watashi wa asa hayaku okitakunai desu. 4. Watashi wa koko ni itakunai desu. 5. Watashi wa dokomo e ikitakunai desu.

Exercise 5: 1. I wanted to draw a picture of the mountain. 2. Last year, (my) grandfather wanted to return to America. 3. During (In) the summer holiday, (my) older sister wanted to work. 4. I wanted to do shopping in town. 5. Kyonen watashi wa Igirisu e ikitakatta desu. 6. Okāsan wa totemo takai doresu ga kaitakatta desu. 7. Watashi wa kuruma ga unten shitakatta desu. 8. Watashi wa kōhī ga nomitakatta desu.

Exercise 6: 1. Watashi wa suika ga tabetakatta desu. 2. Watashi wa Kurisumasu pātī ni ikitakatta desu. 3. Watashi wa asa hayaku okitakatta desu. 4. Watashi wa koko ni itakatta desu. 5. Watashi wa dokoka e ikitakatta desu.

Exercise 7: 1. Last year, I did not want to come to Japan. 2. I did not want to get off the train. 3. (My) younger brother did not want to learn French. 4. (My) father did not want to buy this car. 5. Watashi wa Doitsu e ikitaku nakatta desu. 6. Watashi wa Robert-kun o pātī ni manekitaku nakatta desu. 7. Watashi wa anata ni aitaku nakatta desu. 8. Kinō imōto wa sūgaku ga/o benkyō shitaku nakatta desu (sūgaku no benkyō ga/o shitaku nakatta desu).

Day 27

Exercise 1: 1. ikitai toki 2. ikitaku nai toki 3. ikitakatta toki 4. ikitaku nakatta toki 5. aitai hito 6. aitaku nai hito 7. aitakatta hito 8. aitaku nakatta hito

Exercise 2: 1. c 2. f 3. d 4. h 5. e 6. a 7. g 8. b

Exercise 3: 1. I don't have anything (a thing) I want to do. 2. This is the place I wanted to visit (come). 3. The person I wanted to see (meet) has gone to America. 4. This is the fruit I wanted to eat. 5. The bus that I wanted to get on has gone. 6. Today, I will eat the fruit that I did not want to eat yesterday. 7. Kono mise ni kaitai mono ga arimasen. 8. Watashi wa shitaku nai koto o shimasen. 9. Kinō watashi wa mitakatta eiga o mimashita. 10. Kore wa yomitakatta hon desu. 11. Onīsan wa ikitaku nakatta pātī ni ikimashita. 12. Korekara kinō yomitaku nakatta hon o yomimasu.

Exercise 4:

Meaning	Present	Negative Present	Past	Negative Past
big	ōkii	ōkiku nai	ōkikatta	ōkiku nakatta
red	akai	akaku nai	akakatta	akaku nakatta
busy	isogashii	isogashiku nai	isogashikatta	isogashiku nakatta
healthy	genki na	genki de nai	genki datta	genki de nakatta
convenient	benri na	benri de nai	benri datta	benri de nakatta
(a thing/person) that (I) like	suki na	suki de (wa) nai	suki datta	suki de (wa) nakatta

Exercise 5: 1. (My) younger brother does not like hot (spicy) curry. 2. Yesterday, we watched a boring (not interesting) movie at (our) school. 3. The book store didn't have the book I wanted. 4. I wrote things about (my) unhappy times. (I wrote things about the time that was not enjoyable.) 5. I want to be a splendid doctor. 6. Inconvenient (Not convenient) apartments are cheap. 7. The kind person was Hanako's older sister. 8. Hanako became good at tennis, which she was not good at a long time ago. 9. Nagai ryokō ga owarimashita. 10. Abunaku nai tokoro e ikimashō. 11. Ano inu (Are) wa urusakatta inu de wa arimasen. 12. Watashi wa amari takaku nai doresu o kaimashita. 13. Kinō watashi wa baka na koto o shimashita. 14. Amari benri de nai tokoro ni watashi-tachi wa sumimashita. 15. Suki datta hito wa kekkon shimashita.

Day 28

Exercise 1: 1. Konnichiwa, Good afternoon. 2. Tadaima, I am back. 3. Sumimasen, Excuse me. 4. mikan, tangerine orange 5. ringo, apple 6. yasai, vegetable 7. kudamono, fruit 8. sensei, teacher 9. inu, dog

Exercise 2: 1. ともだち 2. あなた 3. はなこさん 4. ごめんなさい 5. うさぎ 6. にほんご 7. がいこく 8. こども 9. ねこ 10. ねずみ

Exercise 3: 1. u 2. o 3. a 4. o 5. o 6. o 7. o 8. o 9. u 10. o

Exercise 4: 1. おとうさん 2. おじいさん 3. おばあさん 4. いもうと 5. おとうと 6. どうぶつえん 7. にっぽん 8. きっさてん 9. ざっし 10. がっこう

Exercise 5: 1. Koko wa eki desu, This is a (railway) station. 2. Kore wa watashi no inu desu, This is my dog. 3. Anata wa sushi o tabemasu ka, Do you eat sushi? 4. Ashita watashi-tachi wa yama e ikimasu, Tomorrow, we will go to the mountain. 5. Korekara anata wa nani o shimasu ka, What do you do (from) now? 6. Asoko ni kudamono-ya ga arimasu, Over there is the fruit shop. 7. Watashi wa Hanako desu, I am Hanako.

Day 29

Exercise 1: 1. スミス 2. ロンドン 3. アメリカ 4. イギリス 5. パリ 6. フランス 7. ペン 8. クラス 9. ワイン 10. ワシントン

Exercise 2: 1. orenji, orange 2. toire, toilet 3. rajio, radio 4. banana, banana 5. pen, pen 6. purezento, present

Exercise 3: 1. ノート 2. ジュース 3. ニューヨーク 4. テーブル 5. スカート 6. アイスクリーム 7. タクシー 8. コップ 9. コーヒー 10. セーター

Exercise 4: 1. Watashi no okāsan wa Amerika-jin desu, My mother is American. 2. Otōsan wa rajio o niwa de kikimasu, (My) father listens to the radio in the garden. 3. Makoto-kun wa terebi o mimasen, Makoto does not watch TV. 4. Smith-san wa kōhī o nomimasu, Mr. Smith drinks coffee. 5. Watashi-tachi wa sutēki o tabemashita, We ate steak. 6. Toire wa doko desu ka, Where is a toilet?

Day 30

Exercise 1: 1. d 2. a 3. g 4. b 5. e 6. h 7. f 8. c

Vocabulary

A

abunai *dangerous*

achira *that person (a person away from the speaker and the listener)*

agemasu *give (to somebody)*

ahiru *duck*

aidea *idea*

aimasu *meet*

aisatsu *greeting*

aisukurīmu *ice cream*

akachan *baby*

akai *red*

aki *autumn*

amai *sweet (taste)*

amari *(not) very (with negative adjectives and adverbs describing negative verbs); (not) a lot, (not) much (with negative verbs)*

ame *candy*

ame *rain*

Amerika *America*

amimono *knitting*

anata *you*

ano *that (over there)*

aoi *blue*

apāto *apartment*

araimasu *wash*

are *that (a thing away from the speaker and the listener)*

arigatō *thank you*

arimasu *to be located/to exist (to describe a non-living subject)*

arukimasu *walk*

asa *morning*

asa-gohan *breakfast*

asatte *the day after tomorrow*

ashi *leg*

ashita *tomorrow*

asobimasu *play, amuse, enjoy*

asoko *that (place over there) (a place away from both the speaker and the listener)*

atama *head*

atatakai *warm*

ato *(time) after*

atsui *hot (of touch)*

atsui *hot (temperature)*

atsui *thick (of flat things)*

atsumemasu *collect*

B

baka na *foolish, stupid*

-ban *put after numbers to tell the order*

ban *evening*

banana *banana*

ban-gohan *dinner*

banira *vanilla*

basu *bus*

bāsudē *birthday*

basu-tei *bus stop*

benkyō *study*

benri na *convenient*

bentō *meal in a box*

bideo *video*

boku *I, me (for boys)*

bōshi *hat*

budō *grape*

burausu *blouse*

burūsu *blues*

buta *pig*

buta-niku *pork*
byōin *hospital*

C

cha *Japanese green tea (commonly called* ocha*)*
chairoi *brown*
-chan *added after the names of small children, especially girls*
chawan *bowl (rice)*
chekkuauto *check out*
chiisai *small, quiet (sound, voice)*
chikaku *nearby*
chiri *geography*
chizu *map*
chokorēto *chocolate*
chūgakkō *secondary school*
Chūgoku *China*

D

daidokoro *kitchen*
daigaku *university, college*
daikon *large white radish*
dakara *so, therefore*
dakkusufundo *dachshund*
dame na *not good*
dare *who*
dare mo *(not) anyone*
dareka *somebody*
de *in/with/by*
deito *date*
dekimasu *be made, be produced, be possible*
demasu *go out*
densha *electric train*
depāto *department store*
desu *is, am, are*
dewa mata *see you (later)*

dō *how, in what way*
dōbutsu *animal*
dōbutsuen *zoo*
Doitsu *Germany*
doko *where, which place*
doko mo *(not) anywhere*
dokoka *somewhere*
dono *which*
dore *which one*
dore mo *(not) any of them*
doreka *something*
doresu *dress*
dōro *road, way, highway*
do-yōbi *Saturday*
dōzo *please*

E

e *picture, painting*
e *to (motion towards a "place")*
eiga *movie*
Eigo *English language*
eki *(railway) station*
-en *_yen*
enpitsu *pencil*
erabimasu *choose*

F

fōku *fork*
fuben na *inconvenient*
fuku *cloth*
funabin *surface mail*
fune *ship, boat*
Furansu *France*
furimasu *fall (rain, snow)*
furo *bath*
furoba *bathroom*
futoi *thick (of cylindrical things), fat*
futsuka *2nd (day of the month), 2 days*

fuyu *winter*

G

gaikoku *abroad*
gaikoku-jin *foreigner*
gakkō *school*
gakusei *student (in a school)*
-gatsu *put after a number to tell the month*
-gawa *-side*
genki na *healthy, hearty*
getsu-yōbi *Monday*
ginkō *bank*
-go *added to the name of a country for its language*
go *five*
Gochisōsama. *Thank you for the food. (after eating)*
go-gatsu *May*
gogo *p.m.*
gohan *meal, boiled rice*
go-kai *fifth floor*
gōkei *total*
gomennasai *sorry*
goshujin *somebody else's husband*
gozen *a.m.*
gyū-niku *beef*
gyūnyū *milk*

H

hachi *eight*
hachi-gatsu *August*
hai *yes*
hairimasu *come in, enter, join, get in*
ha-isha *dentist*
hajimarimasu *begin*
Hajimemashite. *How do you do?*
hajimemasu *begin*
hajimete *for the first time*
hakarimasu *measure, weigh*
hakimasu *put on (footwear, trousers)*

hakusai *Chinese cabbage*
han *half past (time)*
hana *flower*
hana *nose*
hanashi *talk, conversation*
hanashimasu *speak*
hana-ya *flower shop*
hanbāgā *hamburger*
handobaggu *handbag*
hansamu na *handsome*
hantai *opposite*
hare *fine weather*
haru *spring*
hashi *chopsticks*
hatarakimasu *work*
hayai *quick, rapid, early*
hayaku *quickly, rapidly, early*
hebi *snake*
hen na *strange, suspicious*
heta na *bad (at a particular skill)*
heya *room*
hi *day*
hidari *left*
-hiki *put after a number to count animals such as dogs, tigers, rabbits, fishes and insects*
hikōki *airplane*
hikui *low, short (height)*
hima *free, time to spare*
hiroi *spacious*
hiru *afternoon*
hiru-gohan *lunch*
hito *person*
hō *direction*
hokenshō *health insurance card*
hōkō *direction*
hon *book*
hone *bone*
hon-ya *bookstore*
hoshii *desirous*

hosoi *thin (cylindrical things)*
hoteru *hotel*
hyaku *100*
hyaku-man *1,000,000*

I

ichi *one*
ichi-ban *most, best, number one*
ichi-gatsu *January*
ichigo *strawberry*
ie *house, home*
Igirisu *Britain*
ii *good*
iie *no*
ike *pond*
ikimasu *go*
ik-kai *first floor*
ikura *how much*
ima *at this moment*
ima *family room*
imasu *to be located/to exist (to describe a living subject)*
imōto *younger sister*
inu *dog*
ippai *full, plenty*
ip-pun *one minute*
Irasshaimase. *Hello and welcome. Come in.*
iro *color*
isha *physician, medical doctor*
isogashii *busy*
isu *chair*
Itadakimasu. *Thank you for the gift. (when receiving), Thank you for the food. (before eating)*
itai *painful*
Itaria *Italy*
itsu *when*
itsu mo *(not) anytime*
itsuka *5th (day of the month)*

itsuka *someday*

J

jagaimo *potato*
jazu *jazz*
jidō-kippu-uriba *automatic ticket dispensing area*
jidōsha *automobile*
jikan *(spare) time*
jikokuhyō *timetable*
-jin *added to the name of a country to describe its inhabitants*
jinja *shrine*
jitensha *bicycle*
jōzu na *good (at a particular skill)*
jū *ten*
jūdō *judo*
jū-gatsu *October*
jugyō *lecture*
jūichi-gatsu *November*
juku *cram school*
jū-man *100,000*
jūni-gatsu *December*
jūsu *juice*

K

ka *or, put at the end of a phrase to indicate "?"*
kaban *briefcase/bag*
kaburimasu *put on (hat)*
kaeri *return*
kaerimasu *to return*
kaeshimasu *return (things borrowed)*
kagaku *science*
kagi *key*
kaigi *meeting*
kaimasu *buy*
kaimono *shopping*
kaisha *company*

kaishain *office worker*

kakimasu *write, draw*

kami *hair*

Kanada *Canada*

kanai *my wife*

kane *money*

kangofu *nurse*

kao *face*

kara *from*

karada *body*

karai *spicy*

karate *karate*

karēraisu *curry*

karimasu *borrow*

karui *light (weight)*

kasa *umbrella*

kashimasu *lend*

kata *shoulder*

kawa *river*

kawaii *cute*

ka-yōbi *Tuesday*

kayui *itchy*

kaze *a cold*

kazoku *family*

kēki *cake*

kēki-ya *cake shop*

kekkon *marriage*

kesa *this morning*

keshō *make-up*

kibun *feeling*

kiiroi *yellow*

kikimasu *listen to, hear, ask for*

kikoemasu *be heard*

kimarimasu *be decided*

kimasu *come*

kimasu *put on (dress)*

kimono *kimono*

kinō *yesterday*

kin-yōbi *Friday*

kirai na *detestable, dislikeable*

kirei na *beautiful, clean*

kirin *giraffe*

kissaten *coffee shop*

kitanai *dirty*

kitte *stamp*

kōcha *Indian tea*

kochira *this person (to describe a person near the speaker)*

kodomo *child*

koe *voice, cry*

kōen *park*

kōgyō-daigaku *technical college*

kōhī *coffee*

kōjō *factory*

koko *this place (to describe a place near the speaker)*

kōkō *high school*

kokonoka *9th (day of the month)*

kōkūbin *air mail*

kokugo *the national language*

konban *this evening*

konbanwa *good evening*

kon-getsu *this month*

konnichiwa *good afternoon, hello*

kono *this*

kon-shū *this week*

koppu *cup*

kore *this (to describe a thing near the speaker)*

korekara *from now on*

kōsaten *intersection*

koshō *pepper*

koto *thing (abstract)*

kōto *coat*

kotoshi *this year*

kowai *frightful, frightening*

kowaremasu *break*

kowashimasu *break (something)*
ku *nine*
kuchi *mouth*
kudamono *fruit*
kudamono-ya *fruit shop*
ku-gatsu *September*
kūkō *airport*
kuma *bear*
kumo *cloud*
kumori *cloudy weather*
-kun *added after the names of boys*
kuni *country*
kurashikku myūjikku *classical music*
kurasu *(lecture) class*
kuremasu *give (to me)*
Kurisumasu *Christmas*
kuroi *black*
kuruma *car*
kurushii *difficult*
kusuri *medicine*
kutsu *shoe*
kutsushita *sock, stocking*
kyō *today*
kyonen *last year*
kyū *nine*
kyūri *cucumber*

M

machi *town*
machimasu *wait for*
mada *yet (used with negative verbs)*
made *until, to*
mae *before/to (time)*
mae *front part, position in front*
magarimasu *turn*
-mai *put after a number to count thin flat objects such as stamps, papers, tickets, plates, blankets, etc.*
mai-asa *every morning*

mai-ban *every evening*
mai-nen *every year*
mai-nichi *every day*
mai-shū *every week*
mai-toshi *every year*
māmā *so and so*
man *10,000*
manekimasu *invite*
manga *comics, cartoon*
manshon *high-grade apartment*
massugu *straight through*
mata *again*
matawa *or*
mazui *unsavory taste*
me *eye*
megane *eyeglasses*
mezurashii *unusual, rare*
michi *road, path, way*
midori-no-madoguchi *train reservation office (for shinkansen)*
miemasu *be visible*
migi *right*
mijikai *short (length)*
mikan *tangerine*
mikisā *blender*
mikka *3rd (day of the month); 3 days*
mimai *a visit (to inquire about someom's health)*
mimasu *see, watch*
mimi *ear*
minikui *ugly*
minna *everyone*
miokurimasu *see someone off*
miruku *milk (UHT single pack)*
mise *shops*
misemasu *show*
mizu *water*
mizūmi *lake*
mo *also/too*

mō *already*

moku-yōbi *Thursday*

momo *peach*

mono *thing (article)*

moshi-moshi *hello (used only on the telephone)*

motto *more*

mottomo *most, best*

muika *6th (day of the month); 6 days*

mukashi *long time ago*

muzukashii *difficult*

N

nagai *long*

naifu *knife*

naka *middle, inside*

nakimasu *cry*

nakushimasu *lose*

namae *name*

nan *what*

nana *seven*

nani *what*

nani mo *(not) anything*

nanika *something*

nanoka *7th (day of the month); 7 days*

naraimasu *learn*

narimasu *become*

nashi *pear*

natsu *summer*

naze *why*

ne *... isn't it?, ... don't you?*

negai *appeal, wish*

neko *cat*

nemasu *sleep*

-nen *put after a number to tell the year*

netsu *body temperature, fever*

nezumi *mouse, rat*

ni *two*

ni *at/in/on*

ni *used to indicate motion towards an event and direction of attention or interest*

-nichi *put after some numbers to tell the day of the month*

nichi-yōbi *Sunday*

nigai *bitter (taste)*

ni-gatsu *February*

Nihon *Japan*

niji *rainbow*

niku *meat*

niku-ya *butcher's shop*

-nin *put after a number to count people*

ninjin *carrot*

Nippon *Japan*

niwa *garden*

nomimasu *drink, take (medicine)*

nomimono *drinks*

norimasu *ride (on)*

nōto *notebook*

nyūin *admission into a hospital*

O

obasan *aunt*

obāsan *grandmother*

ohayōgozaimasu *good morning*

oishii *delicious, tasty*

ojisan *uncle*

ojīsan *grandfather*

okaerinasai *welcome back*

okāsan *mother*

okashi *confectionery, sweets, candy*

okashi-ya *confectionery shop*

ōkii *big*

ōkii *loud (sound, voice)*

ōkiku *big*

okimasu *wake up*

okuremasu *be late*

okurimasu *send*

okusan *somebody else's wife*
Ōmisoka *New Year's Eve*
omocha-ya *toy shop*
omoi *heavy*
omoshiroi *interesting, amusing*
omoshiroku *interestingly*
onaka *stomach, abdomen, belly*
onēsan *older sister*
ongaku *music*
onīsan *older brother*
orenji *orange*
orimasu *break (bone, stick)*
orimasu *get off*
osoi *late, slow*
osoku *late*
otearai *washroom (polite)*
ōtobai *motorcycle*
otona *adult*
otōsan *father*
otōto *younger brother*
ototoi *the day before yesterday*
oyasuminasai *good night*
oyogimasu *swim*
ōzei *many people*

P

painappuru *pineapple*
pan *bread*
pan-ya *bread shop*
Pari *Paris*
pātī *party*
pen *pen*
pittari na *perfectly fit*
poppu songu *popular song*
puratfōhōmu *platform*
purezento *present*
pūru *pool*

R

rai- *next*
rai-getsu *next month*
rainen *next year*
raion *lion*
rai-shū *next week*
rajio *radio*
ranchi *lunch*
reizōko *refrigerator*
rekishi *history*
resutoran *restaurant*
rikō na *clever*
ringo *apple*
rippa na *splendid*
risu *squirrel*
roku *six*
roku-gatsu *June*
romanchikku na *romantic*
Rondon *London*
ryokan *Japanese inn*
ryokō *travel*
ryōri *cooking*

S

sabishii *lonely*
saifu *wallet, purse*
sakana *fish*
sakana-ya *fish shop*
sakaya *liquor store*
sake *Japanese rice wine*
sakki *a little while ago*
sakuranbo *cherry*
samui *cold (temperature)*
-san *Mr., Mrs., Ms (after a name)*
san *three*
sandoicchi *sandwich*
san-gatsu *March*

sangurasu *sunglasses*

sansū *arithmetic*

sara *plate (most commonly* osara*)*

sarada *salad*

saru *monkey*

satō *sugar*

sayōnara *good-bye*

se *height, stature*

seito *student (general)*

semai *limited (space)*

sen- *last*

sen *1,000*

sen *(train) line*

sen-getsu *last month*

senpūki *electric fan*

-sensei *added after the names of teachers and medical doctors*

sensei *teacher*

sen-shū *last week*

sentaku *laundry*

sētā *sweater*

shi *four*

shichi *seven*

shichi-gatsu *July*

shi-gatsu *April*

shigoto *work*

shimasu *do*

shinbun *newspaper*

shingō *traffic light*

shinimasu *die*

shinsetsu na *kind*

shio *salt*

shio-karai *salty*

shiroi *white*

shita *lower part, space underneath*

shiteiseki *reserved seats*

shizuka na *quiet, peaceful*

shōgakkō *primary school*

Shōgatsu *New Year's Day*

shōyu *soy sauce*

shujin *my husband*

shukudai *homework*

shumi *hobby*

shuto *capitals*

sō *so, in that way*

sochira *that person (indicates a person near the listener)*

sōji *cleaning*

soko *that place (indicates a place near the listener)*

sono *that*

sora *sky*

sore *that thing (indicates a thing/person near the listener)*

sorekara *after that, and then*

soto *outside*

sūgaku *mathematics*

sugi *after/past (time)*

sugu *immediately*

suiei *swimming*

suika *watermelon*

sui-yōbi *Wednesday*

sukāto *skirt*

sukī *ski, skiing*

suki na *likable*

sukimasu *be empty, not crowded*

sukoshi *a little*

sukūtā *scooter*

sumimasen *excuse me, pardon me*

sumimasu *live at, take up residence*

sumō *sumo wrestling*

sūpāmāketto *supermarket*

supōtsu *sport*

supūn *spoon*

sutēki *steak*

suteki na *lovely*

sutereo *stereo*

sūtsu *suit*
suzushii *cool (temperature)*

T

tabemasu *eat*
tabemono *food*
-tachi *added to make a person into a plural form*
Tadaima. *I am back (now).*
taihen *very (with adjectives and adverbs); a lot, much (with verbs)*
taiin *discharge from a hospital*
taionkei *clinical thermometer*
taisetsu na *precious*
taisō *gymnastics*
takai *expensive, high, tall*
takaku *expensively, highly*
takusan *much, many, a lot, plenty*
takushī *taxi*
tamago *egg*
tamanegi *onion*
tanoshii *enjoyable*
tanoshiku *enjoyably*
tanuki *racoon dog*
tatemono *building*
te *hand*
tēburu *table*
tegami *letter*
ten *mark, score*
tenisu *tennis*
tenki *weather*
tera *temple*
terebi *television*
tesuto *test*
tetsudai *help*
-tō *put after a number to count animals such as whales, cows and horses*
to *and, together, along with*
toire *washroom*

tōka *10th (day of the month); 10 days*
tokei *watch*
tokemasu *melt*
toki *time, moment*
tokidoki *sometimes*
tokkyū *super express (train)*
tokoro *place*
Tōkyō *Tokyo*
tomarimasu *stay (overnight), stop*
tomato *tomato*
tomemasu *stop (something)*
tomodachi *friend*
tonari *next door, position next to*
tonkatsu *pork cutlet*
tora *tiger*
torakku *truck*
tori *bird*
torimasu *score*
torimasu *take*
tori-niku *chicken meat*
tōsutā *toaster*
totemo *very (with adjectives and adverbs); a lot, much (with verbs)*
tsuitachi *1st (day of the month)*
tsukaremasu *be tired*
tsukiatari *T-intersection*
tsukimasu *arrive*
tsukimasu *be accompanied, be included*
tsukue *desk*
tsukurimasu *make*
tsumaranai *boring*
tsumetai *cold (to the touch)*
tsuri *change (most commonly* otsuri*)*

U

uchi *house, home*
ude *arm*
ue *upper part, space above*

uētā *waiter*
uētoresu *waitress*
ugokashimasu *move (something)*
ugokimasu *move*
uma *horse*
umaremasu *to be born*
umi *sea*
undō-gutsu *sport shoes*
unten *driving*
urimasu *sell*
urusai *noisy*
usagi *rabbit*
ushi *cow*
ushiro *back part, position behind*
usui *thin (of flat things)*
uta *song*

W

-wa *put after a number to count animals such as rabbits, and birds such as ducks and chickens*
wain *wine*
wakarimasu *to be understandable; to understand*
wanpīsu *one-piece dress*
warui *bad*
Washinton *Washington*
wasuremasu *forget*
watashi *I, me (except young boys)*

Y

-ya *-shop*
yagate *soon, presently, before long*
yakusoku *promise*
yakyū *baseball*
yama *mountain*
yamemasu *resign from, cease, stop*
yamimasu *stop (rain, snow)*

yaoya *vegetable shop*
yasai *vegetables*
yasashii *easy*
yasashii *gentle*
yasui *cheap*
yasuku *cheaply*
yasumi *holiday*
yasumimasu *be absent from, rest from, take time off from*
yo *put at the end of a phrase to indicate "!"*
-yōbi *denotes the day of the week*
yōchien *kindergarten*
yoi *good*
yōka *8th (day of the month); 8 days*
yokka *4th (day of the month); 4 days*
yoko *side part, position beside*
yoku *well, fully, often, a lot*
yomimasu *read*
yon *four*
yori *(more) than*
yoru *night*
yubi *finger*
yūbinkyoku *post office*
yuki *snow*
yukkuri *slowly*
yūmei na *famous*
yūsuhosuteru *youth hostel*

Z

zasshi *magazine*
zenbu *all, everything, completely*
zenzen *not at all, entirely (used with negative verbs)*
zero *zero*
zō *elephant*
zubon *trousers*

Berlitz®

speaking your language

phrase book & dictionary
phrase book & CD

Available in: Arabic, Brazilian Portuguese*, Burmese*, Cantonese Chinese, Croatian, Czech*, Danish*, Dutch, English, Filipino, Finnish*, French, German, Greek, Hebrew*, Hindi*, Hungarian*, Indonesian, Italian, Japanese, Korean, Latin American Spanish, Malay, Mandarin Chinese, Mexican Spanish, Norwegian, Polish, Portuguese, Romanian*, Russian, Spanish, Swedish, Thai, Turkish, Vietnamese

*Book only

www.berlitzpublishing.com